THE NEW CITIZENSHIP OF THE FAMILY

The New Citizenship of the Family

Comparative perspectives

Edited by
HENRY CAVANNA
Director, Forum International des Sciences Humaines, Paris

Ashgate

Aldershot • Burlington USA • Singapore • Sydney

Published by
Ashgate Publishing Ltd
Gower House
Croft Road
Aldershot
Hants GU11 3HR
England

Ashgate Publishing Company
131 Main Street
Burlington
Vermont 05401
USA

Ashgate website: http://www.ashgate.com

British Library Cataloguing in Publication Data
The new citizenship of the family : comparative
    perspectives
    1. Family - Social aspects 2. Family - Economic aspects
    I. Cavanna, Henry
    306.8'5

Library of Congress Control Number: 99-75547

ISBN 0 7546 1222 8

Printed and bound in Great Britain by MPG Books Ltd, Bodmin, Cornwall

Contents

List of Figures

List of Tables

List of Contributors

Jacques Bichot
University Louis Lumière, Lyon
Président de la Fédération des Familles de France

Allan Carlson
The Rockford Institute, Rockford, Illinois

Henry Cavanna
Director
Forum International des Sciences Humaines, Paris

Jacques Commaille
Fondation Nationale des Sciences Politiques, Paris

Pierpaolo Donati
Department of Sociology, University of Bologna

Sophie Duchesne
CEVIPOF, CNRS, Paris

Wilfried Dumon
Department of Sociology, KU Leuven, Belgium

Kurt Lüscher
Department of Sociology, University of Konstanz

John O'Neill
York University, Canada
Staffordshire University, U.K.

Jan Pahl
University of Kent at Canterbury

Alan Tapper
School of Social and Cultural Studies
Edith Cowan University, Australia

David Thomson
Department of History, Massey University, New Zealand
Cambridge Group for the History of Population and Social Structure, Cambridge

Helmut Wintersberger
University of Vienna

Introduction

HENRY CAVANNA

What is the contemporary family? What is the role of the family in society? Is the family the appropriate analytical entity by which to study society, a legitimate interlocutor of societal institutions and governments? Is it possible to talk about the family without necessarily expressing a partisan viewpoint? Is it possible to defend family policy without taking a political view of the family? Family policies, conflicts between generations, exclusion, the lack of social support for families – these are just some of the questions and topical issues that contemporary societies and governments are increasingly confronted with.

The aim of this publication is twofold. First, it is the duty of the social sciences to juxtapose the political and moralising discourses on the family with a more scientific approach drawing on the fields of sociology, economics and the political sciences using case studies and empirical evidence. But it is equally important to find some kind of middle ground for analysis between simple descriptive methods and official discourse. It is a challenging and exciting task.

Three different but complementary approaches to the subject of the family have been adopted in this volume. First, the family is studied in its sociological dimension. The purpose of this section is to define the family and its functions in society taking into account its historical evolution and problematic nature and to analyse the changing structures of the family, including the tensions and power struggles within the family and the interactions between the family and society and the family and the political sphere. The issue of the family undoubtedly inspires a whole series of reflections and this section proposes new conceptual tools and ways of looking at and studying the family.

Second, the family is examined in its economic dimension. The family unit is a complex entity with a specific economic status based on a budget which needs to be managed and subjected to a particular tax regime. This section looks at the family in terms of capital and the administration of this capital. The economic causes and consequences of social phenomena related to the family, such as the decline in marriage and fertility rates and the increasing number of births out of wedlock are also analysed and possible solutions to these problems are suggested.

Finally, the family is above all a political issue. The question of the family is vast and linked to complex issues such as citizenship, identity and the welfare state. This section focuses on the relationship between the family and the rest of society, the family and the state, the family and the nation and examines the specific role of the family in politics and the need to take into account the nature of the family in the formation of family policy.

The issue of the family is also considered in its European dimension. The questions asked include: does the family have a role to play in the construction of Europe as a political entity? Can a revived and reformulated family policy help forge a European identity? Can the European Union offer a solution to the crisis facing contemporary families?

The contributions presented in this volume are aimed at opening up the debate on the family and at studying the family in its full complexity from various different but complementary angles. The purpose is to provide a better understanding of what constitutes the family by proposing new perspectives and methods of analysing the family and by offering possible solutions to the many difficulties and dilemmas faced by the family as it enters the twenty-first century.

This book is composed of a collection of articles from specialists from around the world on the different aspects of the family in contemporary society. The aim is to study the family under three main headings: the family in its sociological dimension and in particular the changing structures of the family and the tensions within in order to determine the analytical entity that is called the family; the family in its economic dimension looking in particular at fiscal aspects; the family in its political dimension and the question of family policy and the relationship between the family and government including the questions of citizenship and the Welfare State.

PART I
THE FAMILY AND ITS
POLITICAL REGULATION

1 Family Rhetoric in Family Politics

KURT LÜSCHER

Over the last decades, we have been witnessing a rising interest in family politics and family policies, and consequently in public debates on the family. Family reports may be seen as an important institutionalized form of this discourse, and consequently merit special attention within the sociology of the family. The analysis of these reports, especially in the perspective of a sociology of knowledge, may be advanced by comparisons between different forms of reports, their institutional settings, their contents and their impacts. The analysis may also profit from attempts to look at other forms and modes of public discourse on the family and on family politics. A tool for these kinds of comparative analysis – in the two ways just mentioned – may be seen in the conceptualization of family rhetoric. This is the perspective I will take in the following presentation. Its focus is on the general features of family rhetoric, thus it aims to sketch out a theoretical frame of reference. I will start with a definition of family rhetoric and then develop my argumentation in a set of four propositions.

Definition

The concept of family rhetoric refers to texts, images and statements which aim to publicly appraise 'the' family in general, certain forms of families, family behaviours or family patterns in particular in order to judge them, to promote or to reject them, and to impose specific models on individual actors.

Not all types of statements and texts on the family should be interpreted as rhetorical. My definition deliberately excludes:

• private conversations on the family, although these may be influenced by family rhetoric and may merit sociological studies;

3

- scholarly texts, insofar as they are not intended to make normative statements. However, scholarly text may be used (and misused) for rhetorical purposes, and rhetoric may be one of their concerns.

Family rhetoric, as a social phenomenon, has a long history, because public discourses on marriage, family, and household have always had a moralistic component. This is also true for the writings of the founding fathers of family sociology such as Riehl and Le Play.

A new interest in family rhetoric correlates with debates over family developments since the mid-1960s. These changes concern behaviours as well as ideas regarding the family. They go together with new notions concerning family policies and family politics, e.g., the relations among individual, family, state and society. The new interest also correlates with recent developments of the organization and the patterns of all forms of human communication as a consequence of the introduction of new media. Thus we should not be surprised to observe a renaissance of interest in rhetoric in the social sciences, as well as in law, economics, political science and the humanities proper.

The term 'family rhetoric', to my knowledge, first appeared in the 1980s. Thus, Gubrium and Lyott (1985), under the heading 'Family rhetoric and social order', proposed viewing 'family discourse as a form of social action through which aspects of social life are not only assigned meaning, but also are organized and manipulated – that is controlled' (Gubrium and Holstein, 1990, p. 132). Bernardes (1987, p. 691) expressed an interest in '… exploring the predominance of the representation of "family rhetoric" (or the power of "family ideology", in my terms)' implicit in the official statistics.

In our work, we first employed the term in connection with the analysis of different attempts to formulate a definition of the family (Lüscher, Wehrspaun and Lange, 1989). We then used the concept in connection with an analysis of family reports (Walter, 1993). Kaufmann (1993) took up this lead and used the concept of family rhetoric to characterize the different types of arguments employed in substantiating the legitimization of family policy. More recently, we have used the approach to compare publications in the field of family sociology and on the so called 'war between generations' (Bräuninger et al., 1997).

However, in this presentation, I do not wish to elaborate this line of analysis. Instead, I would like to offer a set of propositions based on a general thesis concerning the basic function of rhetoric.

This thesis relies on the leading idea behind Blumenberg's (1981) 'anthropological approach to the actuality of rhetoric'. The latter states that the essence of (philosophical) anthropology can be expressed in the juxtaposition of man as a 'rich or a poor creature'. Man's creativity emerges from the precariousness of his needs or from a playful use of the abundance of his talents. Thus rhetoric reflects either man's possession of wisdom or truth or his inability to achieve them.

If we apply this idea to our proposition on family rhetoric, we may say that the latter serves to express convictions about what the family has been in the past and will be in the future; or it raises fundamental doubts about the reasonableness of such convictions and indicates a genuine openness what the family is or should be. Thus, we may formulate:

Proposition 1

Rhetoric serves to affirm either the possession of truth or to veil basic doubts. Accordingly, family rhetoric either proclaims a particular ideal of the family, or denies the feasibility of defining mandatory models of the family.

The juxtaposition of these two rhetorical positions is meant to be an ideal-type reference for the analyses of public discourse on the family along different themes and topics. I would like to briefly describe three such themes.

A   Family as a Natural Unit

Quite often, orators and writers start from the notion of a profound crisis of the family. Thus radical critics may ask if the family is a dying species, or what will happen to a society whose basic unit, its 'cells', are seriously endangered. These critics draw on a metaphor characteristic of a dogmatic conception of the family. It treats the family as a natural unit, put simply, as natural.

This idea is deeply rooted, first, in Roman Catholic doctrine, where it is related to the conception of marriage as a sacrament. The validity of such religious convictions will not be debated here. We are instead interested in their functions. These functions lie in the fact that a given form may be regarded as normative, and prescriptions may be made concerning what should be considered as natural, therefore as good behaviour, e.g., in regard to contraception or to reproductive medicine. The reference to nature is a rhetorical device serving to devaluate alternative views. The same is true for references to the origins of family, and defining the family and marriage as having been instituted by God.

A related position is held by those ethnologists, social-biologists and others who attempt to draw inferences as to the structure of the family from the study of animal behaviour, especially in regard to mother-child relations. They overlook the fact that such a use of the term family is not free from anthropocentric implications, and they also neglect the great diversity of behaviour found among non-human species.

The rhetorical counterposition conceives the family as an exclusively social construction, intended to serve specific interests, e.g., those of a given social class, as does the so-called 'bourgeois family', or to express male supremacy.

B   What is Meant by 'Normal'?

Rhetorical statements on the family very often contain 'prescription in the form of description' (Finch, 1989, p. 237). Thus politicians in their political speeches often claim that the 'family provides its members security, devotion and warmth'. This is certainly often true. But there are, unfortunately, also instances and cases of family violence, even of homicide. Such cases are used as arguments against the dominance of an ideal model of the family, and estimates of the percentage of undetected crimes within families are used to strengthen the rhetorical impetus.

Any reference to the diversity of family forms is a threat to the notion of normality. Comparisons between different family types seem necessary, and this raises questions of the proper criteria for such comparisons. The topic is much discussed in the USA nowadays, as is demonstrated by the Poponoe-Stacey debate reported by Wilson (1993). Although he himself admits that his conclusions may not be conclusive, he nevertheless claims that there is a best form of the family, because the family 'is not a human contrivance invented to accomplish some goal and capable being reinvented or reformulated to achieve different goals. Family – and kinship generally – are the fundamental organizing facts of all human societies, primitive or advanced, and have been such for tens of thousands of years' (Wilson, 1993, p. 28).

The rhetorical counterposition is again represented by those who propose new labels for different forms of families in order to plead for their recognition. The same purpose may be served by pointing to the diversity of family forms and the lifestyles of politicians, or by quoting exotic witnesses for the value of the family, such as, for example, the pop musician Peter Townsend.

C   Family as 'Value'?

'The family is our future' – this is a dictum which points to the relevance of the family beyond the present. In connection with an idealizing view of the past, it allows us to transcend or to transform the family rhetorically into a value in itself. In turn, this notion also allows us to construct a closer relation between the decline of the family and a general loss of values, without the necessity to explain the reasons for this loss (or this decline). It seems plausible to hope for a remedy for grievances through a return to family-values. On the other hand, the temptation is great to blame parents for societal problems.

Here the rhetorical counterposition to such an idealized view of the family is nourished by radically subjective individualism. Thus a German newspaper states: 'Whoever feels like a family is a family.' According to this position, every kind of enduring relation among persons who care for one another may be called a family. Thus the term should be used only in the plural, and it would be impossible to provide a valid definition.

To summarize: surveying the different topics related to the family, we can identify two basic positions, namely that there is only one correct form of family, and that there is a basic openness or undetermination in the concept of family. The first position is somewhat dogmatic and authoritarian, whereas the second is tied to individualistic and emancipatory ideas. These positions are also reflected in the definitions of family, in the circumscription of family functions or in the ways the patterning of the basic components (subsystems) of family is conceived.[1]

Proposition 2

Family rhetoric is programmatic; family behaviour is pragmatic. Thus the latter necessarily modifies and devaluates the former.

This proposition refers, first of all, to the plausible supposition that 'life' is more complex than the ideologies which are meant to capture it. Indeed, in looking around us, we observe a diversity of forms of family life. As forms or types, they stand for enduring patterns of behaviour and of relations. What are the origins of this diversity? Is it only the consequence of social differentiation?

I would like to offer an alternative line of argumentation. Most social scientists would agree that they arise from the task of caring and educating human offspring over a period of several years. The way this task is to be fulfilled can and must be interpreted. It is not an instinctual given or self-evident truth. It must be creatively formed. From the very beginning, 'nature and nurture' are interwoven. I suggest that we locate here a basic underlying potential for the emergence of a plurality of family forms or types, and we may want to see in this a true anthropological source of family plurality. To state this more explicitly: It is proposed that we begin the sociological conceptualization of 'family' not with the idea of one basic form (Urform), but rather with the idea of an underlying potential for a plurality of forms.

There is an additional dimension to be considered, namely our ability to reflect an understanding of nature and nurture, its interplay and thus to organize the tasks of socialization and of families in general. In a first approximation, we may want to distinguish three modi of reflection, namely experimental, theoretical and dramaturgical. Empirical approaches start with the observation of factual behaviours and interpret them by trail and error, by comparison and generalizations. Theoretical approaches derive from general systems of thoughts. The dramaturgical approach is represented by literary texts and works of art. These approaches are rooted in the social conditions of each culture and subculture, as well as in the subjective abilities of those who act in a socially correct way. Thus the primary potential of plurality is reinforced by a secondary potential inherent in the modes of reflective interpretation. It also concerns the reflection of processes of institutionalization.

As a consequence, different models of the family and of the fulfilment of family tasks have to be compared and will be evaluated. The needs for selection and evaluation derive from the relevance of the family and of family forms for the development of the individual and of societies. Thus the potential plurality of family forms will be restricted. It is a 'relative plurality'.[2]

In sum, we may even want to consider speaking of a contradictory openness of the processes of socialization and of family behaviours. This fundamental ambivalence which characterizes the family as an institution is reflected in the two positions of family rhetoric. This insight is important for family research and for the sociology of the family.

Proposition 3

An important task and an opportunity for contemporary sociological research on the family consists in the analysis, on the one side, of individual family behaviours, knowledges and beliefs, and, on the other side, in the study of (public) family rhetoric. In this way, it becomes possible to reflect the perspective of sociological family research and to determine its place within the many different perspectives on the family.

This proposition assigns to family sociology a 'third' position between what may be called the programmatics of rhetoric and the pragmatics of acting. Of course, doing research is also a way of acting, albeit a special kind of acting, because research reconstructions are guided by theory and methodology, and by other ways of speaking and of acting. This approach applies reflection and, in turn, constitutes specific perspectives. The better this reflection is done, the more the qualities and the singularities of a given perspective become recognizable, and also the differences in comparison with other perspectives. This is the case in regard to different sociological theories, as well as in regard to differences between the two positions and family sociology.

From its historical origins, those working in sociology and particularly in family sociology, at least to the extent they had a concern for empirical data, had to define their position between (simplifying) ideologies and the plurality of behaviours. With the development of perspectives which include the analysis of systems of knowledge and beliefs, both theoretically and empirically, it became possible to reflect the interrelationships among ideologies or belief systems, behaviours and the role of sociology. Major advances became possible with the acceptance of constructivist paradigms, a process still going on. It generates new interests and new insights into the contribution of sociology to public discourses and to politics.[3]

A topic of increasing relevance concerns especially the relevance of socio-logical knowledge, the role of sociologists as political advisors and, as experts and as participants in public discourses. Social reporting is a case in point. The study of this role involves many aspects. With reference to the foregoing general propositions on programmatic of family rhetoric and the pragmatics of family behaviours, I would suggest the following general proposition:

Proposition 4

Social reporting on the family (family reports) may be interpreted as an attempt to overcome the polarization of family rhetoric and to master – pragmatically – the 'contradictory openness' of processes of socialization, as well as the accompanying fundamental ambivalences of the family as a social institution.

Family reports (see the presentation in this session) are specific contributions to the public discourse on the family on a national level which since the 1960s have been available in several countries. Furthermore, reports are available on small political units, and even on cities and communities. In most cases, they have an official character, insofar as they are commissioned by the government or parliament. The situation is different in the United States, due to a fundamentally different understanding and organization of family policy and family politics (cf. the contribution by Walter). In Germany, the boundaries to other forms of public discourse on the family are much more open. But this is also true in other countries. Also, certain interconnections exist between social reports on women and children (for the latter see: Lüscher and Lange 1992). Finally, family reports can be located within the general tradition of social reporting, 'white papers' and similar publications. These correspondences, as well as differences, may well be topics of further discussions and elaborations. Here I would like to suggest, as I did in regard to proposition 4, that we start with the basic functions of the reports.

All reports provide, so-to-speak 'by definition', as an important component, differentiated analytical descriptions of the situation of the family. For this purpose they rely heavily on demographic material, but they also make ample use of the social sciences. In this way, they stress the pragmatic aspect of the public discourse. This entails that these reports must also deal with the notion of plurality and of pluralization.

On the other hand, insofar as they aim to make recommendations for family policy and family politics, these reports must also contribute to a 'reduction of complexity', and in this way they necessarily take positions which ultimately restricts the potential for plurality or which provides reasons (or even legitimizations) for doing so.

Several strategies may be employed in order to deal with this dilemma (and to overcome its inherent ambivalences). I would like to mention three such strategies, namely:

- a strategy of (implicit and explicit) *advocacy*, taking recent developments of family behaviours as point of departure. This strategy was, in my view, followed in the first *Austrian report* (1970), and to some extent in the more recent second Austrian report, which significantly enough bears the title: 'Lebenswelt Familie' ('Life World of the Family') (1990) and pays great attention to the pluralization of family forms. This strategy is characterized by extended descriptive sections and a discussion of the (international) research literature. Policy recommendations are primarily based upon common sense reasoning;

- a strategy of *institutionalized differentiation*, starting from existing family policy. This strategy characterizes French social reporting on the family (see Lamm-Hess, 1993). The analysis and recommendations are developed within the highly elaborated system of family policy, of which the fundamental justifications and legitimization are taken for granted. It goes without saying that this includes references to the pluralization of family forms, yet within the already differentiated system this is not a point of reference of primary (rhetorical) reference;

- a strategy of *systematic reconceptualization*, both of recent developments in the family and of family policy. I find this strategy realized in the most recent German report. It is organized around the concept of *Humanvermögen* (human capital) which is meant to characterize, on a general level, the achievements of the family and serves as point of reference for a fundamental (re)orientation of family policy and its justification. It does account for pluralization on a higher level of conceptualization. This strategy may well be supported both by the fact that this report had the task of taking into account the situation in a reunited Germany; it can also find a basis in a series of recent decisions (judgments) by the Federal Constitutional Court of Germany (Bundesverfassungsgericht). However, the dialectic of reconceptualization may be seen as potentially built into the format of the German reports. With the exception of the first report, they all consist of a group of (independent) experts and the government official position paper (see also Walter, 1993).

What about strategies in the case of a weak institutionalization of family policy - as in the case of the USA? In my judgment, the pluralization of family forms is an important issue in at least two regards. First, it encourages moral arguments on the rightness of certain forms (regardless of their empirical reality), and second, it provokes the comparison of the functioning and of the achievements of the failures of different forms, in the concrete case of the single-parent family.

I am aware that my suggestion to distinguish different types of family and to study the way family reports deal with the inherent ambivalences of the plurality of family forms and patterns is tentative and in need of further elaboration. We may also want to consider the strategies of dealing with other major issues of contemporary family life, especially those which refer to other forms of conflict and contradictions such as arises from the incompatibility of work and family or of gender and family obligations.

I am also prepared to be confronted with the argument that my characterization of family rhetoric and its relevance to family politics overstates the polarization of the two basic models. However, I would suggest that a formal view may provoke a series of arguments and of hypotheses, both theoretical and empirical, in regard to a topic which is only beginning to receive attention.

Notes

1   Those components may be described in reference to the model of the so-called 'traditional family' (*bürgerliche Familie*): partnership (marriage), parenthood, household, relation to kinship, and also: authoritarian vs. egalitarian division of tasks and competences among the members of the nuclear family. Model 1 refers to a strict temporal order and an institutionalized connection, especially between marriage and parenthood. Model 2 challenges this order on theoretical and empirical grounds. For the analysis of family discourses it is also noteworthy to recall the duality of meanings related to the concept of *bürgerliche Familie*, namely as a historical ideal-type, and as a term to be used with polemic intentions (see also Lüscher 1997a).
2   For a further elaboration of this conceptualization of family plurality see Lüscher 1997b.
3   These recent developments may be characterized as a move away from a sociology which took a firm stand against ideologies (thus attempted to be value-free) to a sociology which reflects differentially (and in connection with empirical observations) the relations of all parts involved, including sociology itself, toward elements of ideological thinking, as well as toward all other possible connections among texts, contexts and actors.

References

Bernardes, J. (1987), 'Doing Things with Words: Sociology and "Family Policy" Debates', *The Sociological Review*, 35, pp. 679–702.
Blumenberg, H. (1981), 'Anthropologische Annäherung an die Rhetorik', in *Ders. Wirklichkeiten, in denen wir leben. Aufsätze und eine Rede*, Stuttgart: Reclam, pp. 104–36.
Bräuninger, B., Lange, A. and Lüscher, K. (1997), 'Krieg zwischen den Generationen?', *Die Darstellung von Generationenbeziehungen in ausgewählten Sachbuchtexten*, Konstanz: Forschungsschwerpunkt 'Gesellschaft und Familie', Arbeitspapier No. 26.
Bundesministerium für Familie und Senioren (1994), *Familien und Familienpolitik im geeinten Deutschland*, Bonn: Fünfter (deutscher) Familienbericht.
Finch, M. (1989), *Family Obligations and Social Change*, Oxford: Polity Press.
Gisser, R. et al. (eds) (1990), 'Lebenswelt Familie', Wien: Institut für Ehe und Familie (2. Österreichischer Familienbericht).

Gubrium, J.F. and Holstein, J.A. (1990), *What is Family?*, Mountain View: Mayfield.

Gubrium, J.F. and Lynott, R.J. (1985), 'Family Rhetoric as Social Order', *Journal of Family Issues*, 6, pp. 129–52.

Kaufmann, F.-X. (1993), 'Familienpolitik in Europa', in Bundesamt für Familie und Senioren (eds), *40 Jahre Familienpolitik in der Bundesrepublik Deutschland*, Festschrift (S. 141–67), Neuwied: Luchterhand.

Lamm-Hess, Y. and Wehrspaun, C. (1993), *Frauen- und Müttererwerbstätigkeit im Dritten und Vierten Familienbericht*, Konstanz: Forschungsschwerpunkt 'Gesellschaft und Familie', Arbeitspapier No. 4.

Lange, A. (1995), *Kindheitsrhetorik und die Befunde der empirischen Forschung*, Konstanz: Forschungsschwerpunkt 'Gesellschaft und Familie', Arbeitspapier No. 19.

Lüscher, K. (1990), 'The Social Reality of Perspectives: on G.H. Mead's potential relevance for the analysis of contemporary societies', *Symbolic Interaction*, 13, 1, S. 1–18.

Lüscher, K. (1997a), 'Familienleitbilder und Familienpolitik', in Uta Meier (ed.), *Vom Oikos zum modernen Dienstleistungshaushalt*, Festschrift für Rosemarie von Schweitzer, Frankfurt/New York: Campus Verlag, S. 381–97.

Lüscher, K. (1997b), 'Demographische Annäherungen an die "Pluralität familialer Lebensformen"', *Zeitschrift für Bevölkerungswissenschaft*, 22,2/3, S. 269–309 (Demographie. Festgabe für Karl Schwarz).

Lüscher, K. and Lange, A. (1992), 'Konzeptuelle Grundlagen einer Politik für Kinder: Ansätze und Begründungen aus sozialwissenschaftlicher Sicht', *Zeitschrift für Sozialisationsforschung und Erziehungssoziologie*, 12, pp. 204–18.

Lüscher, K., Wehrspaun, M. and Lange, A. (1989), *Familienrhetorik – über die Schwierigkeit, Familie zu definieren*, Zeitschrift für Familienforschung, 1, pp. 61–76.

Walter, W. (1993), *Vom Familienleitbild zur Familiendefinition. Familienberichte und die Entwicklung des familienpolitischen Diskurses*, Konstanz: Forschungsschwerpunkt 'Gesellschaft und Familie', Arbeitspapier No. 5.

Wilson, J. (1993), 'The Family-values Debate', *Commentary*, 95/4, pp. 24–31.

2 The Control and Allocation of Money Within the Family

JAN PAHL

The aim of this paper is to consider the ideas developed by Professor Donati (1997), in the context of one particular type of family and one particular aspect of family life. So the paper will focus on families consisting of a married couple with at least one dependent child, and on the economic aspects of family life. Over the past 15 years I have been involved in a number of different studies concerned with financial arrangements within families and with the intra-household economy more generally. However, before presenting empirical data from some of these studies there are definitional issues to be considered.

I   Definitions and Theories

Professor Donati defined the family as:

> The symbolic and structural relationship that binds people together in a lifelong project that intersects a horizontal dimension (the couple) and a vertical dimension (relations between descendants/ascendants) (Donati, 1997, p. 6).

As we shall see, symbolic and structural relationships are very powerful when money is concerned. Professor Donati extended his definition by saying:

> Even those who do not share living quarters or wealth can be a family. What identifies a group of people (at least two) as a family is the existence between them of fully reciprocal relationships between genders and generations (ibid., p. 16).

These definitions are very broad and raise many questions. For example, what is meant by 'fully reciprocal relations'? The term might include caring for those who are unable to care for themselves, exchanging support in times of trouble, sharing the pleasure of good times, dividing space and time between

14

the different members of the family, and making arrangements for financial resources to be used equitably. It is not clear from his paper whether 'fully reciprocal relations' means that resources should flow in both directions and in equal proportions between men and women and between parents and children. I would suggest that this is not likely, but that rather we must think of the family as a system for the redistribution of valued resources of several different types. This paper is concerned with the reciprocal relationships which surround the transfer of money between men and women within the family.

In thinking about 'the family' it is important to be clear what definition is being used. In his paper it seemed as if Professor Donati was mainly concerned with the *nuclear family,* and more specifically with that group which consists of a married couple and their children, living in the same household. This is helpful for me, because the evidence which I shall be presenting to you is also concerned with that type of family, but it is by no means the only form which families can take.

Eurostat has implemented the United Nations' definition of the family unit as:

> The persons within a private or institutional household who are related as husband and wife or as a parent and never-married child by blood or adoption. Thus a family nucleus comprises a married couple without children or a married couple with one or more never-married children of any age or one parent with one or more never-married children of any age (Hantrais and Letablier, 1996, p. 8).

'Families' which consist of a married couple living with their dependent children represent a minority among households throughout the industrial world and are continuing to fall as a proportion of all households. In Britain, for example, this type of household made up 38 per cent of all households in 1961, but had fallen to 23 per cent by 1996. Over the same period of time married couples without children increased from 26 per cent to 29 per cent. Lone parents living with dependent children increased from 2 to 7 per cent of all households, but remain a small minority among households and families (Office of National Statistics, 1997, p. 40).

However, in thinking about reciprocal relations between generations we must also consider what has been called the *extended family,* or the wider kin group within which a particular nuclear family is located. Caring, mutual support, financial resources and so on are exchanged within the extended family as well as within the nuclear family, and we shall impoverish our discussions if we forget this.

In addition, more and more people are finding themselves living in *reconstituted families*. This complex but increasingly common type of family is produced by the breakdown of a marital relationship but the continuation of parent-child relationships. Two brief stories illustrate what can occur.

- Laura is a divorced woman in her sixties, living in a stable, long term relationship with Rob, a widower. He is the main carer for the mother of his dead wife, who lives about fifty kilometres away. He accepts the obligation because she helped him so much with the children after their mother died. Laura is also involved in caring, but commented, 'If it was his mother I would feel an obligation to her, but as it is I'm not sure how much I should do'.

- Helena and her husband had two children. When the marriage ended she went on to live with Martin and his two children from a previous marriage. She is now in her forties and her relationship with Martin has ended, but she continues to give help to his children and his parents. 'I can't end those relationships just because Martin and I are not together any more,' she said.

Both these examples fall within Professor Donati's definition of the family, in that both involve reciprocal relationships between genders and generations, and both represent continuity over time, but neither is based on an existing marriage. There has been very little research about flows of resources within reconstituted families, though some work is taking place at the University of Exeter (Burgoyne and Morison, 1997; see also Burgoyne and Clark, 1984).

From a historical perspective it is clear that reconstituted families have a long history and that 'the family' has never been as stable as Professor Donati implies. Estimates today suggest that up to one-fifth of children under 16 are likely to see their parents divorce. By comparison a study of family life in England in the seventeenth century showed that one-third of children had lost one or both parents by this age, leading to the conclusion that 'we are hardly justified, in historical terms, in sympathising with ourselves for the prevalence of broken marriages and its deplorable effects on children' (Laslett, 1977, pp. 169–70).

Family policy inevitably reflects assumptions about the nature of family life. This can be seen, for example, in the rules related to entitlement to social assistance or income maintenance. Most European social protection systems set up after the Second World War assumed that the normal family would be composed of a breadwinner husband, with a dependant wife and children. The man was to be the claimant, while the woman and children were seen as his dependants. These schemes are now having to be adapted to cope with the increases in women's employment and in the diversity of family situations. (see for example Bradshaw et al., 1993; Ditch et al., 1996; Hantrais and Letablier, 1996). Some benefits, in some countries, are directed at mothers and paid directly to them, but these tend to involve relatively small sums of money. It seems that a woman may become a claimant in her role as mother, but that family policy has found it harder to see her as the claimant in a family which also contains an adult man.

Within economics, theories about the allocation of money within the family have also taken as their norm the ideal of the breadwinner husband and the dependant wife and children (see, for example, Becker, 1981). These theories assume that in general individuals pursue their own economic interests, that is, they have independent utility functions, but that within the family these utility functions are modified by altruism, and in particular by the altruism of the main earner. Becker argued that the money which enters the household is distributed by the 'altruistic benefactor' to the 'selfish beneficiaries': in a footnote he explained that 'to distinguish the altruist from the beneficiary, I use the masculine pronoun for the altruist and the feminine pronoun for the beneficiary' (Becker, 1981, p. 173). Thus, the theoretical foundations of the new home economics do seem to imply an association between breadwinning, masculinity and altruism. In this chapter we shall see whether the assumptions stand up to empirical and sociological investigation.

II   Sources of Data

Since the paper on which this chapter is base was presented at an international conference the aim will be to draw together research from a number of different countries, and to consider whether there are any generalizations about our topic which apply across cultures. However, the two main data sets on which I shall draw come from Britain.

The first data set comes from my own study of money and marriage (Pahl, 1989). This involved interviews with 102 married, or as-married couples, all with at least one child under 16. The sample was randomly selected from the general population in Kent, in southeast England, and though a sample of this size cannot be regarded as representative, the study couples had many of the characteristics which one would have hoped to find in a representative sample, in terms of employment patterns, social class, housing tenure and ownership of consumer durables. Because I was interested in the different perspectives of husband and wife, each couple was interviewed first together and then separately, but at the same time. This method was quite complicated and expensive, since two interviewers were required for each couple interview, but the disparities which emerged between the views of some husbands and wives more than justified the costs.

The second main source of data for the paper is the Social Change and Economic Life Initiative (Anderson et al., 1994). This focused on six different parts of Britain with contrasting experiences of economic and social change, with respondents being randomly selected from the population aged 20 to 60. The data presented here come from the 1,235 interviews with couple households. Interviews were conducted jointly with both partners, but a large proportion of questions were answered by means of self completion booklets, which individuals filled in without conferring with each other. The Social Change and Economic Life Initiative (SCELI) provided quantitative data with which to test out some of the ideas which had been developed in the course of qualitative research; for a more extended account of the analysis presented here see Vogler and Pahl (1993 and 1994).

III   The Meanings of Money

In my own study I was interested in how married couples defined the money which entered the household. Table 2.1 shows the answers which husbands and wives, being interviewed at the same time but in different rooms, gave to the question, 'How do you feel about what you earn: do you feel it is your income or do you regard it as your husband/wife's as well?'. Many respondents amended the question, explaining that they saw their main income as belonging to 'the family', rather than to themselves as a couple. Table 2.1 shows that there were substantial differences between husbands and wives on this issue, and also between answers relating to the income of the respondent and the income of the other partner. Men's income was more likely to be seen as belonging to the family than was women's income: the idea of the male breadwinner is still powerful. However, both men and women were more likely to see their partner's income as belonging to the individual, while they preferred to think of their own income as going to the family as a whole. A very similar pattern was found in Australia by Edwards (1981).

Table 2.1   **'How do you feel about what you earn: do you feel it is your income or do you regard it as your husband/wife's as well?'**

	Husband's income		Wife's income	
	Husband's answer	Wife's answer	Wife's answer	Husband's answer
Income belongs to:	%	%	%	%
the earner	7	24	35	52
the couple/family	93	76	65	48

N = 102

Source: Pahl, 1989.

The evidence in Table 2.1 is very relevant to debates about the meaning of money. In general, both men and women seemed to define the family as a unit within which money is shared, but this was particularly so among men, and especially when they were thinking about their own money: only when husbands were thinking about their wives' earnings did more than half of the sample earmark the money as being for the use of the individual rather than the family. Both partners tended to see the husband as the main earner, the breadwinner whose income should be devoted to the needs of the family, in contrast to the wife whose earning were seen as more marginal. It was interesting to see that both partners tend to regarded their own money as belonging to the family to a greater extent than their partner's money: this suggested that earners welcomed the role of breadwinner and the power attached to it.

Anthropologists have documented the social nature of exchange and the central role of money as a medium of exchange. They have also, of course, emphasized the enormous variety of family forms which exist in the world, among which the European nuclear family is very much in a minority. An interesting collection of papers on money and the morality of exchange explored this point in a variety of different cultures. The editors of the collection suggest that 'In order to understand the way in which money is viewed it is vitally important to understand the cultural matrix into which it is incorporated' (Parry and Bloch, 1989, p. 1). They show that while in some societies money is seen as morally neutral or positively beneficial, in others it is associated with danger, selfish individualism or antisocial acquisition. Recent research in New Zealand has suggested that there are important differences between the Pakeha (white) and Maori communities in the significance attached to money. In particular many Maori interviewed in the course of the study did not associate control of money with power in the way that many of the white couples said they did. Instead the Maori found their self worth in giving rather than accumulating wealth. The accumulation of material possessions, which is so much part of the Pakeha consumer society, does not seem to have been a part of the pre-colonial Maori experience (Taiapa, 1994, p. 11).

In thinking about the control and allocation of money within the family, and the power which particular individuals have over financial resources, it is important to have regard to the meanings attached to money and the extent to which money is earmarked for specific purposes. At the point where it enters the household economy 'male money' is regarded rather differently from 'female money': is this translated into differences in how the money is managed and spent?

A   *Systems of Money Management*

The disparity in income between men and women, particularly during the child rearing years, means that there has to be some sharing of resources if the women and children are not to have a lower standard of living that the men. Every couple has to devise some arrangement by which this transfer of resources takes place. Though many never consciously decide to organize their finances in one way or another, in every case there is a describable system of money management. There are a number of questions which help in distinguishing one system from another. To what extent is money pooled? Who has overall control of financial arrangements and big financial decisions? Who takes responsibility for managing money on a day-to-day basis?

Over the past few years many typologies have been devised with the aim of making sense of the complexities of money management within couple households (see, for example, Brannen and Wilson, 1987; Edwards, 1981; Gray, 1979; Morris and Ruane, 1989; Pahl, 1989; Wilson, 1987). The typology used in this paper is that developed for the SCELI questionnaire (see Vogler and Pahl, 1993 and 1994). Respondents were asked to identify which of six systems of money management came closest to their own. The six system were the female whole wage, the male whole wage, the pooling system, the housekeeping allowance system and the independent management system. The independent management system is defined by both partners having their own source of income and neither having access to all the household funds. In the SCELI research only 2 per cent of couples opted for independent management and so this category has been omitted from the main analysis presented here.

What do the different allocative systems mean in practice? In the *female whole wage system* the husband hands over his whole wage packet to his wife, minus his personal spending money; the wife adds her own earnings, if any, and is then responsible for managing the financial affairs of the household. In the *male whole wage system* the husband has sole responsibility for managing household finances, a system which can leave non-employed wives with no personal spending money. The *housekeeping allowance* system involves separate spheres of responsibility for household expenditure. Typically the husband gives his wife a fixed sum of money for housekeeping expenses, to which she may add her own earnings, while the rest of the money remains in the husband's control and he pays for other items. Finally the *pooling system* involves complete or nearly complete sharing of income; both partners have access to all or nearly the money which comes into the household and both spend from the common pool. Couples adopting this system often explain that 'It is not my money or his/her money – but our money', and this phrase expresses something of the ideology which underlies pooling. There has always been an issue about the extent to which the ideology becomes reality.

Table 2.2   Household allocative systems showing different forms of pooling

	%
Female whole wage	27
Female managed pool	15
Joint pool	20
Male managed pool	15
Male whole wage	10
Housekeeping allowance	13
Total %	100
Total number	1,235

Source: Vogler and Pahl, 1994.

The SCELI data showed that half of all couples claimed to pool their money, a proportion very similar to that found in other studies. However, questions about who had ultimate responsibility for organizing household money and paying household bills made it possible to distinguish female managed pools and male managed pools from the genuinely joint pools. Table 2.2 shows that only 20 per cent of couples agreed that both were equally responsible for the management of their pooled money, while the male and female managed pools were each used by 15 per cent of the sample. The remainder of the sample were divided between the female whole wage (27 per cent), the male whole wage (10 per cent) and the housekeeping allowance (13 per cent). As we shall see, the system of money management adopted by the household had significant implications for the living standards of individuals within the household.

Table 2.3   Mean standardized household income for different allocative systems

N = 1235
Standardized income: £s per month

Female whole wage	624
Female managed pool	658
Joint pool	719
Male managed pool	728
Male whole wage	755
Housekeeping allowance	697

Source: Vogler and Pahl, 1994.

Table 2.3 shows the mean standardized household income for each allocative system. The two female managed systems were associated with the lowest income levels, while the male managed pool and the male whole wage system were associated with relatively high household incomes. Thus the study confirmed that in low income households it was women who were likely to have the difficult task of making ends meet. A regression analysis which examined the factors associated with joint pooling of money showed that this system was associated with the wife being in full time employment and making a substantial contribution to the household budget; by contrast the housekeeping allowance system was associated with the man being the sole or main earner, and with his perceiving himself as the breadwinner for the family.

B   The Relationship between Money and Power

Professor Donati did not say much in his paper about power relations within families, but it is important to remember the very real power differences between men and women, parents and children: the divisions of gender and generation, which he mentioned in his paper, represent fundamental distinctions between the more and the less powerful. The relationship between bringing money into the household and having power within the household has been documented ever since the pioneering study by Blood and Wolfe (1960; see also Bird, 1979). It seems that this association holds across a wide range of cultures, so that a collection of papers on inter-household resource allocation concluded, 'the greater the proportion of household income contributed by the woman, the greater her power in making decisions' (Rogers and Schlossman, 1990). My own study showed that husbands dominated decision making where wives did not have a job; wives who were dominant in decision making were usually in paid work.

More recently research has examined the relationship between managing money within the household and having power. In particular there has been an issue about whether managing money in very poor households, where life is a struggle for existence and there is no surplus for discretionary spending, is also associated with having more power. The SCELI interviews included questions designed to identify the relative power of husband and wife in two different spheres. The first question was concerned with who had the final say in 'big financial decisions' made in the household, while the second was concerned, more generally, with the 'most important decisions' made in the household. Both questions were included in the self completion questionnaire and so were asked of each partner separately. In order to construct an index of power within the household the answers to the two questions were combined. Table 2.4 shows the results. The category 'female power' includes households where both husband and wife agreed that wives exercised power in both spheres, or where there was disagreement about whether power was exercised by the women or shared. The category 'male power' includes households where both partners agreed that husbands exercised power in both spheres, or where there was disagreement about whether power was exercised by the man or jointly.

Just over half of all households were egalitarian in both spheres; one third were characterized by male control and just 9 per cent by female control. There was a significant association between the balance of power within the household and the way in which the couple organized finances. Couples using

Table 2.4   Household allocative systems and marital power

N = 1235

	Female whole wage %	Female managed pool %	Joint pool %	Male managed pool %	Male whole wage %	House-keeping wage allowance %
Greater male power	7	21	26	41	53	61
Equality	61	69	69	56	45	37
Greater female power	33	9	5	2	2	2

Sig < 0.0000

Source: Vogler and Pahl, 1994.

the joint or female managed systems were markedly more egalitarian than those using male managed systems. The management of money and the control of household finances were linked in important ways. When husbands managed finances, they were also likely to control them and to have power over financial and other decisions within the household. However, when wives managed finances, or when finances were jointly managed in a pool, there was likely to be joint control. The implication is that male control is typically exercised though male management, whereas other forms of management, notably joint or wife management, are circumscribed by joint control.

C   *Access to Resources within the Household*

What are the implications for individuals within households of particular systems of money management? Is there a relationship between the intra-household balance of power and the distribution of resources? In this analysis we used two different measures of intra-household inequality. These were concerned, first, with levels of financial deprivation and, secondly, with inequalities in access to personal spending money.

In order to provide a general picture of *financial deprivation*, SCELI respondents were asked to indicate what 'you yourself have had to do over the last two years to make ends meet when your household was short of money'? The focus of the question was clearly on the individual. The list which was presented included 14 different items, running from having missed a meal or turned down the heat, to borrowing money or selling the car. The commonest things on which people had cut back were social activities, buying clothes and holidays. Much rarer were reductions in heating and expenditure on food, together with measures such as getting into debt and borrowing. The chief differences between partners were that wives were much more likely than husbands to have experienced cuts in spending on meals and clothing.

Respondents were given a score of one for each action which they had taken in order to cope with financial difficulty. A measure of the difference in financial deprivation between husbands and wives living in the same household was then obtained, by subtracting husbands' financial deprivation scores from those of their own wives. A minus score indicated that husbands experienced higher levels of financial deprivation than wives, whereas a positive score indicated that wives experienced higher levels of financial deprivation than husbands.

As Table 2.5 shows, all the scores were positive, indicating that wives generally experienced more financial deprivation than husbands, but the extent to which this was the case varied markedly with the system of money management.

The largest differences between spouses emerged among couples using the female pool, the female whole wage and the housekeeping allowance systems, with index scores of .55, .52, .44 respectively. Differences between spouses were smallest among couples using the jointly managed pool where the score was .07. The greatest inequalities between husband and wife were therefore associated, first, with low household income and, secondly, with households in which the husband had a high degree of control over finances and a high level of power in the marriage.

The second way in which a system of money management may be associated with inequalities between spouses is through their access to *personal spending money*. In the SCELI research access to personal spending money was measured by asking individuals who in their household had the most personal spending money: the male partner, the female partner or both equally. Given the strong normative emphasis on the importance of sharing and equality in marriage, people may have been reluctant to admit to having different amounts of personal spending money, which means we may be underestimating possible inequalities in this respect. In the sample as a whole, just over half of all couples both perceived personal spending money as equally distributed. A further 12 per cent agreed that the husband had the most personal spending money, a tiny 4 per cent agreed that the wife had the most personal spending money, while the rest disagreed. In the analysis couples who disagreed over whether the wife had more personal spending money or whether they had

Table 2.5   Differences between husbands and wives in financial deprivation

$N = 1235$

Allocative systems	Differences between spouses in financial deprivation (mean .33)
Female whole wage	.52
Female managed pool	.55
Joint pool	.07
Male managed pool	.11
Male whole wage	.15
Housekeeping allowance	.44

Sig < .01

Source: Vogler and Pahl, 1994.

Note: higher positive score = greater deprivation for wives.

equal amounts were coded as 'female more PSM'; disagreement over whether the man had more or whether personal spending money was equally shared were coded as 'male more PSM'.

As Table 2.6 shows, inequalities in access to personal spending money varied markedly with the type of allocative system used in the household. Couples using the joint and male pools were characterized by the highest level of equality: 67 per cent of joint and 70 per cent of male pool couples agreed they had the same amount of personal spending money, compared with 61 per cent of those using the female pool, 55 per cent of those using the male whole wage, 50 per cent of those using the female whole wage and 47 per cent of those using the housekeeping allowance systems, where husbands clearly had greater access to personal spending money than wives. These differences were remarkably persistent within income groups and within classes. Inequalities between spouses in financial deprivation and personal spending money thus tended to coexist.

The housekeeping allowance system and the two female-managed systems were clearly associated with the largest inequalities between husbands and wives, both in terms of financial deprivation and in access to personal spending money. The joint, and to a lesser extent, the male-managed pools, on the other hand, were associated with greater equality, both in terms of financial deprivation and in access to personal spending money.

Table 2.6   Household allocative systems and differences between spouses in personal spending money (PSM)

	Female whole wage %	Female managed pool %	Joint pool %	Male managed pool %	Male whole wage %	House-keeping allowance %
Male more PSM	34	24	18	20	26	42
Equal PSM	50	61	67	70	55	47
Female more PSM	15	15	15	11	20	13

N = 1235

Sig. < 0.0000

Source: Vogler and Pahl, 1994.

Similar results have been found in other studies (see, for example, Wilson, 1987; Pahl, 1989). A recent study carried out in New Zealand concluded that, 'overall men were more likely to command large areas of the collective income for their personal spending and to spend on major items without consultation. The strongest and most persuasive form of control of spending we recorded among couples in the study was the practice of self control by women' (Fleming and Easting, 1994, pp. 54 and 68). The parallel study carried out among Maori couples reported that there was a tendency for men to have more access to personal spending money than women, and for women to put extra money into general standard of living rather than into individual pursuits (Taiapa, 1994, p. 31).

IV   Spending on the Family

There is a growing body of evidence to suggest that women are more family-focused in their spending than men. My earlier study showed that an increase in the woman's earnings had more impact on the amount spent on food and household living expenses than a similar increase in the husband's earnings. Despite husbands defining the wife's earnings as being for her own, individual use, in reality wives typically chose to spend their income on the family. A pound which entered the house through a woman's pay packet was more likely to be spent on the children than a pound which came in through the husband's pay packet (Pahl, 1989). My current research is showing that women are responsible for over 80 per cent of all expenditure on food and on goods and services for children. Men tend to be responsible for most of the spending on alcohol, motor vehicles, repairs to the house, meals bought away from home and gambling. When women are in full time employment the household not only spends more overall, but it tends to spend more on the sorts of goods which women buy (Pahl and Opit, 1997).

Recent evidence suggests that this is a worldwide pattern. For example, a review of research on female headed and female maintained families concluded:

> Several careful empirical studies of the distribution of income and expenditure within the household provide direct evidence for the contrasting expenditure responsibilities of men and women and support the hypothesis that women in a variety of household types are more child oriented in their spending (Bruce and Lloyd, 1992: see also Blumberg, 1991; Gonzalez de la Rocha, 1994).

A report from the World Bank argued that the growing body of evidence on this topic has important implications for the health and welfare of children, and gave examples from a number of different countries:

> The distribution of income within households also affects health. Increasing women's access to income can be especially beneficial for the health of children. In Brazil income in the hands of the mother has a bigger effect on family health than income controlled by the father. In Jamaica households headed by women eat more nutritious food than those headed by men. In Guatemala it takes fifteen times more spending to achieve a given improvement in child nutrition when income is earned by the father than when it is earned by the mother (World Bank, 1993, p. 41).

These findings have significant implications for policies for families. In particular, they underline the importance of policies which increase women's income. This income may derive from employment, in which case appropriate policies would focus on equal opportunities policies for recruitment and selection, provision for the care of children and other dependants, parental leave, more flexible hours of work and so on. When families depend on income maintenance schemes, in general the money is likely to be used more efficiently if it enters the household through the hands of women rather than men. Aid agencies working to enhance the living standard of children in developing countries should not assume that income generation schemes directed at men will necessarily benefit families. This is especially so in those parts of the world, such as Africa, where there is a tradition of 'separate purses' for husband and wife. Depending on the circumstances, the living standards of children may be enhanced, either by protecting the subsistence farming carried out by their mothers, or by developing income generation schemes aimed at women.

Conclusion

The research presented here suggests that treating 'the family' as a unit can be problematic. 'Families' come in a variety of different forms and they manage their money in a variety of different ways. Different systems of money management reflect broader social structural inequalities and can lead to inequalities within the family. There can be conflicts between the financial priorities of individuals within a family, and in those conflicts the interests of the more powerful tend to dominate.

There is a discrepancy between theory and practice in the control and allocation of money within the family. In theory the man is seen as the breadwinner, while any money a woman earns tends to be seen, especially by men, as external to the family budget, hers to spend on herself. In practice things are more complicated. In absolute terms, men may contribute more to the family, since in general men earn more than women. However, in relative terms women contribute more because they are more family-focused than men in their spending: they are more willing to make sacrifices when money is short, they claim less for their own personal spending, and they devote a higher proportion of their earnings to spending on the family and the children. If there is an association between gender and altruism, as Becker implied (1981), the data presented here suggest that, in the context of the distribution of money within the household, the altruist is more likely to be female than male.

These results also pose questions for those who are concerned with family policy. Professor Donati said:

> In patriarchal society the family was recognised and supported with specific benefits to the extent to which the family head accepted the delegation of functions from the state for the social control of women and children. The new family citizenship, on the contrary, consists of access to certain rights, which are positive and relational rights granted to the family nucleus as such, in addition to and without reducing individual rights (Donati, 1997, p. 18).

But who will be entitled to claim these new rights to which the family is to be entitled? Dependent children cannot claim for themselves. So who will be identified as 'the family nucleus'? As we have seen, the family is a site of power inequalities which reflect, not just gender and generation, but also employment and income differentials: even if the family were entitled to receive welfare benefits as a unit, in many families there would not be consensus about how the resources should be used.

Professor Donati does not see the traditional patriarchal 'family head' as the appropriate person to represent the family. The results presented here suggest that in general women are more reliable than men in directing scarce resources towards the family group, as opposed to themselves as individuals. Perhaps implementation of 'the new family citizenship' will involve giving women the right to claim financial benefits on behalf of the family nucleus?

References

Anderson, M., Bechofer, F. and Gershuny, J. (1994), *The Social and Political Economy of the Household*, Oxford: Oxford University Press.

Becker, G. (1981), *A Treatise on the Family*, Cambridge, Mass · Harvard University Press.

Bird, C. (1979), *The Two-Paycheck Marriage*, New York: Pocket Books.

Blood, R. and Wolfe, D. (1960), *Husbands and Wives*, New York: Free Press.

Blumberg, R.L. (1991), *Gender, Family and Economy*, London: Sage Publications.

Bradshaw, J., Ditch, J., Holmes, H. and Whiteford, P. (1993), *Support for Children: a Comparison of Arrangements in Fifteen Countries*, London: HMSO.

Brannen, J. and Wilson, C. (1987), *Give and Take in Families: Studies in Resource Distribution*, London: Allen and Unwin.

Bruce, J. and Lloyd, C. (1992), *Finding the Ties that Bind: Beyond Headship and Household*, Working Paper No 41, New York: Population Council.

Burgoyne, C.and Morison,V. (1997), 'Money in Re-marriage: Keeping things simple – and separate', *Sociological Review*, 45, 3, pp. 363–95.

Burgoyne, J. and Clark, D. (1984), *Making a Go of it: a Study of Stepfamilies in Sheffield*, London: Routledge.

Ditch, J., Barnes, H., Bradshaw, J., Commaille, J. and Eardley, T. (1996), *A Synthesis of National Family Policies 1994*, York: University of York.

Donati, P. (1997), *Family Citizenship: Concepts and Strategies for a New Social Policy*, paper presented at the Forum International des Sciences Humaines, Grenada, 8–12 October.

Easting, S and Fleming, R. (1994), *Finances, Money and Policy*, New Zealand: Social Policy Research Centre, Massey University.

Edwards, M. (1981), 'Financial Arrangements made by Husbands and Wives: Findings of a survey', *Australian and New Zealand Journal of Sociology*.

Fleming, R. and Easting, S. (1994), *Couples, Households and Money*, New Zealand: Social Policy Research Centre, Massey University.

Gonzalez de la Rocha, M. (1994), *Fighting for the Family: Resource Management Among Households in Mexico*, paper presented at the Convegno Internazionale Mutamenti della Famiglia nei Paesi Occidentiali, Bologna, 6–8 October.

Gray, A. (1979), 'The Working Class Family as an Economic Unit', in C. Harris (ed.), *The Sociology of the Family*, Sociological Review Monograph, 28, University of Keele.

Hanatrais, L. and Letablier, M. (1996), *Families and Family Policies in Europe*, London: Longman.

Laslett, P. (1977), *Family Life and Illicit Love in Earlier Generations*, Cambridge: Cambridge University Press.

Morris, L. and Ruane, S. (1986), *Household Finance Management and Labour Market Behaviour*, Aldershot: Avebury.

Office of National Statistics (1997), *Social Trends 27*, London: HMSO.

Pahl, J. (1989), *Money and Marriage*, London: Macmillan.

Pahl, J. and Opit, L. (1997), *Patterns of Spending within Households*, paper presented at the Royal Statistical Society, London, April.

Parry, J. and Bloch, M. (1989), *Money and the Morality of Exchange*, Cambridge: Cambridge University Press.

Rogers, B.L. and Schlossman, N.P. (1990), *Intra-household Resource Allocation: Issues and Methods for Development, Policy and Planning*, Tokyo: United Nations University Press.

Taiapa, J. (1994), *Ta Te Whanam Ohanga: the Economics of the Whanau*, New Zealand: Department of Maori Studies, Massey University.

Vogler, C. and Pahl, J. (1993), 'Money, Power and Inequality within Marriage', *Sociological Review*, 42, 2, pp 263–88.

Vogler, C. and Pahl, J. (1994), 'Social and Economic Change and the Organisation of Money in Marriage', *Work, Employment and Society*, 7, 1, pp. 71–95.

Wilson, G. (1987), *Money in the Family*, Aldershot: Avebury.

World Bank (1993), *World Development Report: Investing in Health*, Oxford: Oxford University Press.

3 Recent Trends and New Prospects for a European Family Policy

WILFRIED DUMON

A preliminary remark refers to the title, the style in which the three terms family, policy and Europe are not well defined. As to family, the notion by itself, both on structural and cultural level, has been the core centre of the sociopolitical debate. On the structural level one can identify growing diversity of family types with single parenting, cohabitation and more important even, the so-called reconstituted or stepfamilies. These developments do not refer only to emergency of new types, but to growing numbers and more particularly adaptation of these forms over the social stratification. As a result they become accepted and the stigmatization associated with some forms is disappearing and regarded as unjustified, even qualified as intolerant and discriminative. The latter element, norms, values, in sociological terms, the cultural element is as important as the mere morphological element, which is reflected in social action and in social policy, with as solution on the semantic level, in which the term 'family' is gradually replaced by a plural form of 'families'. Yet, all these forms have one characteristic in common, they all can be defined as 'person supporting groups' (Dumon). In this respect K. Lüscher has coined the term 'pluralities of the family' rather than plurality of families.

As to Europe, the entry of additional member states into the European Union makes for expansion and thus growing complexity. The phenomena of changing families and changing family policies do not coincide with the boarders of the European Union, they overlap and they are vaster and wider, they tend to be more universal. Yet, the diversity within Europe, the intra-European diversity, can be accentuated and even the regional differences (intraregional perspective) within a given European Union member state can be highlighted. Two differentiated perspectives can be taken.

A first one is to highlight differentiation and to characterize Europe as a patchwork in which differences in demographic and family issues can be identified between North and South, for instance the Scandinavian versus the Mediterranean countries, and between East and West, for instance, the actual member states versus applicant states of Eastern Europe. This represents rather a static view. An alternative approach, a more dynamic view, attempts to identify convergencies and divergencies in the middle and long run. If one takes time into perspective, the more dynamic approach, one tends to observe, as far as demographic and family changes are concerned, more similarity.

It is not unlikely that the shaping of Europe will be affected by similar developments in the domain of demography; family and technological changes, which will call for social and political responses in all member states, some of which might be addressed adequately on the local or regional level, others on the national level, and still others on the supra-national, i.e. European, level.

As to policies also major changes in policy formation, in the process of policy-making as in the process of policy exertion, can be observed. As far as family policies are concerned, some elements will be mentioned, as far as necessary, in the course of this address. A distinction can be made between policy as a product and policy as a process.

I will structure this short chapter in three sections:

- changes in demography and their effects on family;

- changes in family structure and their effects on family policies;

- changes in relationship between family and society (including technological changes).

I   Demography

By now, we all are well aware and well informed on demographic changes in Europe due to many efforts of member states thanks to international efforts such as the European Population Conference (Geneva, 23–26 March 1993) and lately the annual demographic by the European Commission. Therefore I will not repeat any of those well documented developments, but try to draw some conclusions which might bear policy relevance.

The first refers to the so-called fear of population decline, i.e. the numbers of population. The second refers to the structure of population: on the one hand, dejuvenation and ageing as major characteristics, the ethnic pluriformity due to migration on the other hand (which will not be treated here).

Fear of Population Decline

Gauthier has documented that some European countries have, even before the First Word War, developed family policies, based on the fear of population decline. This movement has been accentuated after the first world war (in concerning parts of Europe) due to the devastating effects of this war on population, which has effected some countries even more than others, for instance France and Belgium.

The current situation in Europe, characterized by fertility rates tending to be below replacement level, has been met by two types of strategies among the member states. A first strategy can be identified as an intervening strategy, a second as an adaptive strategy. Examples of the intervening strategy encompass programmes having the third child in focus in some countries.

Lately, however, concern is not so much on this direct numbers of population but on the morphological structure of population. The issue of dejuvenation and ageing becoming part of the sociopolitical debate.

What one can observe is that next to the gender issue (division of society according to gender and the issue of emancipation, nondiscrimination, equality or equity), a new type of stratification, i.e. age stratification, might be occurring: the aged, the children becoming recognized as a social category. Ever since 1985 (Preston) the issue of redistribution of wealth (societal transfers of wealth) between the children versus the aged and the balance between them has been in the core centre of the sociopolitical debate. (Where should society invest: in the children or in the aged?) In demographic terms: the active population versus differentiation within the dependent population. The question reads not only: who is paying for whom?, but is posed in terms of investment: who is investing in children? investing in future or in the past? These are the terms in which the issue is being debated.

(a) Children As to children, on global level, the Convention on the Rights of the Child, adopted in 1989, and more particularly monitoring of children's rights has been developed on a global scale. The emergency of children policies in member states, respectively development of children policies, can be identified. The advocacies of childhood policies originally define children in terms of a separate social category, even in terms of social class (Oldman), and some still do so. In this respect, child policy tends to be crosscutting and even in opposition and conflict with 'family policy'. Lately one can observe some tendency indicating growing convergencies between those policies. There is growing recognition that children are capable to cope with difficult

situations within the family and with stressful events such as divorce etc. If one takes care of maintaining the social and ecological context in which children are living. One can observe some tendency to growing recognition to keep children at home and monitor them in difficult family situations. In quite a few member states debate is on whether children should be placed in homes, or whether all efforts should be made to assist families, in order to enable them to maintain them at home.

This movement is paralleled in some member states by actions of the so-called fourth world (*quatrième monde*) which is voicing its claim on its children. This tendency is not limited to 'families in distress' but is to be situated in a general tendency of empowerment of families, giving them representation rights and even management duties in kindergartens, schools and other institutions such as child hospitals – families as representatives of children.

(b) The aged As to the aged and ageing as a social phenomenon one can identify similar tendencies in policy developments. A first tendency can be characterized 'aged as a social category', a second one is more family oriented, under the style of 'solidarity among generations'. Although, as Lüscher has pointed out, the notion 'solidarity' can be characterized as ambivalent, yet in policy terms it has been institutionalized, even to the effect that in one of the member states (France) at a certain point in time, a Cabinet Minister has been appointed under the title of 'Solidarity between the generations'.

I will not address any of the ageing policies but limit myself to three developments relating to family and ageing, bearing policy implications.

The first, indeed, relates to family solidarity. The concern for the ageing population coincides with the so-called crisis of the Welfare State. This development in some countries has been legitimized under the title of: from a Welfare State to a 'caring' society, implying a greater role of the informal sector, with great emphasis on family 'responsibilities'.

In this respect the element of gender has been widely developed (women as care-givers versus men as care-receivers), so has the notion of sandwich family, families which have simultaneous responsibilities for the aged (the emergence of the over 80s and 90s as large groups) and for younger generations, not of children but of young adults (the delay of home-leaving). Although the notion of the 'sandwich family' is not very well defined yet, the problem of caring – capacities of families versus (growing) caring – responsibilities remains.

A related policy issue very much at stake is on the location of societal support, whether this should be addressed to the care-giver or the care-receiver. They define themselves and their work in terms of exploitation (the exploitation of home care workers' labour). In some member states family members group themselves under the style of home carers and claim recognition and governmental support, e.g. in terms of pension rights. In other member states provisions are to the effect that the aged persons are given financial or other support enabling them to hire or pay for help (informal or on the market). (Parallel systems can be identified as far as child care is concerned.)

Turning to the second development, on an individual as well as on a societal level, the prolonged longevity is leading to separation between pensioning and old-age. Due to the scarcity of labour places, one could observe a tendency to retirement at lower ages (in some countries systems were engineered for persons aged 55), although lately some counter-tendencies are emerging (Germany). Yet the vitality and social and physical well-being of persons around the 1960s, means that they can hardly be labelled as 'aged' but rather as 'late adults' (in opposition to young adulthood), in individual terms; a new 'leisure class' in societal terms. This vitality expresses itself, in terms of family, on two levels:

• increasing tendency for renewed family life and family formation at late age, more particularly LAT-relations, which, according to some sociologists (Trost), might become the most expanding form of family formation;

• a second element relates to grand-parenthood in which grandparents not only play active role, in many societies, in informal care for children (it remains to be seen if this might be decreasing in post-modern society), but are requesting new rights in their status as grandparents, such as is expressed by tendencies to have legal rights of access, i.e. visiting rights to their grandchildren in case of divorce of their children.

The third issue relates to a growing number of one-person households, so-called isolation and the recognition that ageing is not an illness, but a condition in which human beings (over 80) require care, such as younger persons (e.g. under 6). The family aspects in this respect are related to material and non-material issues. As to material issues, the whole question of inheritance is here at stake, more particularly as in the domain of social (public) assistance for persons possessing (economic) capital, either in terms of real estate (own home) or in terms of savings. The significance of private transfer of capital regulated formerly by birth, marriage and death, has dramatically decreased.

Yet, the prolonged longevity may result in reversed investments of middle-aged and older-aged persons having to invest in the very old (80–90 years old), due to the fact that the latter tend to need extra care and monitoring.

As to non-material issues, the issue of self-determination and autonomy in terms of entering into parenthood is expanding to a growing tendency for autonomy in terminating life situations under 'unacceptable' life conditions. The latter element is partly due to the growing expansion and developments into health care and technological innovations (which will be referred to later). The issue of family responsibility and family involvement in these developments tends to become an issue with policy relevance.

II   Family

As to family, dramatic developments and changes have taken place in recent decades which call for some changes and adaptations in family policy.

These changes involve the family as a group, intra-family relations (inside the family), as well as the relationship between family and society, external family relations.

A   Intra-family Relations

As to intra-family relations, major changes have occurred in family life-cycle as well as in family organization, i.e. division of power and labour within the family.

In the family life-cycle, as indicated previously, more particularly the beginning of the family life-cycle, i.e. family formation, and the ending of the life-cycle, i.e. family dissolution, changes are most visible and recognized, and by now, rather well understood. The important matter, however, is not so much that these phases have changed (even if they would have changed dramatically), nor that some phases such as the empty-nest phase have been extended considerably (which has occurred), but the important element lies in the fact that many actors no longer follow a linear or curvilinear path, to the effect that a dissociation occurs between the so-called family life-cycle and so-called life course analysis. The semantics here are important: family cycle, life course. 'Course' not 'cycle' refers to the fact that, firstly, the sequence of life events such as cohabitation, childbirth, divorce, etc. is not in a cycle but that the sequence of events is not totally prescribed (one can become mother (or parent) before (in sequence) being spouse or partner or even becoming mother without being spouse or partner). Secondly, the notion of phases reflected in family cycle can be repeated, one can form a new partner relationship (turnover of partners) and form a reconstituted family (remarriage/re-cohabitation). As a result, the notion of 'cycle' is less adequate than the notion of 'life course'. Both elements are to the effect that one can identify a dissociation between parenthood and partnership. Both subsystems, the spousal or partner subsystem on one hand, the parental subsystem on the other, regain some autonomy. If this is reflected in the formation of family, it is also reacted in the dissolution of the family. Moreover it should be noted that in many instances the same actors are involved from one family form into another (the notion of reconstructed families might serve as an example).

The policy implications are relevant to the debate on family versus individual as unit of policy-making on several levels.

- As to the partner subsystem both in civil and social law (law concerning social protection), two strategies can be identified, which are not mutually exclusive; they tend partly to overlap and partly to crosscut each other. A first strategy consists of associating cohabitation with marriage, of granting equal benefits to persons in cohabitation and/or in marriage. A second strategy is to stress individual rights and social protection based on individual status rather than on family status. As to social protection, e.g. the issue of the so-called derived rights is here at stake, an important issue in the current debate on the reform of the social security systems, which is at the core centre of the sociopolitical debate in quite a few member states.

- As to the parental subsystem, currently the debate tends to be focused on two issues. One tends to be male-oriented, the other tends to be female-oriented. The former relates to the continuation of the relationship between father and child after divorce, fathers claiming the rights to protect the father-child relationship. This tendency is paralleled by a societal claim that child support should be established and that child support adequately should be collected. In many member states the collection of child support has been enforced, which has led to some criticism and controversy, due to the fact that transfer is not only from father to child but often from one reconstituted family to another reconstituted family. The issue is that of private versus societal transfers. From a perspective of family policy as a process, the latter development illustrates a broader issue regarding the role of the state in post-modern society. The theory of the withdrawal of the state in social welfare might be a misleading concept. The providing role of the state tends to be partly and fractionally replaced by securing regulation (Wintersberger).

The female-oriented issue relates to lone parenthood and lone motherhood, with the question of whether support should go to the child in special family circumstances or to the person (mother) with special family responsibilities. Labelling the former issue as male, the latter as female, is not entirely adequate (and may even lead to accusations of gender-bias). These issues are in fact not gender-specific by definition, yet in the morphological structure males/men/ex-husbands/fathers are more the target group, in the latter, females/ex-wives/mother tend to be more the target group. Whatever the case, both elements shed some lights on family versus individuals as unit of policy-making. One might suggest that neither of these notions can be put in absolute terms but that it is the person in its relationship to familial rights/obligations, who is the target group of civil and social protection as one form of solution. (The other alternative is to grant civil and social rights to all human beings, including children. Yet, a child, at least an infant, should be represented by an adult, which again leads to a parent, To the effect that the relationship parent-child, however established, calls for social and civil protection.)

Changes in Family Organization

Modes of decision-making For decades now, the changes in family organization have been documented, suggesting a dramatic change from an organization characterized by hierarchy and a command structure, to an organization characterized by decision-making through processes of negotiations: families as a negotiating structure relates to both subsystems, to the spousal or partner subsystem, as well as to the parental and sibling subsystem. As stated, all this has been well documented and is by now fairly well understood. However, policy implications are not yet fully recognized.

One of the consequences, is great emphasis on quality and intolerance of inadequate family functioning, to the effect that domestic violence has become a societal problem, being transferred from a juridico-penal system into the realm of social assistance and welfare.

The negotiation element is also reflected by changing divorce procedures with emphasis on so-called family and divorce mediation. However, from a scholarly point of view, one can argue *pro* and *contra* the adequacy of such procedures. Yet, the mere fact that such procedures get such prominence, in quite a few member states, reflects a change from decision-making by courts towards involving the partners themselves in decision-making by forms of supervised and assisted negotiation among themselves.

Modes of task allocation Task allocation within the family has become a governmental concern on the European level. The whole issue of 'new parenthood' is here at stake, with policy implications regarding care-giving. However, this concern is not limited to the parent-child relationship, but to the partnership relationship. Governments tend to concentrate on the intra-family relationships, for instance by launching public awareness campaigns. This can be seen as an intrusion of governments into family life (paralleled by similar actions on individual behaviour: smoking/sexual relations: safe sex, etc.). Yet, it also can be defined in terms of giving support to the weaker position inside the family (micro level) as a form of backing new cultural norms in society (paralleled by campaigns combating domestic violence) (macro level).

B   External Family Relations

Family policy in itself can be defined as the link between family and society. In this respect (as indicated above) two elements can be distinguished:

- family policy as a product relating to issues addressed, policies engineered to cope with problems or in order to structure society, identifying the actors involved, i.e. identifying policy-makers, gaps targeted; and

- methods engineered in order to obtain the objectives put forward.

Family policy as a product As to the external family relations, family and employment offers a good example of the relationship between family and policy-making.

The old family model on which family policy, more particular in the realm of social protection, was engineered is that of the husband/father in the providing role, and the wife/mother in the caretaking role. This model has been portrait by sociologists (Parsons) in the 1950s in terms of 'instrumental role'/male; 'experimental role'/female; division i.e. of power and task allocation by gender and age. In cultural terms, this model as 'ideal' type has prevailed even after profound changes in the structure have occurred (as indicated above). As a result, currently the one-earner/the one-income family has become a situation of potential social and economic insecurity. The two-earner family, or at least the two-income family has become the model for middle- and working class Europe.

The policy implications are manifest and deal directly with the main features of family policy as it originally was introduced in the 1930s and consolidated in the 1940s, relaying heavily on tax-rebates and on child allowances (in Germany, the system of *Familienlastenausgleich*, in France, *le système des prestations familiales*). It should be noted that there are overflows between the tax-systems and child benefits or child allowances systems, as documented by the work of the European Observatory on National Family Policies. However, the difference between the two systems is that tax allowances can relate to the division of labour between husbands and wives (partners) (even the semantics are important here), as well as to the burden a family has in raising children. Child allowances (of course) only relate to the latter.

The changes occurring in the family system have resulted in changing tax systems. Yet, the relationship can be inversed and many groups, more particularly from the female emancipatory movements, have argued that joint tax systems hinders female occupation, a claim which has been largely substantiated by economists. As a result, in major European member states, such as France and Germany, one can observe, over time, a tendency towards individual taxation. Yet, the issue remains on the political agenda and family and fiscality still is one of the major issues in the sociopolitical debate, both in feminist groups as in family organizations.

Two remarks are relevant here:

- the focus of attention regarding tax rebates has been somewhat more towards division of labour male/female than it has been focusing on children;

- secondly, as far as child allocations are concerned, one can notice a general trend and claim of child benefit as a parental right (in some member states related to the status of the father/mother as worker) to a right of children, not related to the occupation of the parents, but related to the family situation of the child, for instance one-parent family. Yet, the so-called economical crisis or economical restraints has led to an opposite result, to the effect that child allowances, in many member states, tend to be reduced and/or linked to the (family) parental income. The issue of child allowances has become in the 1990s a major element in the debate on restraining social welfare, under the title of adequate redistribution of income, with the debate in many member states, whether benefits should be universal or selective.

The issue of tax reforms and child allowances and its potential importance, reflects our difficulty of coping with the past more than it reflects our ability to structure the future and respond to the current situation and new challenges, as represented by the actual family situation, and the actual work situation. With elements of flexibility, scarcity of jobs (working places), which in turn are the reflection of very profound changes in the economic system, under the title of globalization of economy, changes in mode of production (from manufacturing to service economy) and new technologies, e.g. communication highway. In this respect, for more than a decade, focus has been on the reconciliation between family and work, under the title of balancing, harmonization, etc., as reflected by the recent introduction of the European network 'Families and Work' with emphasis on best practices. Out of the debate, two elements have emerged:

- first, it has been recognized that the reconciliation of family and work can not be restricted to the position of women only. Results only are acceptable if men in their capacity as husbands and fathers are involved. Recently this relatively old, ideological or cultural stand, has gained support from research evidence, suggesting that mere measures facilitating the combination of family and work do not automatically result in more gender equity. Indeed, to some extent, the reverse can occur cementing a skewed redistribution;

- secondly, the issue of balancing family and work cannot be dealt with in a restrictive way. As has been recognized by seminars (some organized by the European Commission), the relationship is not bipolar but at least tri-polar: family, work and citizenship. Indeed, a person (male/female) cannot be, whatever status, limited to her/his role as a worker or family member, but plays a role in society in terms of citizen and consumer/producer of social goods.

The reconciliation of family and work only represents part of a more comprehensive and fundamental element, related to the division between paid and unpaid work. The question of 'what is work?' is reflected in expressions such as 'the exploitation of home care workers'. As mentioned above, this issue relates to the problem of task allocation (male/female) but goes far beyond it and relates to questions of 'minimum income for all' (social protection) or 'basic income for all' as one of the options being debated. But it also involves the element of the amalgamation of work and education (permanent education) and the redistribution of work over the life-cycle. The latter issues call for attention to the family dimensions involved, more particularly in the societal context of the demographical situation and more particularly to issues such as childbirth in periods later in life (average age: 27 in some member states) which call for measures such as maternity leave (or the issue of having children) in the stage of mid-career, as one example of an issue to be addressed.

New technologies and advancements of science have greatly influenced society in its structure and organization (relationships).

- For decades now, new technological developments in medicine allowed couples/individuals to take almost complete control on their fertility, in negative terms, to avoid unwanted pregnancies. The debate on pregnancy interruption or abortion can be defined as an extension of the unacceptance of unwanted pregnancy. For more than two decades now, positively, gradually steps have been made to the effect that couples (heterogeneous or homogeneous) or persons (female) can receive medical assisted fertility regulations. It is a paradox that the latter developments have an impact that, from a demographic perspective, is almost negligible and certainly will not cause a new demographic solution (positively or negatively) to the replacement issue. Yet, symbolically the impact is enormous. From a sociological point, it puts the notion of fatherhood into question, with a distinction between biological and social fatherhood. Some methods put also the notion of motherhood into question, such as surrogate motherhood. It is noteworthy to remark that the latter element has lost some of its potential in the socio-public debate, whereas the medical assisted and medical controlled methods are gaining attention. Society has reacted to these developments by the establishment of so-called bio-ethical commissions in order to control the application of the techniques. From a sociological point of view, this means that the social control of entry into society, which was in the hands of families (and controlled by the institution of marriage) (illegitimacy as a social stigma), gradually is being replaced by notions such as responsible parenthood, controlled by individuals and medical assisted fertility controlled by the medical profession, which in turn is controlled by governmental approved commission. In the latter, usually the medical profession, the legal profession and ethical expertise is represented. Family organizations or women organizations usually are absent. From a certain feminist perspective, lately some critique to these methods has been voiced, blaming the 'heavily medical approach to the problem and the neglect of the socio-psychological elements' involved.

Fractionally women are portrayed as victims rather than persons being served. Yet, this criticism is to be situated on the level of opinion-making and the sociopolitical debate. On the level of practice, although statistical evidence is not abundant, this type of fertility regulation seems to be expanded rather than to be curtailed. On the cultural level, the bio-social and more particularly the ethical dimensions tend not to be loosening importance, but to be widened and expanded to other domains, from the beginning of life to the termination of life (as mentioned above).

- Ever since the 1950s overwhelming research attention has been devoted to the relationship of family and new means of mass-communication. The influence of television on family life, particularly on children, has received a lot of attention. Society has reacted by formulating some rules of conduct for programme makers or broadcast corporations, such as timing of commercials in respect to children's programmes, avoiding explicit sex on times children are likely to watch TV, etc.

Less attention has been devoted, to the influence of computers, more particularly PCs, which have been introduced widely in the households since the 1980s. (Moreover, television and computers tend to be combined into one machine.) Although the latter developments tend to entail more dramatic changes, or at least visible changes, and call for political action to the effect that in many member states certain provisions already have been made.

Most attention has been devoted to the issue of telework and home-based business. Telework influences families in a dramatic way to the effect that:

- separation between home/family and work: typically a product of the industrial bureaucratic society, tends to be replaced by amalgamation of work and family, typical of a former agrarian pre-industrial society;

- the gender issue, more particularly the issue of division of paid and unpaid labour/the division of formal and informal labour between partners tend to re-emerge as part of the discussion, as is the issue of career-making versus securing income;

- the issue of family-time versus working-time is at stake;

- the new technological developments certainly relate to the gender issue, as indicated above, but also to the age issue, not only to generational differentiation (older generations tending to become new types of illiterates) but also intra-family in youngsters, especially young adults, tending to be more knowledgeable than parents, as has been the case for a long time with other cultural trends such as music styles, pop culture and other modern forms of mass media related products.

This might lead to new forms of age and gender stratification, but more important contribute to a new balance to be reached between the tripolar family, work and leisure time (citizenship).

Family policy as a process The relationship family-labour not only relates to new issues in family policy as a product, but also to new issues in family policy as a process. Three elements are at stake here:

- new actors;

- the question of dual society;

- family impact and family monitoring.

Family policy no longer belongs to the exclusive realm and authority of governmental power (legislative, executive, juridical) but, as (implicitly) illustrated above, belongs partly to the negotiations between the so-called social partners (trade unions, employers). The recent provision relating to parental leave results from an agreement between employers and employees 31 January 1996). It is noteworthy to remark that family organizations, also on the European level, have expressed their concern not to be involved in this decision-making process. The situation described above reflects a far wider element i.e. that family policy is to be situated in a totally new context, with not one major player, i.e. governments. But a situation in which three major elements are competing for power and are interwoven in the process of decision-making and policy-making, i.e. government, the market and the social sector. These three have being referred to under the style of 'welfare mix'. However, the three parties are unequally developed, the market being better equipped than the third sector. Under the title of market one can situate an emerging and expanding corporate family policy, in which policies go way beyond reconciliation of family and work, but involve family dimensions in selection, promotion and career orientation of employees (as suggested by an expanded field of research results). As far as the third sector is concerned, family organizations tend to be the weaker partner, whereas governments tend to occupy some of the domain formally reserved to the social partners.

As has been demonstrated for some years now, family policy in its origin was geared at the able-bodied blue-collar worker, and not a device for the poor. In this respect, it has been argued that family policy was a major tool preventing poverty, rather than combating it. The current developments with the emergence and expansion of corporate family policy is by definition geared at the able bodied worker, more particularly on the level of female/male middle management. The unemployed, the fourth world, the persons grouped under the title of 'social exclusion', and the persons involved in professions lagging behind in social protection, by definition lag behind.

In combination with a social context in which governments are, for good reasons, trying to balance the (public) budget, resulting in selective measures in social protection, more particularly in the family sector (child allowances, as an example), two unintended situations might appear:

- corporate family policy geared at the able bodied prosperous part of population;

- governmental family policy tending to be part of a welfare system (social assistance). These two elements would then contribute to the development of a so- called dual society. Although there is no research evidence suggesting that we are evolving towards such situation. Yet, it might suggest that;

- we are facing new forms of social stratification; and consequently

- perhaps more to the point, that we need a thorough and overall evaluation of the family situation and monitoring of policies, i.e. family impact.

The new developments are calling for new types of family policy. Two elements are here at stake. A first one concerns family monitoring, a second concerns families as actors and re- actors in formulating and evaluating family policy. As to the former, the dramatic events in Belgium regarding the so-called 'Dutroux' case, the great societal debate on child sexual abuse can be identified as a manifestation of 'parent empowerment'. Indeed, not the authorities (government, church) nor the third sector were involved, on the contrary they were rejected as untrustworthy entities. They were the parents themselves who constituted the so-called 'white movement'. As to the latter:

- First, the old American notion of the late 1960s and early 1970s of family impact could be given a new and critical reappraisal. It should be noted however that, in order to assess family impact, one needs adequate social statistics (role of Eurostat) and adequate methodology of measurements of family impact. Yet, we are beyond the modernistic approach characterized by naive trust in such indicators. Although recognizing their importance and vital function, the post-modern society recognizes that policy evaluation cannot be reduced to mere scholarly or scientific operation. It is increasingly being understood that all actors should be involved: policy-makers, scholars, third sector, taking part in a permanent assessment process.

- Secondly, and even more important, families tend to be recognized as partners in policy-decisions. The latter element has been referred to as empowerment of families. The new technologies, especially the new means of communication which tend to be home-based, could serve as elements in which families are not only seen as consumers of material products and goods, but also as consumers of non-material goods. Moreover, the new developments lead to types of interactive communication, to the effect that families will not only be objects of policy-making, but will become active actors, which, due to the new technology, have direct access to the decision-makers. Consequently one could envisage a stronger individualization and autonomization of society, but not necessarily. It could mean that the role of the third sector, more particularly family organizations, becomes more crucial. The latter might act as a kind of clearing houses and transfer mechanisms, functioning as brokers between the impact that policies have on families on one hand and family issues calling for attention, family needs to be met in the context of the welfare mix, on the other hand.

Conclusions

1 Change has become a feature of our society, therefore, family monitoring on a permanent basis becomes necessary, as it does permanent monitoring of family impact of measures taken by governments, market and third sector (representing families).

2 The growing process of differentiation of our society, which has led to specific policies addressing the issues of gender and age-stratification

(emancipation policy, child policy, youth policy, policy for the aged, policy for the handicapped, policy combating social exclusion) cannot be amalgamated into one large family policy. Yet, the family dimension should be taken into consideration when dealing with all these specific areas. As it should be taken into account in general policies addressing social, economic and cultural issues.

3 Reshaping and adaptation of old-type family policy has been overdue for a long time. The old purpose of prevention of poverty and prevention of social exclusion should be given adequate consideration. However, the former emphasis on mere economic aspects is gradually being supplemented by the recognition of the importance of relational aspects (quality of life). In this respect, the notion of family policy as a specific domain within policy making, is being gradually supplemented by the recognition that, in all types of policy, the family dimension should be adequately addressed.

PART II
ECONOMIC ASPECTS OF THE FAMILY

4   A Social Policy for All Ages? The Declining Fortunes of Young Families

DAVID THOMSON

Introduction

No one can doubt the dramatic scale of recent changes in early family life. During the last quarter century or so marriage has been avoided by growing numbers. Cohabitation has become widespread, as either a precursor to or an alternative for formal marriage, and marriage ages have risen by several years. Parenting has been put back into people's 20s, and even more into their 30s. Few children are born, and choosing not to have children has become increasingly common. Rising portions of all births occur outside of marriage. Marriage breakdown has become frequent, and single parenting is now a common experience. During my classes on the history of West European population and family, I ask my students to consider when, in the past 1,000 years, the most significant or rapid changes have occurred in family life. They weigh the break-up of feudal society, the rise of capitalism, the emergence of the nation state, the population explosion of the nineteenth century, industrialization, urbanization and much more. But they conclude – with a good deal of justification – that the most dramatic changes of all have probably occurred during my lifetime, perhaps even during their own shorter ones.

What underlies these changes is much debated, and still little understood. The rise of consumer society, feminist demands, extreme individualism and many others have been proposed. Here I want to investigate a key issue, which has been given surprisingly little attention – the rapidly shrinking economic fortunes of young adults and their children. The decline in young adult incomes through the last quarter century is something that is often remarked upon, but lightly and in passing. Commentators in the USA note as a matter of course that the earnings of young adults have been falling for 20 or so years.[1] Swedish data points to something similar, and this has drawn a few remarks.[2] Australians note that incomes of the young have fallen behind those of others.[3] But with very few exceptions, the significance and the implications of these insights are then ignored, and in popular discussion are all too often swept aside with an 'of course, young people today are so lucky, they have everything we never had'. This is not true: as the following discussion will show, in the last 25 years the economic fortunes of young adults and their children have fallen a great deal more than even the gloomiest of current figures might suggest.

There are, I suspect, many reasons why this subject remains so unfashionable and underdeveloped. The constant arrival of new products – portable CD players, the Internet, the latest sporting goods – makes it hard for anyone to judge what is significant change. Our faith in progress as an inevitability is still immensely strong, and blinds us to much of what goes on: 'to be born later is to be born luckier' is remains a dominant, unspoken assumption in developed societies. Further, the political implications of acknowledging serious youth decline are too disturbing for many of us to face, and ignoring or denying it all is a comfortable and appealing option for the middle aged and elderly in particular. And the economics profession must accept a good deal of the blame for our ignorance. Its general distaste for the real world and its measurement, in favour of theorizing, has served us badly. So has an arid and esoteric concern with 'poverty' and 'inequality', which has been allowed to dominate what little work does get done on income distribution. Our understanding of who actually has what, at this stage of life or that, in this decade or the last, is disappointingly poor.

I Policies for the Young and the Old

This analysis of historical trends in the incomes of young adults and families forms part of a larger study of the changing fortunes of successive generations during the twentieth century. Alan Tapper's paper for this gathering discusses this work, in which we have each been involved both singly and together, and I will not dwell upon it here. The central argument, very briefly, is that through the last 60 or so years, the priorities of developed societies have undergone a crucial inversion. From the 1930s to the 1960s, the concern was for the young, and the incomes and freedoms of the middle aged and elderly were held down, very deliberately, in favour of investing in youth. But in the last quarter century those priorities have been abandoned, maximal income freedom for older adults has come to the fore, and the young have lost out badly.[4]

That reversal can be seen in many areas of our economic, social and political life. It is most obvious in the 'welfare state', with the closing down or eliminating of family benefits, while payments to the aged have been made more widespread and generous. But those are only a few, and by no means necessarily the most important of the reversals, though they are what claim political attention. Public spending beyond social security shows a similar historical refocus, most obviously perhaps in housing. The post-war states invested heavily in housing, either in public rentals for young families, or in subsidizing private home ownership for new buyers. The percentage of national income going into these activities was often greater than all spending upon the aged – now it is a mere fraction as much, and so great has been the shift that few can now imagine how different things used to be.

Perhaps more important in shifting resources from younger to older citizens has been the 'reform' of taxation. In the 'youth state' of the 1930s to the 1960s, taxation was steered carefully away from young adults and families, and on to the later stages of life, by means of penal taxes on 'unearned incomes', and by spouse and child tax exemptions in particular. Now, in the 'elder state', taxes fall firmly upon early adult and family life, and decreasing fractions are collected from the incomes which predominate in the later half of life – company income, self employment, high earnings, or investment income.[5] New 'user charges' of the last 20 years, for public services once free, have also been placed much more readily upon things used earlier in life – tertiary education is an example – than upon the nursing homes of later years.

Beyond taxing and spending to redistribute in favour of the young went a much wider use of collective power to the same end. Entire financial sectors were regulated heavily, with the prime effect that lenders (persons in later life) had to give their money on very favourable terms to borrowers (persons in earlier life). Tight rent control had a similar consequence. Imports were managed rigorously, to protect jobs, pay packets and career promotions: again, the effect was to limit the freedoms of older consumers, and to advance younger workers. Government investment was managed to secure employment at the expense of lenders' returns, and debt was repaid so as not to fall to those coming later. Workplace policies emphasized security and continuity of earnings. But in the last 25 years these and many other regulatory programmes have been abandoned. The argument for this is that all will benefit in time, but the most immediate beneficiaries have been the middle aged and elderly of the late twentieth century.

II   The Measurement of Personal Income

How extensive has been the resulting shift in resources against the interests of the young? That is my question for the rest of this paper. The analysis offered is experimental, since little has been done in this area. The example I will use is New Zealand, for it offers the researcher a number of distinct advantages. Most unusually, at least within the English-speaking world, it has held regular censuses of individual incomes from the 1920s.[6] Only the published tabulations remain – New Zealand destroys all census papers a few years after each count, and gives independent researchers no access to computerized data about individuals. Even so, the published data permits the reconstruction of a history of personal income for different age and gender groups across the last 70 years: the 1996 results are not yet available.

New Zealand has other advantages as a case study among modern societies. Its history this century, of depression, war, post-war prosperity and more recent stagnation, of baby booms and baby busts and more, is fairly typical for developed nations. So, too, has been the nature and scale of its welfare state, and the managed – now increasingly de-regulated – economy which accompanied it. But the country's smallness also makes for unusual ease of analysis. For example, all taxes and cash benefits, and all education, housing or health services, have been set and managed nationally, with little or no regional variation. The society has, too, been relatively homogeneous, with few variations of wealth or lifestyle. All this means that it is possible to weigh the 'impact' of the state upon individual lives, or to talk of the 'average' person or family as doing this or that, with an accuracy not possible in larger and more complex nations. No one country is 'the developed world' in microcosm, of course, but New Zealand appears broadly typical of the pathways followed in Europe and North America. Despite its insignificant size and remoteness, it offers an important window on to historical processes which have been at work widely through the twentieth century.

Standard studies of the history of personal income downplay age as a variable – indeed, they ignore it altogether. The results are indices such as national income per capita, or average male wage rates. Figure 1 shows the New Zealand versions of these, and it suggests a fairly predictable linear long-run rise in personal purchasing powers. But such tools are too crude to have much use, and are especially unhelpful when we want to understand the income movements faced by a specific group – young adults, at the key decision-making stages of life, when they marry and raise children or choose not to do so.

For one thing, averages across age groups miss the obvious fact that different age groups have different incomes, that these have all varied over time, and that there is no fixed relationship through time between, say, the wages of 20 year old men or 50 year old women or 80 year old pensioners. An average cannot be used as a proxy indicator for the income history of any particular group.

Second, taxation falls unevenly on different groups from one decade to the next. In 1945, for instance, the 'effective income tax take' from a two-child, single-income New Zealand family, and on the average wage for men aged 25 to 34 years, was negative 11 per cent. That is, the two universal cash family benefits received were larger than the income taxes paid, so that final or total net income was 111 per cent of original gross earned income. By the 1980s an identical family would pay an 'effective' income tax of positive 18 per cent – its total net income was just 82 per cent of its gross income, so much had tax rates and exemptions and family benefits changed in relative value. But over the same time the tax rate for middle aged couples barely doubled, and for aged pensioners changed even less. Both 'ageless averages' and considerations of gross income alone are a nonsense in such a world.

Third, averages miss the differing interplay of movements over time in wages, in tax rates, exemptions and credits, and in social security benefits, for more and less affluent persons, even when of the same age. This means that a worthwhile incomes history must watch for differential trends at the higher and lower ends of all income spectrums. And incomes histories must treat distinct ethnic groups separately, so far as is possible. New Zealand's indigenous Maori, for example, now form about one in seven of the population, and have long had lower than average incomes, earlier marriage and larger families (these last have ceased to be true of late). This meant that they were especially exposed, first to the family-favouring policies of the post-war decades, and second to the family-penalizing ones of the last 25 years. Their more-than-usually violent swings in marriage and parenting patterns through recent decades suggest that they have been particularly hit by the economic changes, but sadly, this cannot be investigated here.[7]

III   Residual and Underlying Fortunes

In what follows I focus upon two age groups, 20 to 24 years, and 25 to 34 years, because these are the groupings dictated to us by the surviving data. I have selected four points within each income range for special attention – the

10P or 10th percentile point, at each date being the income of the person who was just 10 per cent of the way up from lowest to highest income for his or her group; the 25P or 25th percentile point, the 50P or median point, and the 75P or 75th percentile point. These give us a means to gauge movements in income among lower, middling and higher-earning young persons.

I also focus attention upon young men, for a number of reasons. For most of the last 70 years – and much longer as well – few young families have had dual incomes, or even one-and-a-bit earnings. Male earnings accounted for 88 per cent of the total personal income enjoyed by all New Zealanders aged 25–34 years in 1951, and still 62 per cent by 1991. Among the married, the male income dominance was and remains substantially greater. Female earnings are of course of growing importance, in part because young women have more jobs and earn more at them, and in part because the incomes of younger males have collapsed. Among those aged 20–24, males now earn just 54 per cent of the total, and females 46 per cent. But the focus upon male incomes is central to our historical study, where the search is for what I shall call 'underlying' economic fortunes, or the deeper forces which in turn may be leading to greater female employment, smaller families and the like.

The procedure, briefly, has been to first calculate for every census the gross incomes of men at the 10P, 25P, 50P and 75P points in the income ranges for men aged 20–24, and 25–34 years. Each man is then assumed to have been single, and his after-tax net income is calculated. These are adjusted to constant dollar values, using the official all-groups Consumer Prices Index (CPI), and trends in real net income are plotted with the purchasing power of 1951 set as the base of 100. Next, each man is assumed not to be single, but instead to have a Standard Family to support, consisting of a spouse without earnings of her own, and two small children. The total net income (TNI) or after-tax-after-social-security cash income of each Standard Family is calculated, and the trends in real purchasing powers traced. Later stages involve similar calculations for other groups, as a way of exploring the relative historical fortunes of young adults and families and others.

There are several reasons for following these modelling procedures. One is that the New Zealand census asks only about individual and pre-tax incomes, and not about household or family income. We cannot follow actual families by this means, but only the model or theoretical families which individuals might form. An annual household sample survey, conducted each year since 1973, provides an alternative tool which does report actual families, and I will refer to it from time to time. But it in turn has a number of drawbacks, its brief time span being the most obvious.

There is, however, a deeper reason for adopting the 'model individual' and 'model family' approach. Household surveys report only what I shall call 'residual' change. They show income changes from year to year for young households, as the people in them made all sorts of changes and adaptations along the way. The incomes they report are thus a composite or 'residual' product, or the net outcome of two quite different types of change over time. One is 'behavioural' change, or the changes in economic fortunes which are brought by new actions or lifestyles among young persons, such as having more women in employment. The other is 'underlying' change, or the changing economic fortunes which society delivers to young adults, regardless of what they may do.

Our interest here is with this underlying change, and our question is 'what would have been the historical trend in the incomes of young men and families, had all been trying to lead similar lives at each moment in time'. We seek, in other words, the path of economic fortune when it is stripped of behavioural adaptations and modifications along the way. For underlying fortunes, I am arguing, are crucial to understanding the plight of young families at the end of the twentieth century, and the need for a new 'citizenship of the family'. For them, income trends look nothing like the comforting averages familiar from such graphs as Figure 4.1.

IV   Real Incomes of Young Men and Families

Figure 4.2 shows movements in after-tax real purchasing power for men aged 20–24 years, if all had been single taxpayers. It shows, perhaps not unexpectedly, that real incomes have proven more volatile at the lower than the upper ends of the earnings range, but also that the historical pattern is fairly consistent across richer and poorer alike. Real incomes reached a nadir in the 1930s – much more so for younger men and women than for older ones – then rose steeply through the 1940s, 1950s and 1960s. Just how steeply is seldom now appreciated, and New Zealand, it might be recalled, had one of the 'mildest' of 1930s' depressions seen anywhere. By the mid-1960s real spending power for single young men was about four times what it had been for similar young men in 1936, or close to double what it had been just 20 years before, at war's end. But since the later 1960s after-tax incomes have fallen, by 20 or 30 per cent for the better-paid of young men, and by 50 per cent for the lower paid. For them, real spending powers by 1990 were back to 1940s levels, and for the higher-paid to 1950s levels. And the indications are that

Figure 4.1   Two indices of long-run movements in real incomes, New Zealand, 1916–91

Sources: real GDP per capita: calculated from population, GDP and Consumer Price Index data in Statistics New Zealand, annual. Nominal real gross adult male wage rates: as reported annually in the *New Zealand Official Yearbooks*. New Zealand has never had an official long-run wage series. The nominal rate, the closest to a wage rate that exists, refers to the minimum rates of wages as set in awards by the Arbitration Court.

since 1991 incomes of young men have fallen more sharply than in the 1970s or 1980s.[8]

This refers to all men aged 20–24 years. The pattern is almost identical if we restrict the analysis solely to a somewhat privileged and shrinking fraction of them – to those who hold full-time employment. Figure 2.3, a repeat of Figure 2.2 but this time for men aged 25–34 years, reinforces the general point: young men have incomes now back at 1940s or 1950s levels. Moreover, I will argue presently that these procedures still underestimate the decline to a serious degree.

With Figures 2.4 and 2.5 our attention shifts to more complex patterns in the underlying economic fortunes of Standard Families. Figure 2.4 records trends in inflation-adjusted total net income, if we assume that all the young men reported in Figure 2.2 had each had a Standard Family to support. At mid century the patterns for Standard Families were fairly similar to those for

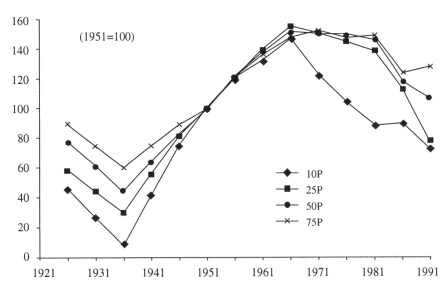

Figure 4.2 Index of real net income for all men aged 20–24 years, if all were taxed as though single, New Zealand, 1926–91

Notes:

1 No censuses were held in 1931 or 1941, and the census due in 1946 was held in 1945.
2 Straight lines have been drawn between 1926 and 1936, and 1936 and 1945, to make the trend lines continuous.

Sources: incomes data is drawn from Department of Statistics, 1926–91, Volumes on Incomes, Wellington. Taxation and social security data is from Department of Statistics, annual.

single men, though the rise in family incomes from the 1930s was even more massive than that for single men. For low-income men with Standard Families at the 10P point in the income range, for instance, total net family income in 1926 or 1945 was only about one quarter of what it would be for a similar low-earning, single income young family in the 1960s: in 1936 it was, according to the figures, about one tenth the 1960s level, though some problems with low income reports from the 1930s must be suspected. From the 1930s to the 1950s the real incomes of young families were doubling every few years, even on these 'minimal' estimates, in part because earnings were improving, in part because substantial tax reliefs were being offered to families, and in part because large universal family benefits were introduced.

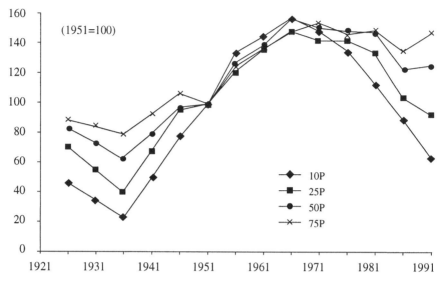

Figure 4.3   Index of real net income for all men aged 25–34 years, if all were taxed as though single, New Zealand, 1926–91

Notes and sources as for Figure 4.2.

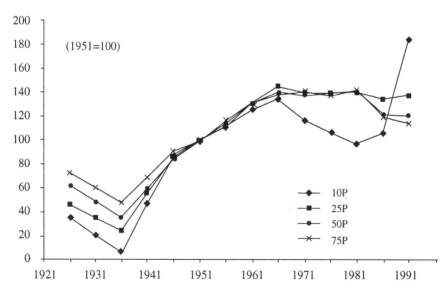

Figure 4.4   Index of real net income for Standard Families of all men aged 20–24 years, New Zealand, 1926–91

Notes and sources as for Figure 4.2.

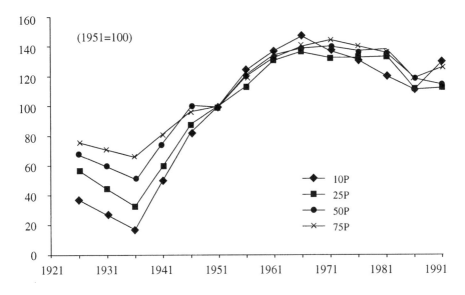

Figure 4.5   Index of real net income for Standard Families of all men aged 25–34 years, New Zealand, 1926–91

Notes and sources as for Figure 4.2.

And from the mid-1960s or soon thereafter, family incomes began to fall, as earnings faltered, tax rates rose steeply, exemptions for non-earning spouses and dependent children were narrowed then eliminated altogether, and as cash family benefits slid in value, then were abolished late in 1991 (after the income census of that year). However, governments have in the last 20 years responded with a variety of new tax credits and special cash supplements for low income families. This slowed but did not halt the retreat, except for the small group of families still being formed by young men with minimal earnings. For the larger block of young families, that is those of men in the age range 25–34 years, total net income by the 1990s was down 10 or 20 per cent below late 1960s or early 1970s levels, and were back to 1950s' purchasing powers. Figure 4.6 shows the parallel calculations, if we assume that men aged 25–34 had been raising four rather than just two children, since for the 1950s and 1960s at least four was closer to the New Zealand norm than was two. Once again, it points to the same historical pattern – the multiplying by several times of real incomes through the 1940s, 1950s and 1960s, and the quiet decline since, back to 1950s spending powers.

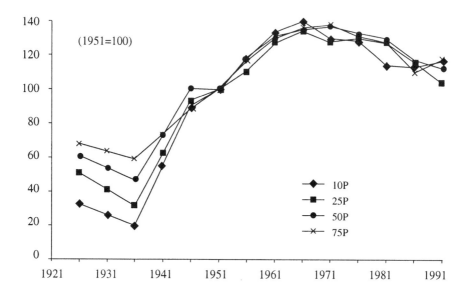

Figure 4.6   Index of real net income for Standard Families of all men aged 25–34 years, if children number four, New Zealand, 1926–91

Notes and sources as for Figure 4.2.

V   Model and Actual Incomes

This begs many more questions. One is to wonder how close these trends for model families might have been to trends for actual families – in other words, how closely might underlying and residual economic trends match, after young adults had adopted all sorts of new behaviours through the last 25 years? The household surveys from 1973, though the published reports on them are brief, suggest that residual incomes for young adults have followed underlying ones through the last 20 years: the key results appear in Figure 4.7. Only average income and expenditure figures are available, for all the households in which the householder was aged under 25 years, 25–29 years, and 30–39 years. Because sample sizes are small, year-by-year figures can be erratic, and I have grouped annual figures for three or four years to smooth these out. Adults and children have been given a weighting as so many fractions of the income or expenditure needs of a standard 'adult equivalent'.

Figure 4.7 makes clear that the actual resources of younger households

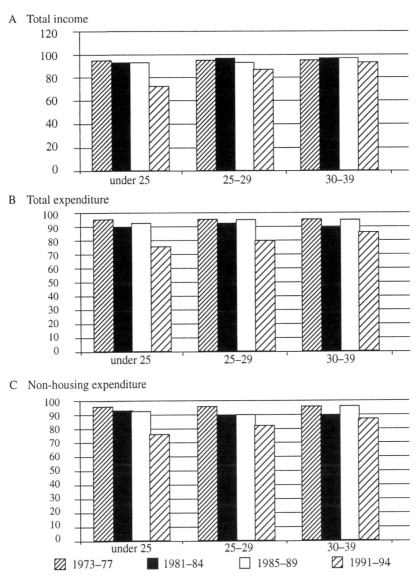

A Total income

B Total expenditure

C Non-housing expenditure

☑ 1973–77   ■ 1981–84   ☐ 1985–89   ☑ 1991–94

**Figure 4.7   Indexes of inflation-adjusted resources per adult-equivalent,
in households of different ages, New Zealand, 1973–94**

Notes:

1   Income is gross: no data is collected in income taxes.
2   Data for 1978–80 and 1990 is not compatible with that for the other years.

Sources: Department of Statistics, annual since 1973.

shrank per person, regardless of which measure of 'resources' we care to use – gross income per adult-equivalent, expenditure per adult-equivalent, or non-housing expenditure per adult-equivalent. In households where the 'head' was aged under 25 years, resources per person fell by about a quarter between the mid 1970s and the early 1990s, and by 10–15 per cent in slightly older households. In other words, behavioural changes – we might call them a fight back against unfavourable underlying economic fortunes – seemed only to slow the decline. By the 1990s the proportion of women in their 20s or 30s, both married and unmarried, who held full-time employment was now double what it had been in the 1960s. The fraction holding part-time employment had increased even more, by a factor of perhaps six. There were now only about half as many children to every 100 adults in their 20s or 30s as there had been in the 1960s. And young adults by the 1990s, in addition to their extra employment, now claimed at least 10 social security benefits per 100 persons, of a type simply not available to young adults in the 1970s and earlier. The most prominent of the new benefits was the single parent allowance, but sickness, invalidity and unemployment benefits were also paid in numbers and values without precedent in earlier decades. Even so, the collective real incomes of younger persons were down 20 or so per cent on those of the earlier 1970s, so powerful were the adverse underlying currents against them.

VI   Income Estimates Much Too Conservative

All of the above, I have hinted, must be seen as minimal or conservative estimates of the underlying post-war rise and post-1970 decline in resources for young men and families. There are many reasons for thinking that the true loss of position has been rather greater than our figures suggest.

A first reason concerns income taxes. Only personal, spouse and child exemptions and rebates have been considered. But until the 1970s young New Zealanders had lowered their actual tax payments, quite legitimately, through a wide range of further claims and allowances. These included tax relief for work expenses and equipment, overtime work, shift work, contributions to superannuation schemes and life insurance, support for dependent relatives, membership dues for trade unions or professional associations, and charitable donations. But only the last on this list is now claimable, since most tax exemptions were pruned away during the 1980s. This means that actual tax payments in the late 1980s and 1990s would have been close to those assumed in our model. But earlier actual taxes would have been smaller than what we have assumed here, and so after-tax incomes higher, by a few percentage points on average. The rise and fall of post-war incomes was in consequence a little steeper than indicated by Figures 4.2 to 4.6.

A second, wider concern is the changing 'context' in which youthful incomes are received. There are various aspects to this, and we can raise only a few. One involves certainty, predictability, and 'future prospects'. Most would agree, I venture, that $100 a week has one use and worth, if it arrives regularly, without doubt, and with prospects of being followed in future by even greater earnings and secure state retirement pensions. Such, broadly, were the circumstances in which younger adults received their weekly incomes in the first post-war decades. But we would also agree that the same $100 a week has quite another and lesser worth if received, as so often by younger adults today, amid doubts as to whether it will come again next week, or without expectations of leading to rising earnings in the years ahead, or with dimming likelihood of a secure state pension in old age. The causes of this new uncertainty are many – declining wage protection, short-term contracting, free trade, globalization of economic activity, worries about population ageing and many more. The effects are to lessen further the shrinking spending powers and freedoms of younger adults relative to their predecessors, but again in ways not captured in Figures 4.2 to 4.6.

One simple means to put some figures to just one, immediate facet of these declining future prospects is to look at what we might call income progression. Between 1945 and 1956, for instance, the real median net income for men aged 20–24, assuming all were single, rose by 50 per cent. But actual rather than model young men of course aged in this period – those who had been 20–24 years old in 1945 were in the 25–34 years group by 1956. They did not in reality remain at age 20–24 and so experience 'only' a rise in income of 50 per cent. The real median net income for men aged 25–34 in 1956, assuming all were single, was 92 per cent greater than for men aged 20–24 in 1945. In other words, young men in any period face a 'future prospect' of two types of income rise. One is the general improvement that may take place in incomes for men in their 20s or 30s. The second comes from moving from one's 20s to one's 30s, and so to the higher earnings that normally go with being further on in a career. The net effect for the young men of 1945 was that they had a 'future prospect' of a 92 per cent lift in real spending powers across the next 10 years. Those of below-median earnings had even better prospects – a 168 per cent rise for low-income earners at the 10P point for instance.

But their successors, in making the same ageing transition from their early 20s to their early 30s, gained very much less. Those on median earnings who made this transition from 1961–71 had a 37 per cent rise in real spending power, from 1971–81 a 23 per cent rise, and 1981–91 just a 7 per cent increase. Even more dramatic falls in future prospects are evident, if we move our models yet closer to real life. In the immediate post-war decades, it was not normal for men to remain single through their 20s and 30s, but to form families rather like the Standard Family. Figure 4.8 reports income progression, as single young men became men with Standard Families a decade later. The comparison is between real net income for single men aged 20–24, and the real total net income of the Standard Families of men aged 25–34 10 years later.

Figure 4.8 shows that total net income of a Standard Family in 1936 was no better than had been the income of a single young man in 1926. But it also shows that from 1936 to 1945 the same ageing progression brought an enormous surge in real incomes – a 200 per cent increase for men at median earnings, and increases of 600 and more per cent for low earners. The 1950s and 1960s, too, brought substantial though more modest increases, in the 30 to 100 per cent range. In the last 20 years such progressions have ceased. A

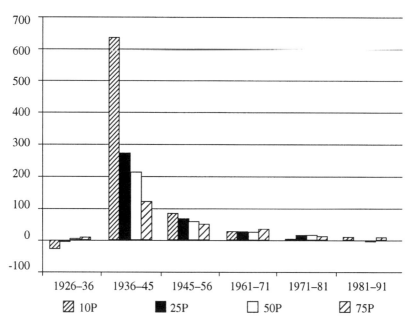

Figure 4.8   Percentage income rise as single young men aged 20–24 years became married men with Standard Families 10 years later, New Zealand, 1926–91

Note: sources and procedures explained in text.

young couple contemplating forming a Standard Family in the 1980s, we might say, would have to anticipate that in 10 years time the four of them (two adults and two children) would be living on a real net income that was merely equivalent to that which the young man alone already had to himself. This is just one illustration of the collapse in 'future prospects', which are part of the economic context in which young adults must make their decisions about family. Figures 4.2 to 4.6 capture nothing of this.

Then there is the crucial part of the 'context' of personal incomes that is formed by public services. In the immediate post-war decades, free or heavily subsidized public services for young families were very considerable, and expanding. These meant, of course, that young adults were able to spend their rising personal incomes on other things. In New Zealand, for example, there was public rental housing for young families of low or middling income, or interest-free grants and low-interest loans for young buyers. There was free education at the primary and secondary levels: tertiary students paid minor fees, and received substantial living allowances, regardless of personal or parental income. Public health services were free, as was dental treatment for the young: visits to doctors were not free, but almost so for children.

This had not been the case in the 1930s and earlier, and has not been the case in the 1980s or 1990s either. In the last 20 years, public housing rentals have been lifted to 'market rates', and state assistance to young house buyers has ceased. Health charges have been introduced for younger (but not older) adults and children, dental treatment is not free, and tertiary education has become a substantial personal expense. In short, the rapidly rising personal incomes of the 1940s to the 1960s had been boosted yet further by generous public expenditures upon families. The collapsing personal incomes of the young in the last quarter century come in addition to falling public support for them. Once again, the rise and fall of our graphs of income should in reality be considerably steeper than they have yet been drawn.

Relativities form one other crucial 'context' for youthful incomes, and here too the young have lost out compared to others. Different groups have followed different income paths, and where young men and families once had incomes which compared well with those of others in their society, they now do not. This loss of place has important emotional and psychological consequences for young adults and the families they might or might not form. But it also affects them economically, though again in ways not measured by or even hinted at in our figures thus far. An income which now puts a person low in the pecking order of incomes, regardless of whether its real purchasing power has risen or fallen, leaves that person increasingly disadvantaged in commanding a share of the goods and services of the society. Relative place matters.

Several comparisons will illustrate this loss of place by young men and families. One is with those who depend upon state benefits for their living, and here the changes are particularly striking. Figure 4.9 illustrates the contrasting income histories for young men and families, and for aged pensioners and for widows, this last group being broadly representative of non-aged state beneficiaries as a whole. The after-tax value of a basic age pension for a single person in the 1920s was about half of the 1950s one, and the pension actually rose in purchasing power during the Depression as prices fell. It rose further through the 1940s, 1950s and 1960s, though more quietly than did incomes of young men and families. But in the 1970s it surged to a new level of spending power, even as incomes of young men and families were moving in the opposite direction. An elderly person today, with no income other that the state pension, has about 60 per cent more net purchasing power than had a similar elderly person in 1951 – young men and families have returned to the spending powers of about 1951.

The long-term rise in state support for a widow with two small children has been even greater, though the timing of the increases has been different. This reflects greater ambivalence towards the deserts of sole parents, especially in the interwar years and in the last decade or so. Even so, the consequence is an income rise quite unlike that for young men or two-parent families. A widow with two children now receives benefits with about four times the real spending power of half a century ago, and almost half as much again as in 1950.

We should remember, too, that access to these state benefits has also been liberalized greatly over time. At mid century, New Zealand's age pensions were still means-tested, and only about half of the elderly collected them. From the mid 1970s they were made universal, without any tests, and payable from age 60. At mid century the elderly could have little income in addition to a pension: now they can and do have substantial occupational pensions or investment incomes as well. Similarly, an even greater opening up of state benefits to the non-aged has taken place. At mid century widows still had to face a 'moral character' test as well as a means one, and there were no benefits for single, deserted or divorced mothers. Now a Domestic Purposes Benefit (equivalent in value to the Widows Benefit) is payable to all sole parents alike, whether never-married, separated or divorced. The loss of relative position by young men and two-parent families, then, has two components – a loss of relative spending power compared with state beneficiaries, and a

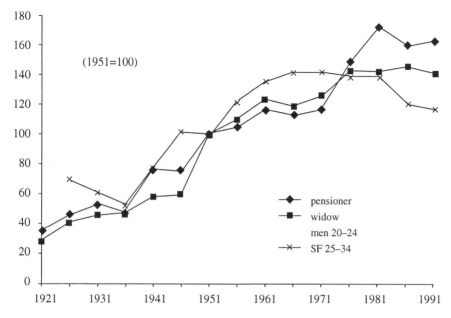

**Figure 4.9   Trends in real net income for young men and families, and
those dependent on state benefits, New Zealand, 1921–91**

Notes:

1   'Pensioner' means net real income for an age pensioner who has no other income.
2   'Widow' means net real family income for a woman with two small children who was in
    receipt of the Widow's Pension.
3   'Men 20–24' means median real net income for all men aged 20–24 years, assuming all
    men had been single.
4   'SF 25–34' means median real total net income, if men aged 25–34 years were assumed
    each to have a Standard Family.

Source: as for Figure 4.2.

loss of relative access to these incomes compared with the growing access of
state beneficiaries. Figures 4.2 to 4.6 miss all of this.

A second relevant comparison is with older workers, and this points to a
rather more modest if still real loss of place over time by young men and
families. Older workers in general have experienced less volatile swings in
earnings over time, as Figure 4.10 illustrates. They faced a more minor loss
of purchasing powers in the Depression of the early 1930s, less of a surge in
the 1940s, a quieter climb in incomes in the 1950s and 1960s, and a modest

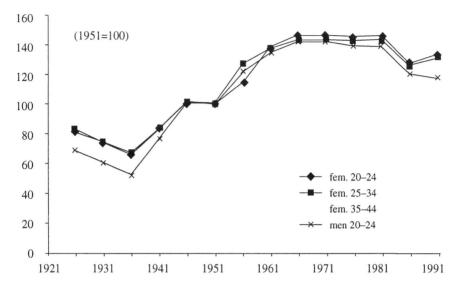

**Figure 4.10 Trends in real net income for younger and older male
workers, New Zealand, 1921–91**

Notes:

1   'Men 35–44' means median real net income for all men aged 35–44 years, assuming all
    men had been single.
2   'Men 45–54' means median real net income for all men aged 45–54 years, assuming all
    men had been single.
3   'Men 20–24' means median real net income for all men aged 20–24 years, assuming all
    men had been single.
4   'SF 25–34' means median real total net income, if men aged 25–34 years were assumed
    each to have a Standard Family.

Source: as for Figure 4.2.

fall in earnings of late. There has for them been no return in the 1980s and
1990s to the real spending powers of the 1940s or 1950s.

Our third comparison to illustrate loss of position is with the earnings of
women, which have had a very different history from those of men, as Figure
4.11 makes clear. Only a minority of New Zealand women in each age group
have held full-time paid employment, though the fraction has been growing
markedly. For them real net earnings have jumped faster than for any other
group, except perhaps the elderly, whose pension-plus-other incomes have
risen in something of the same order. Young men now have real earnings

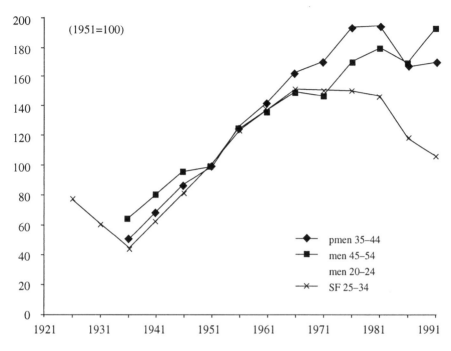

Figure 4.11 Trends in real net income for young men and single women in full-time work, New Zealand, 1921–91

Notes:

1 'Female 20–24' means median real net income for all women aged 20–24 years and in the full-time labour force, assuming all women were single.

2 'Female 25–34' means median real net income for all women aged 25–34 years and in the full-time labour force, assuming all women were single.

3 'Female 35–44' means median real net income for all women aged 35–44 years and in the full-time labour force, assuming all women were single.

4 'Men 20–24' means median real net income for all men aged 20–24 years, assuming all men had been single.

Source: as for Figure 4.2.

comparable to those of young men around 1950: women workers commonly have 70 per cent higher earnings than did their working contemporaries of 40 years ago. In short, the average real income trends suggested in Figure 4.1 are a product of very different histories for different groups, and young men and families have been the clear losers in this. Figures 4.2 to 4.6 pick up only some of this.

There remain a number of further reasons for thinking that other losses are also being missed. We will consider just one more of them – the question of whether or not different age groups buy different things, and whether these separate purchases face variable rates of inflation. We have assumed thus far that they do not, and that the official all-groups CPI reflects accurately the rise in prices confronting young adults and families. But there are good reasons for questioning whether this has been so, and to suspect that inflation for young families has been much faster than we have allowed – and hence that their real purchasing powers have fallen further in the last 25 years than we have yet allowed.

Little research attention has been given anywhere to age-specific inflation rates. Elder lobbyists have insisted, in New Zealand as in a number of countries, that the aged face more fierce cost escalation than do others. In 1994 Statistics New Zealand began a new index of prices faced specifically by the elderly to test this matter, and found the opposite to be true – inflation on things bought primarily by the aged was less than inflation for younger persons. The government was swift to assure the aged that the new report would be ignored, and that the old adjustment of pensions according to the CPI would be retained. Statistics New Zealand did not repeat the exercise, and no more was heard on the subject from elder spokespersons.

But the issue should not be left there, for the CPI likely masks the true rise in the costs faced by younger households to a very considerable degree. For one thing, some cost of living indexes, such as New Zealand's CPI, includes interest charges upon home mortgages. A rise in interest rates (whether nominal or real) means in reality that a portion of households – those younger ones with substantial, recent mortgages – will have confronted all of the new costs: most older households will experience no change in their housing charges. In the calculation of the CPI, however, these new expenses are averaged out as a small general rise in costs for all households – and age pensions are raised automatically in compensation.

Another, related difficulty with such cost of living indexes concerns the handling of new charges. In 1970, for example, university students in New Zealand such as myself paid trifling fees, and received substantial tax-free living allowances from government as an automatic right. Now my students pay about 25 per cent of the total costs of their courses, or around $2,500 a year on average, or the equivalent of about one month of gross average wages, and receive no living allowances at all. Again, the CPI index handles this awkwardly, by assuming that a generalized new charge – for higher education – has emerged and now falls equally upon persons of all ages. In reality a much larger-than-generalized charge actually falls to a particular, youthful minority (and perhaps to their parents). The rising costs of things used by the young, yet again, tend to be underassessed, those of the middle-aged and elderly over-assessed, and the aged are compensated with rising pensions for costs they will never face.

Still more critical questions surround the interacting or compounding consequences of changes in economies and government policies, for again these cumulative effects are largely missed in current cost-of-living procedures. The young do not buy 'goods in general', but spend large portions of their income on a few specific things – children and a home are obvious examples. What, we must then ask, are the compounding effects upon the costs of these particular purchases, which have resulted from such things as changes in young adult earnings, taxes and charges, state benefits to families, prices, rising mortgage interest rates and more. Existing statistical procedures and incomes analyses overlook many of these compounding effects, whose hidden cumulative impacts may well have been massive.

The following paragraphs outline a modelling exercise which illustrates some of these issues. It is designed to test the compounding effects of a range of factors which influence the cost of a first home, New Zealand being a society of private home ownership for the great majority. The data available allows the experiment to run from 1960 only, and the broad approach has been to cost out the most common process by which young adults acquired a first home in the 1960s, then to watch what happened to costs, as successors tried to buy the same houses at the same points in life and by behaving in the same ways. The results, expressed in Figure 4.12, are of the costs of mortgage repayment in the first year of ownership, expressed as a fraction of total net household income.

The first step, determining the prices of homes of a fairly fixed quality and quantity, is relatively easy. Annual Valuation Department publications record the sale prices of what are known as R2 houses, being that substantial body of bungalows built between 1914 and 1929 which in the post-war era have formed an important target for first-time buyers. Even more valuably, the same sources detail the average sale prices of building sections in urban areas, along with the costs of erecting a new 'modal house', that is a fixed, modest-quality, single-storey house of 1,000 square feet, which is constructed and finished to an unchanging standard.[9] The next steps were to calculate total net incomes for Standard Families at the 10P, 25P, 50P and 75P income levels at each of the census years; to determine that portion of the purchase price that could be met by each Standard Family from the interest-free

A   All families buying a new modal house

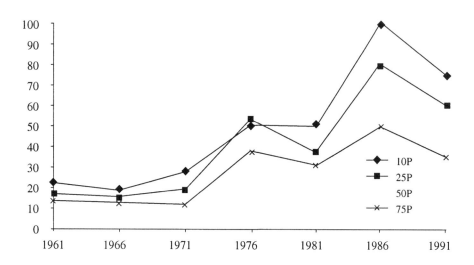

B   All families buying an average price R2 house

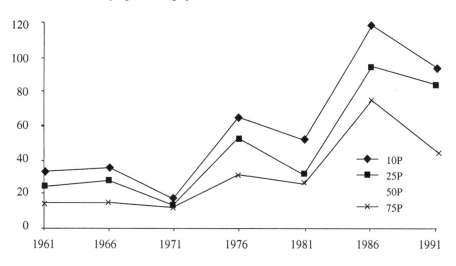

Figure 4.12 Percentage of total net income required to meet mortgage repayments after all Standard Families have bought the same house, New Zealand, 1961–91

Sources: explained in the text.

government grants available to it at that date; to assume that all Standard Families would put into the purchase personal savings equivalent to one year of total net income; and to calculate annual mortgage payments if each Standard Family were to borrow the remainder of the purchase price from the most favourable government or private (non-family) sources open to it.[10]

The striking conclusion from Figure 4.12 is that Standard Families at all income levels have seen the costs of a basic first home rise several times across the last quarter century, relative to their total net incomes. In the 1960s and early 1970s, most first-time buyers were steered by government towards new houses very like the modal home, since new houses were seen as right and proper for new families, and since this would boost construction and employment. For a small, single-income young family of median earnings, mortgage repayments on such a house would absorb 14 or 15 per cent of total net income in the first year of ownership. Lower-income, single-earner young families could buy the same house with 20 to 25 per cent of income going into repayments – higher-income families with little more than 10 per cent.

This changed swiftly in the 1970s, as house and land prices rose, tax rates increased and exemptions shrank, family benefits were not lifted to counter inflation, mortgage lending terms tightened, interest rates for borrowers multiplied, and government loan facilities dried up. Our optimistic assessment of their cumulative impact is that costs of a new modal home trebled, relative to income. In all likelihood they rose a good deal more still, for the model is, once again, highly conservative in a number of its assumptions. The costs of an R2 house followed a more complex path, though to similar general effect.

It is important to lay these estimates along side some more standard and widely-quoted indicators of the changing costs of housing. One such measure is the house price/wage ratio. In 1971, for instance, the cost of a new modal house on a section of average sale price was $11,120, the median gross income for men in the full-time work force was $3,150, and one was 3.5 times the other. The comparable ratio for 1991 was 4.0, which suggests that house prices had risen by perhaps 14 per cent, relative to earnings, across these 20 years.

Another familiar indicator of housing cost movement is the household expenditure survey. At the time of the first survey in 1973–74, 22 per cent of all household spending was on housing, with the figures for households under 25 years and 25–29 years of age being 27 and 32 per cent. Twenty years later the overall figure was 20 per cent, for households under 25 years 26 per cent, and for those 25–29 years 30 per cent. This suggests that actual spending on housing changed very little, even as the size and quality of many New Zealand homes improved substantially.

But neither of these familiar tools tell us anything about underlying trends in housing costs for young adults. The first, the price/wage ratio, misses all the interacting effects from movements in the earnings of young adults, taxes, benefits, loan subsidies, or interest rates. The second, based on the household survey, captures only a residual effect, or the product of underlying and behavioural changes, and indicates 'no change'. The more comprehensive model of housing cost to young families suggests underlying cost rises of 300 and more per cent over 20 years. That underlying rise has been countered and masked by enormous and rapid adaptations on the part of younger adults. They are, for instance, staying at home with parents longer, forming into larger groups to share housing costs, marrying and parenting later so as to retain two full incomes for more years, having fewer children and going back to work earlier in their childhoods, or buying older or smaller or more rundown houses in less desirable neighbourhoods.

Two conclusions are pertinent here. One is that the CPI proves quite inadequate for measuring the underlying costs facing particular age groups in the population. A second is that the compounding consequence of numerous changes in the last 25 years has been a massive fall in the real incomes of young men and families, on a scale that goes well beyond anything indicated in Figures 4.2 to 4.6, let alone by standard measures such as those in Figure 4.1. Just how much those figures still miss is unknown, and a possible subject for a future project. But this discussion suggests that we are still a long way from grasping the true pace and scale of the retreat.

Comment

In the face of such powerful historical forces, families cannot be left simply to their fate. I make no claim that economics alone have driven the changes in early family life – that would be quite wrong. But declining fortunes are central to any account of what has happened in the last quarter century, just as improving ones were to the decades before that. For we are talking here about massive and rapid rather than marginal or slow shifts in fortunes, even before we might consider the cumulative or lifetime incomes that result for persons born in one decade rather than another.[11] At mid century modern societies voted for a 'new citizenship for the family', though they did not call it that. They agreed, in other words, to a range of strong 'family friendly' economic programmes, which both directly and indirectly penalized the middle aged, the elderly and single persons so as to favour young families. In the last 25 years we have tossed those aside, with enormous consequences, both immediate and yet to come.

The first-round effects, as the economists like to put it, have been greater freedoms and resources for the later half of life, and the reverse for the first half. A great many responses and adaptations in the face of these pressures have become apparent among the young. Some are clearly worrying from any viewpoint – rising youth suicide, drug-taking or violence are examples. Others may be viewed or argued away as successful or welcome adaptations, which improve the lot of young adults in some way – gains by women relative to men might fall into this category. But non-marriage, marriage breakdown, wide sole-parenting, or having few children will have lasting consequences for all, whatever we think of the first-round results. A few of these consequences, such as the financial costs of ageing populations, are beginning to be considered. Others, including the transformation of family structures and relations within ageing populations, are not yet catching our attention.

Fifty or 60 years ago Western societies chose a new 'citizenship for the family', out of concern at the then-shrinking prospects of young families and the wider social implications of these. No new citizenship for the family now can or would want simply to repeat that earlier venture: too much is too different for that. But the goal, to foster the institution that remains crucial to the well-being of our societies, will be much as before. The choices made half a century or so ago did much to shape the late twentieth century world. A new citizenship for the family will do no less for the twenty-first century.

Notes

1 One useful work that goes further than most is Levy, 1987.
2 See, for example, Vogel, Anderson, Davidsson and Hall, 1988.
3 See, for instance, Bradbury, Doyle and Whiteford, 1990.
4 My own contributions to this analysis are developed further in Thomson, 1991, and in a later edition of that work, Thomson, 1996. Various aspects of the work are explored in, for example, Thomson, 1989; Thomson, 1992; or Thomson, 1993.
5 Very little has been done on the changing incidence of taxation upon particular age or other social groups. An earlier study which pointed some of the way into this subject is Pechman, 1985.
6 The question about income was added to the population census in 1926, as part of an inquiry into the need for family allowances. It has been asked at each of the five-yearly censuses since that date – New Zealand takes its population censuses in each year ending in the digit 1 or 6. However, no censuses were held in 1931 (an economy measure) or 1941 (a wartime measure), and the planned 1946 census was brought forward to 1945.

7   Maori were asked the income question at each census from 1951, but the results have been tabulated and published only a couple of times in the last 40 years.
8   The household survey, for instance, as reported below in Figure 4.7, indicates that income and spending among young households fell sharply between the later 1980s and the early 1990s.
9   Valuation New Zealand. Figures for the 1960s are estimated from data in the *Report of the Commission of Inquiry into Housing in New Zealand*, 1971.
10 Details on the size and nature of government grants, mortgage lending criteria, and interest rates is taken from several government publications, including the annual reports of the Department of Social Security and of the State Advances Corporation (later the Housing Corporation of New Zealand), and from Department of Statistics (later Statistics New Zealand), *New Zealand Official Yearbook*.
11 Alan Tapper considers some of these in his paper to this symposium.

References

Bradbury, B., Doyle, J. and Whiteford, P. (1990), *Trends in Disposable Income of Australian Families, 1982–83 to 1989–90*, Sydney.
Department of Statistics, *Household Income and Expenditure Survey*, Wellington, annual since 1973.
Department of Statistics, *Census of Population and Dwellings* (1926–91), Volumes on Incomes, Wellington.
Department of Statistics, *New Zealand Official Yearbook*, Wellington, annual.
Levy, F. (1987) *Dollars and Dreams: The Changing American Income Distribution*, Washington.
Pechman, J. (1985), *Who Paid the Taxes, 1966–85?*, Washington.
Report of the Commission of Inquiry into Housing in New Zealand (1971), Wellington.
Statistics New Zealand, *New Zealand Official Yearbook 1990*, Wellington, annual
Thomson. D. (1989), 'The Welfare State and Generation Conflict: winners and losers', in P. Johnson, C. Conrad and D. Thomson (eds), *Workers versus Pensioners: Intergenerational Justice in an Ageing World*, Manchester.
Thomson. D. (1991), *Selfish Generations? The Ageing of New Zealand's Welfare State*, Wellington.
Thomson. D. (1992), 'Generations, Justice and the Future of Collective Action', in P. Laslett and J. Fishkin (eds), *Justice Between Age Groups and Generations*, New Haven.
Thomson. D. (1993), 'A Lifetime of Privilege? Ageing and Generations at Century's End', in V.L. Bengtson and W.A. Achenbaum (eds), *The Changing Contract Across Generations*, New York.
Thomson. D. (1996), *Selfish Generations? How Welfare States Grow Old*, Cambridge.
Valuation New Zealand (formerly Department of Valuation), *The Urban Real Estate Market in New Zealand*, Wellington: half yearly.
Vogel, J., Anderson, L.-G., Davidsson, U. and Hall, L. (1988), *Inequality in Sweden: Trends and Current Situation*, Stockholm.

5 Cultural Capitalism and Child Formation

JOHN O'NEILL

> A society is rich when material goods, including capital, are cheap, and human beings dear; indeed, the word 'riches' has no other meaning (R.H.Tawney, 1924).

It is a paradox of the human sciences that they lead to the conclusion that human beings are unsure of their own worth. Demographers, economists and ecologists in various ways regard human populations as imbalanced, insufficiently scarce, or excessively damaging to their environment. Even humanists can combine their love of humanity with pessimistic findings on the unteachability, the irrationality and self-destructiveness of our kind. Worse still, when the two sciences of humanity overlap, as they do in psychoanalysis, we find that the human heart is at bottom murderous, rejecting divinity, paternity and the burden of intergenerationality (O'Neill, 1996). Amid so much human ambivalence, the birth of each child is received as both a blessing and a curse. No child escapes the double burden of our psychic and cultural ambivalence towards it. We cannot otherwise understand how we are at once sentimental and cruel to our children nor how some children are so well protected while others are so desperately abandoned. The fate of children is, however, the same fate that we have reserved for ourselves in the divisions of rich and poor, or of the mighty and the vulnerable. For while we are moved to soften inequities among ourselves, we still lack the political will to erase them.

I   The Idea of Cultural Capitalism

Every society institutes its own cognitive and moral map. It does so over a long period of time drawing upon the materials of myth, religion, philosophy art and science. However a society does this, its effect is to constitute what we may call its *cultural capital*. This notion will immediately convey our view that while cultural capital is productive on both the collective and the individual level of conduct, it is everywhere unevenly distributed and thus the subject of political struggle (Bourdieu, 1984). For a considerable time, political struggle in industrial democracies has been phrased in terms of a conflict between capital and labour, or between men and machines. It is now clear that the terms of this conflict are ill-phrased.

Neither capital nor labour is a mere physical entity. Rather, each embodies such considerable cultural capital that their *complementary intelligence* is what should define an industrial society:

> It is my contention that economic thinking has neglected two classes of investment that are of critical importance under modern circumstances. They are investment in man and in research, both private and public (Schultz, 1971, p. 5).

But this hard-won cultural insight has still to be given its proper weight so long as it is the ownership of capital (since formally labour is not owned unless enslaved) that exercises dominance in the conduct of industrial democracies.

However reluctantly, the perspective of *cultural capitalism* has been forced upon us by the restructuring of industrial production, financing and marketing flowing from computerized globalization. The result is that capitalism is less challenged by its differences with communism than it is by the different paths that it may take towards its own civic sustainability. Any political agenda that does not address the infrastructural needs of cultural capitalism, as defined here, is dancing in the dark. Worse still, such negligence serves only to barbarize society from within itself. The essence of the current shift toward the institution of cultural capitalism is the change in the capital/labour relationship from a Fordist to postFordist regime. Broadly speaking, this adaptation has involved two capital strategies, realized to different degrees in different sectors and countries responding to technological change and global competition (Table 5.1).

On balance, the post-Ford strategies of *social capital* appear to have won over the defensive strategies of private capital versus labour that first appeared to be demanded by the new market. The approach of social capital is more long-term in its perspective on labour relations, retraining, wages and incentives. Social capital has learned that there is a *solidarity* component in systems that are defined by their need to learn in order to maintain efficiency.

Of crucial importance to the expanded concept of cultural capitalism, for which we are arguing, is the *complementarity between the strategies of social capital and the strategies of welfare capital*. The latter have displayed both

**Table 5.1   Capital strategies involved in capital/labour relationship
from a Fordist to postFordist regime**

	Private capital	**Social capital**
1 Work organization	Exporting old Fordist methods Reinforcing controls via new technologies Marginally improving Fordism	Modernizing even mature industries Enhance workers' commitment Use information technologies to find alternative
2 Wage formation	Two-tier contracts Deindexing of wages Weakening of unions	Homogeneous labour contract Genuine wage formula (e.g. profit sharing) Joint bargaining of wage employment and welfare by firms or national unions
3 Collective bargaining	Decentralization of bargaining Make wages more sensitive to individual financial situation Relative wages become adjustment variables	Possible centralization Solidaristic wage policies Rather stable wage hierarchy
4 Welfare and Keynesian	Reduction in unemployment benefit Budget cuts Goal of private insurance	Intensive training state programmes Investment in infrastructure (education, transportation, communication) Rationalization of welfare state

Source: Schor and You, 1995, p. 35 (modified).

weaknesses and strengths in the struggle between private and social capital adaptations to globalism. Overall, the cutbacks to public spending in the name of deficit reduction have not altered the basic formula of capitalism:

(A)   *CAPITALISM = Private Capital + Social Capital + Welfare Capital*

What will continue to change in this formula is how we understand the complementarities between the three components of capitalism. In particular, we are concerned to introduce two further modifications that shift the strategy of social capital by treating labour and welfare as specifically *human capital* and *civic capital*.

(B)   *CULTURAL CAPITALISM (Human Capital + Civic Capital)*

With this amended capital formula, we can envisage an expanded concept of cultural capitalism that offers the most relevant context for studies of child and family formation in industrial societies. On the basis of comparative studies of capital/labour relations (Schor and You, 1995), we assume that any analysis and policy recommendations with regard to child formation and family support systems must be directed towards civic developments in cultural capitalism. This demands a hybrid model of social exchanges between the family, school, economy and state, answering to a civic principle of institutional compromise in order to respect the basic social covenant between classes and generations. Apart from such a civic covenant, the prospects of children are likely to be sacrificed in the struggle between market forces, corporatism and social democracy.

II   Cultural Capital and Child Formation

In view of my opening comments upon the harshness of the human sciences towards human ideals, it might seem self-contradictory to propose a capital theory approach to child formation. This would indeed be so on a narrow view of capital. Historically, children have been bred to supply both farm labour and factory labour – and some would say, to supply school labour (Qvortrup, 1994). But we may regard the familization and schooling of labour as an early social learning process shaped by industrial conflicts between capital and labour. Here patriarchy, unionism and Christian reformism all played their part in the reduction of child labour. While the horror of the child's working day can never be forgotten, what must be grasped from the history of the Factory Acts in England, for example, is that such legislation constituted – along with the public health and urban improvements to housing and sanitation – an expansion of the concept of capital towards what we call cultural capitalism:

Factory legislation, that first conscious and methodical reaction of society against the spontaneously developed form of the process of production, is ... just as much the necessary product of modern industry as cotton yarn, self-actors, and the electric telegraph (Marx, 1887, p. 480).

What Marx is saying here is that cultural capitalism can only evolve through alterations in the fit between a given mode of production and its relations of social reproduction, e.g., family relations and the laws that intervene to protect children from abuse or to ensure their schooling in industrial society. In short, Marx saw very clearly that the essential claim in cultural capital theory is *the complementarity between social intelligence and technology.*

Thus the capital value of children will vary according to the shifting contexts of family authority. Once the traditional family had lost its economic base in the shift to industrial production, its traditional authority became the parents' last resort in selling their children into the slavery of the factory system. The desperation of parents in turn fed into the raw exploitation of child labour which early industrialists regarded as a quasi-natural need of competitive capitalism. But, as Marx insists, once industrialism works its full effects upon family relations, the overall effect on the family is to open up possibilities for the expression of individual personality in both sexes, adult or child:

> However terrible and disgusting the dissolution, under the capitalist system of the old family ties may appear, nevertheless, modern industry, by assigning as it does an important part in the process of production, outside the domestic sphere, to women, to young persons, and to children of both sexes, creates a new economic foundation for a higher form of the family and of the relations between the sexes (ibid., pp. 489–90).

I am attributing to Marx an implicit concept of cultural capital theory to make the point that the cognitive and moral formation of the child cannot be understood apart from the child's location in a more or less intelligent and ethical society. It is the exchanges between the family, school, economy and the state, that work to capitalize child development. Thus we can treat childhood as the focus of an institutional matrix (Figure 5.1).

What I also want to convey here is R.H. Tawney's vision that any child must be seen as a richly capitalized subject whose formation is the work of family and state provision of assurances of well-being and learning that will foster its membership in a civic society. This broadens the economist's human capital concept of childhood where emphasis is reduced to the connection

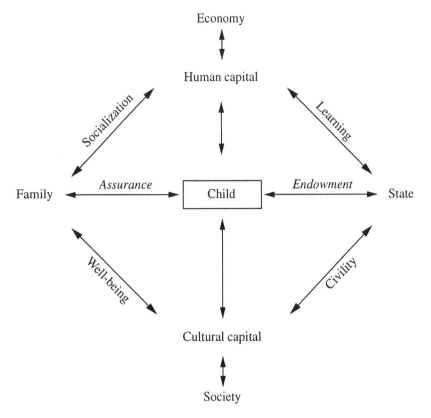

Figure 5.1 Childhood as the focus of an institutional matrix

between schooling and work future. The larger concept of cultural capital includes the state's provision of the endowments of well-being and civility to support family school and community environments that foster child socialization and citizenship. The aim of these civic provisions is to cut across the exclusionary practices of class, race and gender in order to underwrite 'childhood' as a civic achievement rather than to float it as a natural fiction (O'Neill,1994). The same civic strategy, of course, must be held out with respect to parenthood, household, community, school and workplace since childhood is a function of their social coherence.

III   Child Poverty

I began by phrasing the prospects of childhood in terms of a *psychocultural aporia*, namely, our inability to save all children from poverty, illness and ignorance – let alone from cruelty and abuse. Our everyday treatment of children is the limit of our political will:

> it is not a concern about justice between age cohorts that motivates intergenerational – equity protagonists but the fiscal implications of ageing: the so-called 'burden' of economic dependency in the form of pension costs and the 'burden' of physical dependency in the form of health and social care costs. In short, population ageing is regarded as a threat to capital accumulation (Walker, 1993, p. 153).

It is therefore essential that we set aside the ideological veils of dependency and ageing politics to account for the plight of children. These arguments treat the young, the elderly and single mother as welfare state induced drags upon raw capital accumulation. Their ultimate aim is to eliminate the civic component of cultural capitalism by treating welfare as an unearned and therefore illegitimate increment to individual worth. Only the market, it is argued, can establish human worth. It does so by rewarding efficiency and punishing inefficiency. As such, the market is the only mechanism we have for the exercise of blind justice.

Children are the poorest of the poor (Lichter and Eggebeen, 1993). They are poor because their parents are to be found among young people who are less employed and less favoured by government transfers than other population groups. Children fare less well than elders because their young parents do not benefit from inflation adjusted benefits, are subject to low wages and unemployment, aggravated by minority status and gender inequality (Table 5.2). This is not to say that all elders are without exception better off than all children, nor does the well-being of elders conflict directly with the improvement of children.

Children who are not in families headed by a member of one of these groups are included in the totals for all children. This group includes Asian-Americans, Native Americans, and other groups (Danziger and Gottschalk, 1995, p. 90).

It is a common assumption, at least in the United States, that poverty is due to a dysfunctional family structure (headed by never-married single females) that now raises about a million American children. Nevertheless, this new family structure, even when its minority status is weighed in, does not account as much for the increase in the *official poverty rate* (1965–91) as does the decline in family incomes (1973–91) due to slow economic growth and increased social inequality. Worse still, recent economic growth is now

Table 5.2   Child poverty rates, selected years, 1949–91

	1949	1969	1973	1991
All children (A)	46.9 %	14.9 %	14.0 %	19.7 %
White	40.6	9.9	8.1	11.6
Black	86.7	41.2	39.4	42.4
Hispanic	72.9	31.2	26.5	35.5
White children living in families headed by				
Men	38.6	6.9	5.1	6.4
Women	72.1	42.2	36.5	39.3
Black children living in families headed by				
Men	85.0	29.9	20.8	15.3
Women	94.1	66.9	65.7	63.8
Hispanic children living in families headed by				
Men	71.2	27.2	16.0	24.6
Women	87.5	61.1	65.4	65.3

Source: US Bureau of the Census, Current Population Reports, Sct. P–60.

uncoupled from poverty reduction in both the private and public sectors. It is, however, the *child poverty rate* that has been raised by the increase in single parent family structure aggravated by the overall decline in family income. What has happened is that in the period 1949–69 economic growth reduced poverty. But in the period 1973–91 the growth factor was submerged by increased inequality. The latter accounts for about 50 per cent of increased poverty in the more recent period while the rest is attributable to changes in household structure. However, the increase in *child poverty* is about two-thirds driven by family structure and the remainder due to increased income inequality:

> we find, as other researchers have, that demographic changes, particularly the shift toward more female-headed families, contributed to the high poverty rates of recent years. Changes in family structure raised the poverty rate by 1.6 percentage points over an eighteen-year period, or by roughly 0.1 percentage points per year.
>   Economic changes, however, were even more important. The slow economic growth from the 1970s to the 1990s was only enough to decrease poverty by about 0.16 points per year. Meanwhile, the poverty-reducing effect of this growth was offset by increased inequality of family income, which had a stronger

poverty, increasing effect than did changes in family structure. Our findings strongly point to the importance of changes in labour markets, especially the slow growth and increased inequality of men's earnings (Danziger and Gottschalk, 1995, p. 110).

IV Child Formation and the New Household

We need a clear picture of the emergent household economy that now provides the socio-psychological environment of so many children whose futures are not yet fully known to us. In the past 20 years or so, the US poverty rate for children has increased by more than 50 per cent. These children are found in two low income groups – relatively young, two-parent couples and single mother households. These groups have suffered from unemployment, low wage jobs and associated socio-psychological and cultural disadvantages that are more complex than their material base. Here, it is our task to focus upon their interaction with the changing household structures within which children are likely to suffer from under-resourcing or disinvestment.

The structural fact is that there is a marked decline from the all-American family median income of $32,551 to $15,672 for households headed by divorced females and to $8,332 for households headed by never-married females (the median income for two parent households is $39,076).

It is essential, however, to translate the material economy of the new households into a socio-psychological framework. A useful translation device is to think in terms of a social network/resource perspective with focus upon the life-chances of children rather than on the legal-moral status of the parent(s) or on the structural location of single parent households in the overall economy. We may summarize the research findings as follows:

1.0 the greater the number of adults who provide economic resources, support, regulation, and positive role models to children, the more positive is children's development;

1.1 regular contact within long-term, stable relationships increases the potential of adults to provide children with resources;

1.2 co-residence with children maximizes contact and increases relationship stability; as such, co-residence increase opportunities for adults to provide children with resources;

Thousands of dollars

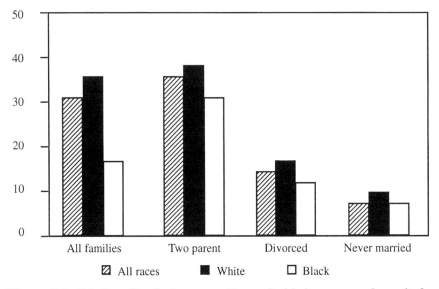

Figure 5.2   Median family income of households by race and marital status (1990)

Source: US Department of Commerce (1991a, Table 6, pp. 45–60), in Darby, 1996, p. 34)

2.0 stable single-parent households with additional resident adults have the same potential to provide children with resources as do two-parent households;

2.1 single-adult households restrict children's access to adult networks; consequently, they are structurally weaker settings for children's development than are two-adult households;

3.0 the extent of disadvantage associated with single-parent households depends on the particular historical, social, and political context;

3.1 in collectivist societies, in which children have close, frequent, and stable contact with large numbers of adults, the loss of one parent from the child's social network may not be especial problematic (Amato, 1995; modified).

To fully comprehend the child's family circumstance, it is necessary to supplement the child network approach with a similarly structural approach to the bio-psychological and socio-psychological structure of parental pre- and postnatal risk:

(i)   child exposure to bio-risks in the uterine environment;

(ii) child exposure to bio-psychic and socio-psychological risks in the domestic environment;

(iii) child exposure to socioeconomic risks on the class environment of the family;

(iv) child exposure to global environmental risks in the family and community (O'Neill, 1994).

Families in poverty are structurally disposed to provide inadequate developmental resources for children's social, cognitive and emotional development. To the extent that the parents of underprivileged children are themselves young, unemployed and under-educated, the socially structured incompetence of such parents aggravates child deprivation. It is important, however, not to treat this cycle of deprivation by politicizing single parent dependency – nor by moralizing the inherent potential of children once their parent(s)' disabilities are removed. Both moves have occurred in the current despair over the inefficacy of the US war of poverty.

V   Community Capital and Family Disinvestment

Our concern for child futures is raised not only by the increased number of children living in poverty. Such concern can only produce a constructive response if we understand the increased severity of the differences that threaten to institutionalize a dual economy of childhood. It is for this reason that we have tried to rework the grammar of human capital theory. Otherwise, there is a considerable chance that the majority of the world's children will be sacrificed to *undercapitalization* in:

(i)   the family;

(ii) the schools;

(iii) the workplace.

Poor children may be regarded as an underclass whose condition condemns them to intergenerational injustice while privileged children are enjoyed and celebrated as the rightful legatees of the world's goods:

> The family in its legitimate definition is a privilege instituted into a universal norm: a de facto privilege that implies a symbolic privilege- the privilege of becoming *comme il faut*, conforming to the norm, and therefore enjoying a symbolic profit of normality. Those who have the privilege of having a normal family are able to demand the same of everyone without having to raise the question of the conditions (e.g. a certain income, living space, etc.) of universal access to what they demand universally. (Bourdieu, 1996, p. 23).

In simple terms, every society must invest in itself as a moral order. That is the *civic capital* problem, as I understand it. Ordinarily, this work falls to families who produce moral agents sufficiently often that the job of policing their failures is not impossibly large. An individual is socialized to the extent that s/he achieves identification with the institutional values and practices that characterize the family itself, schools, workplace and community. In turn, these institutions are concerned to foster socialization. The latter proviso is important because the exclusivity or scarcity of institutional resources will constitute a restriction upon successful socialization and thereby reduce the level of moral order.

Coleman (1990, p. 294) raises a question that goes to the heart of '*rational*' capital theory. He asks, who is to bear the cost of child socialization weighed against the 'discounted future cost of policing to bring about the same degree of compliance'? Coleman's concern is that the less authority a given household exerts over its child's internalization of institutional norms (including its own family), then the more likely is the capital cost of maintaining moral order to be shifted to policing. In so far as parents are rational theorists, this outcome is all the more expectable since it is 'third parties' rather than parents themselves who stand to gain from family investment in socializing children! Coleman concludes that parental disinvestment in child socialization is perfectly congruent with corporate disinvestment in human capital. In both cases, management avoids expenditure of time and effort that is more likely to benefit the larger society than itself due to 'turnover' among its members. Coleman's conclusion is that human capital disinvestment is due to a structural trend in modern family relations. It is, moreover, impervious to social policy claims that parental education would strengthen child formation.

This is the gloomy conclusion to be expected on the assumption that rational transfer theory (Becker, 1981) governs family conduct. Coleman does not say so outright, but what he is implying is that society is impossible when regarded as a by-product of rational individual behaviour. Meantime economists themselves (Loury, 1981, 1987; Ben-Porath, 1980) have had to adjust rational choice theory to modify its atomistic and egoistic assumptions. What matters here for our concern with child formation is that economists have recognised that social capital has its own laws of reproduction which in fact subsidize a good deal of economic behaviour! Child socialization, then, must be considered in terms of a broader concept of human capital which Coleman (1988) calls social capital but which I think is better understood as *community capital*. The two concepts work together as Figure 5.3 shows.

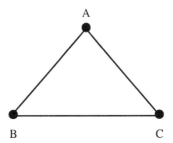

Community capital

A

B   C

Figure 5.3   Three person structure: human capital in nodes and community capital in relations

Source: Coleman, 1990, p. 305 (modified).

Once we recognize that labour and capital are mutually enriching, then the concept of human capital (Schultz, 1961) is ready for expansion through recognition that an individual's social relationships or networks, also facilitate capital formation. This is the function assigned to community capital. Notice, however, that Coleman's community capital is restricted to possessive advantage; it is treated as a resource (obligations, trust, credit) rather than as a complex moral environment. Social relations are regarded as capital relations of control over items of interest between the parties, short of the inalienability of the public good dimension of community capital. Yet, even here, Coleman has to introduce the further (rational choice) restriction that it is not in any individual's interest to invest in community capital since it is largely 'others' who benefit from it!

The paradox of rational choice capital theory emerges fully in the case of parent-child relations. It would enhance child socialization if the parent-child relation were reinforced by parent-parent or community relations similarly directed towards the child's education. Without such 'intergenerational closure' (Coleman, 1990, p. 319) the success of each parent raising a child in a community without inter-parent relations is considerably reduced. Clearly, where family and community relations have less closure (due to time restraints, variations in household type, personal ideology), then it is even less likely that investments in community capital inputs will occur.

The major restriction in Coleman's concept of social (community) capital is that it is undermined on one side by affluence and on the other side by welfare. As I see it, the American concept of community capital is divorced from the larger concept of *civic capital* that is required for a fully viable concept of *cultural capitalism*. Indeed, one can almost measure this ideological difference. Thus, in estimating the cost of what he calls 'compassionate capitalism', i.e., bringing the poor to 40 per cent of the median income threshold by 2020, Kuenne (1993) calculates that the per capital tax increase would be about $700 over 1986 levels. He notes, however, that it took the US Congress eight years to raise per capita taxes $203 to reduce the budget deficit in 1990! In other words, the American ideology of possessive individualism, privatized familism and communitarianism blocks the transition towards a civic concept of cultural capitalism. Coleman argues that the deterioration of inter-generational relations is to be expected inasmuch as corporate institutions are not family-friendly and so undermine even more the provision of child investments. Business and government have stripped families of a number of primordial functions of education and reciprocal care, reducing both the birth rate and the value of children to parents. The latter claim is strongly disputed by Rossi (1990). In any case, it does not mean that the primordial value of parents to children is any less.

Coleman's emphasis is on generation-gapping and parental disinvestment due to structural changes in the composition of households:

(a)   shifts in parent-child relations and extended adult relations;

(b)   shifts in marital relations, child care and school, community relations;

(c)   shifts in temporal commitments in parent-child, school, community relations.

In short, Coleman envisages considerable future child neglect – 'no one to claim the body' – unless either family structures are strengthened or corporate actors are found to assume responsibility for 'the whole child'. But since corporations can hardly treat their child customers or audience as corporate stakeholders, little is to be expected in this direction. Children are left to their family's interest in them which may be strained by

(a) cultural conflict between the family and society;

(b) conflict between parental consumption and investment in child education;

(c) intergenerational conflict between parental enjoyment and deferment on behalf of future generations.

Coleman seems resigned to the America case where social policy with respect to family support conflicts with the dominant 'individualizing and rationalizing' trends, and the government has failed to substitute state care for primordial care of children with any success. The challenge to the social sciences is to discover compensatory strategies to resist the erosion of social capital. Even so, Coleman unwittingly phrases the American dilemma as a class aporia:

> All these questions regarding the replacement of the vanishing primordial capital with constructed social organization are forced on social theory by change. A failure to address these questions does not merely leave society where it was before. It places each of us and each of our children in the position of 'poor little rich kid', having an abundance of material resource but without the social resources necessary for satisfactory lives (Coleman, 1990, p. 655).

Coleman finds little to hope for any policy of shifting the capital functions of the family and community on to the corporations and state and even less hope of these corporate actors investing in the reconstitution of primordial capital. Everyone loses. But the principle of rational individualism is honoured! Meantime, under affluent capitalism the path toward fully developed cultural capitalism is blocked and the civic future of its children lies in the shadow of injustice. Thus, as I would summarize the picture:

AFFLUENT CAPITALISM = INVESTMENT IN CORPORATE CAPITAL + HUMAN CAPITAL - DISINVESTMENT IN COMMUNITY CAPITAL

Conclusion

A   *Child Capitalism*

Child capitalism functions no differently than does the rest of capitalist society. Class location, inequality, affluence and poverty will shape the nature of the social capital available to a given household. The sociopsychic and bio-social elements in human capital will be enriched or deprived depending on household, school and community resources directed towards the child's physical, cognitive and social development. The more these formative elements work towards communicative coherence, the more assured is a child's passage from infancy to adulthood. The richer, i.e., the more extensive and intensive, is a child's adult network, the more likely it is to find sustainable ideals of socialization and personality. However, all such observations remain blocked by the limits of rational choice capital theory. From this perspective, capital investment in children's socialization and schooling as a public good must be discounted from the standpoint of the individual's rational calculation of cost/ benefits. Community capital formation is further limited because corporations and families reinforce one another's short-term and individualized perspective. Both agents expect to be able to buy out from the public consequences of their bias toward disinvestment in children, schools and communities. This a-civic agenda in turn distorts the state's public agenda. More is invested in policing and imprisoning an underprivileged youth than might be spent to educate that youth, supposing other civic institutions like the family, school and community were also regarded as productive civic capital investments.

The contradiction at the core of rational choice capital theory is not simply that its disinvestment bias may lead to less secure enjoyment of individual savings and even considerable negative family income. The fundamental contradiction in the rational choice theory of family formation is that it ignores the fact that family is itself a privileged resource. Whatever a family costs, some families will be able to afford it better than others. Yet under-resourced families are expected by richer families to produce capable recruits to society and the economy. Among the hidden injuries of class (Sennet and Cobb, 1972) is the sacrifice made by under-resourced yet hard-working families to meet the norms of family life set bourgeois families. But these norms are met at far less cost to the bourgeoisie since it can also afford considerable domestic help from the working class, in addition to the enriched socialization available to its children through private schooling and segregated communities.

Child futures are heavily dependent upon the political culture of capitalism.

At times, capital ideology treats market forces and capital accumulation as quasi-rational effects of individual talent that thrives with minimal state intervention. In this vein, capital ideology is opposed to state welfare because it creates dependent groups that are a drag on capital accumulation. Capitalists are even opposed to state interventions that facilitate capital formation, e.g. education and health, whenever these basic elements of human and civic capital formation appear to infringe on property rights. Capital interests may even push the national state into fiscal crisis. Possessive capitalists then risk a civil crisis rather than work through the institutional steps necessary to reach the more viable prospect we are calling cultural capitalism.

From our standpoint, the expression 'late capitalism' may be given a developmental rather than terminal interpretation by expanding its components to include human capital and civic capital as complementary formative processes:

CULTURAL CAPITALISM = CIVIC CAPITAL + CORPORATE CAPITAL + HUMAN CAPITAL

This would define cultural capitalism as a post-Keynesian institutional innovation of general benefit and one of particular importance to the civic assurance of child futures. The divisionary tactics of dependency politics contribute to anti-governance which deepens privatized affluence but spreads civic decay. This is the political formula that breeds *child carelessness.* The current privatization of responsibility for child abuse of any kind does not relieve child neglect. The politics of child abuse cannot be successful on the level of voluntaristic community response without a supportive state policy. *The child's place in cultural capitalism is a civic place.* Here the family's reproductive optimism is assured because it is held to be unacceptable that we should render childhood either a sorrow or an irreparable misfortune. A civic childhood is not an imaginary event. It is a political event for whose inauguration too many children are still waiting.

The shift towards cultural capitalism cannot be fully achieved without a renewed child covenant that will sustain children through a civic investment in institutions that operates as an enabling endowment to underwrite their personal contributions to society. These institutions must be defended on the level of politics and morals as a civilizational matrix from which no child may be excluded.

B   Civic Childhood

The human capital approach to children has no answer to the excesses of over- and under-investment that divides childhood. Only a civic state can provide children with an initial endowment confirmed in family and school and community interaction to avoid the public shame of impoverished childhood. This claim is not made out of nostalgia for a myth of childhood. It is a claim upon our political imagination, upon our will to improve the civic fiction of viable family and child assurance owed to anyone of our own kind – short of barbarism. A civic state need not be identified with welfare dependency, the feminization of child care and paternal delinquency. In a civic state families are located in the public domain where adult members interact with the market economy and where child members interact with the educational system. A civic state is committed to the support of the moral economy of families in interaction with the political economy within which families are both a productive and reproductive element. In a civic state the child is both a moral and a political subject whose voice is heard only when adults subordinate their present selves to their future selves (O'Neill, 1994). This is an exercise in the civic citizenship and not a confirmation of existing ideologies of familism and privatism. We seek rather to offer to any child a number of basic civic assurances. These narrative principles are rounded in the best child research (Bronfenbrenner and Neville, 1994) which we cast as follows:

1   a child's development is more secure (cognitively and ethically), the more complex and intensive are its interactions with its primary caretakers – i.e., a child benefits from those conditions that sustain the narrative of parental love;

2   a child's development is more secure, the more its home culture overlaps with its civic environment (physical, cultural and emotional) i.e., a child benefits from those home conditions that sustain the narrative of social competence;

3   a child's development is more assured, the more its parent(s), sibling, school and neighbourhood culture are congruent, i.e., a child benefits from those institutional conditions that sustain the narrative of civic transitions;

4   a child's development is more assured, the more its home, its care institutions, its school and its parent(s)' workplace are in communication to balance their competing demands upon the child, i.e., a child's benefits from the communicative practices that sustain the civic fiction of a child's worth;

5   a child's development is more assured, the more the state adopts child – focused family support policies, i.e. a child benefits from national policy that sustains the narrative of the civic value of children;

6   a child's development is more assured, the more nation states enforce the United Nation's Convention on the Rights of Children as an index of national achievement, i.e. a child benefits from those international laws that enforce the narrative that children are the world's treasure.

References

Amato, P.R. (1995), 'Single Parent Households As Settings For Children's Development, Well – Being, And Attainment: A Social Network/Resources Perspective', *Sociological Studies of Children*, Vol. 7, pp. 19–47.

Becker, G.S. (1981), *A Treatise on the Family*, Cambridge: Harvard University Press.

Ben-Porath, Y. (1980), 'The F-Connection: Families, Friends, and Firms and the Organization of Exchange', *Population and Development Review*, 6, pp. 1–29.

Bourdieu, P. (1984), *Distinction: A Social Critique of the Judgment of Taste*, trans. Richard Nice, Cambridge: Harvard University Press.

Bourdieu, P. (1996), 'On the Family as a Realized Category', *Theory Culture and Society*, Vol. 13 (3), pp. 19–26.

Bronfenbrenner, U. and Neville, P.R. (1994), 'America's Children and Families: An International Perspective', in S.L. Kagan and B. Weissbourd (eds), *Putting Families First: America's Family Support Movement and the Challenge of Change*, San Francisco: Jossey-Bass Publishers, Inc., pp. 3–27.

Cohen, B. and Fraser, N. (1991), *Childcare in a Modern Welfare System: Towards a new national policy*, London: Institute For Public Policy Research.

Coleman, J.S. (1988), 'Social Capital in the Creation of Human Capital', *American Journal of Sociology*, Vol. 94 ,Supplement S95–S120.

Coleman, J.S. (1990), *Foundations of Social Theory*, Cambridge: Harvard University Press.

Danziger, S. and Gottschalk, P. (1995), *America Unequal*, Cambridge: Harvard University Press.

Darby, M.R. (ed.) (1996), *Reducing Poverty in America: Visions and Approaches*, Thousand Oaks, CA: Sage Publications.

Garbarino, J. and Kostelny, K. (1992), 'Child Maltreatment as a Community Problem', *Child Abuse and Neglect*, 16, pp. 455–64.

Garcia, Coll, C.T. (1990) 'Developmental Outcome of Minority Infants: A process oriented look into our beginnings', *Child Development*, 61, pp. 270–89.

Kuenne, R.E. (1993), *Economic Justice in American Society*, Princeton: Princeton University Press.

Lichter, D.T. and Eggebeen, D.J. (1993), 'Rich Kids, Poor Kids: Changing Income Inequality Among American Children', *Social Forces*, 71 (3), pp. 761–80.

Loury, G. (1981), 'Intergenerational Transfers and the Distribution of Earnings', *Econometrica*, 49, pp. 843–,67.

Loury, G. (1987), 'Why should we care about group inequality?', *Social Philosophy and Policy*, 5, pp. 249–71.

Marx, K. (1887), *Capital: A Critical Analysis Of Capitalist Production*, Vol. 1, Moscow: Foreign Languages Publishing House.

O'Neill, J. (1994), *The Missing Child in Liberal Theory: Towards a Covenant Theory of Family, Community, Welfare and the Civic State*, Toronto: University of Toronto Press.

O'Neill, J. (ed.) (1996), *Freud and the Passions*, University Park: Penn State Press.

Parcel, T.L. and Menaghan, E.G. (1993), 'Family Social Capital and Children's Behavior Problems', *Social Psychology Quarterly*, Vol. 56, No. 2, pp. 120–35.

Presser, H.B. (1989), 'Can We Make Time For Children? The Economy, Work Schedules, and Child Care', *Demography*, Vol. 26, No. 4, pp. 523–43.

Qvortrup, J., Bardy, M., Sgritta, G. and Wintersberg, H. (eds) (1994), *Childhood Matters: Social Theory, Practice and Politics*, Aldershot: Avebury.

Rosenheim, M. and Testa, M.F. (eds.) (1992), *Early Parent-hood and Coming of Age in the 1990s*, New Brunswick, NJ: Rutgers University Press.

Rossi, A. and Rossi, P.H. (1990), *Of Human Bonding: Parent-Child Relations Across The Life Course*, New York: Aldine de Gruyter.

Salzinger, S. (1990), 'Social Networks in Child Rearing and Child Development', in S.M. Pfafflin, J.A. Sechzer, J.M. Fish and R.L. Thompson (eds), *Psychology: Perspectives and practice*, New York: Academy of Science, pp. 171–81.

Schor, J. and You, J.-I. (eds), *Capital, the State and Labour: A Global Perspective*, Aldershot: United Nations University Press.

Schultz, T.W. (1971), *Investment in Human Capital: The Role of Education in Research*, New York: The Free Press.

Sennett, R. and Cobb, J. (1972), *The Hidden Injuries of Class*, New York: Knopf.

Tawney, R.H. (1924), *Secondary Education For All: A Policy For Labour*, London: George Allen and Urwin Ltd.

Walker, A. (1993), 'Intergenerational Relations and Welfare Restructuring: The Social Construction of an Intergenerational Problem', in V.L. Bengston and W.A. Achenbaum (eds), *The Changing Contract Across The Generations*, New York: Aldine de Gruyter, pp. 141–65.

6 A Method for Reducing Mandatory Social Taxes and Contributions: Organizing Intergenerational Exchange

JACQUES BICHOT

Could a reform of the social insurance system lead to a reduction in the rate of mandatory levies on wages? The present contribution to the Forum International des Sciences Humaines symposium answers this question in the affirmative. It aims to demonstrate that when family allowances and other expenditures which benefit children are no longer considered to be independent of the contributory retirement system, it is possible both to improve justice towards families and to reduce the total amounts levied and redistributed.

At a time when most European countries are vying painfully with the problem of mandatory contributions, trying to reduce fiscal and para-fiscal pressure, the proposal sketched out in the following pages merits examination. It has the added advantage of simplicity, as it consists in bringing legal measures back into accord with social and economic realities, from which they have unfortunately drifted widely in past decades.

I The Foundations of Intergenerational Exchange

A Analyzing the Economics of Child-raising and Education Does Not Imply Neglect of other Important Dimensions

There is sometimes a reluctance to consider the relations between successive generations from the viewpoint of economic exchange. If applying ordinary tools of economic analysis prevented us from recognizing and appreciating all that which, in parents' love for their children and vice versa, transcends the purely economic, then this reluctance would be legitimate. However, excepting a purely unidimensional vision of man, the idea that raising and educating children constitutes an investment in human capital, that is, in an essential production factor, does not exclude other possible conceptualizations of the same activity. In a business also, there are human relations, even friendships, but treating the company as a production unit does not mean denying the reality of this human dimension to shared work activity.

We therefore assume that our listeners and readers will maintain an open mind regarding this economic approach to education and to intergenerational relations, with the assurance that our analysis does not in any way postulate the primacy of the purely economic.

B   *Children are First Supported by their Elders, and on Reaching Adulthood, they Support their Elders in Turn*

All human beings begin their lives by receiving a great deal from those who have come before them: the child is fed, housed, cared for and educated by adults, who dedicate rare resources to these tasks. Everyday language expresses this by saying that raising children and young people costs money. In fact, it is common for adults to limit the number of their descendants for this very practical reason, as they consider themselves unable to assume their parental responsibility of meeting the financial cost of additional children. Budgetary constraints, the very essence of economic reality, exist in most families and play a role in the decision to procreate.

After having benefited from these contributions by their elders, the young person enters active working life. Perhaps he or she has trouble finding employment; this is often the case today in Spain, in France and in other countries. Perhaps, on the contrary, finding work is easy, as it tended to be in the past. In either case, the tree of unemployment, however huge and leafy it may be, should not hide from us the forest of jobs: even with an unemployment rate of 20 per cent, as in Spain, 80 per cent of workers are in paying jobs. Naturally, our economic reasoning is based in its first approximation on the situation of 80 per cent or 90 per cent of adults, even if we recognize the problem of those who do not work.

Once the adult acquires official employment, he or she is subjected to mandatory payments on behalf of his elders. It is of little matter whether these amounts are levied in the form of taxes, social contributions or intermediate types of payment such as the French CSG (Contribution Sociale Généralisée); it matters little, also, in the case of social taxes, whether these are technically levied on the company or on the employee; and finally, it is of little importance whether these amounts pass through the employee's own bank account or are paid directly to the relevant social insurance institutions by his or her employer. In every case, a portion of the fruit of the adult's work is made available to his or her elders. If the worker's parents' generation were less numerous at retirement, he or she would conserve a larger purchasing power. All of these forms of payment constitute contributions.

Thus, all human beings begin life being supported by their elders, and, as adults, go on to support these elders when they have reached retirement age.

C   *This Succession of Payment and Repayment can be Organized as an Exchange*

It is theoretically possible to raise and educate children while expecting nothing from them in exchange. We could postulate that this is what parents do, motivated purely by altruism towards their own children. However, even within the framework of the family, we can observe in various civilizations of the past and the present that the parents' contribution to their children's welfare is usually acknowledged by the latter; the children feel they owe something to those who have given them so much, and even if this debt of gratitude is not concretely defined, it is understood that aging parents have certain rights regarding their children, and that the latter have certain responsibilities. The Napoleonic Civil Code calls this economic relationship between children and their parents the *obligation alimentaire*, implying a responsibility to provide for necessities of food and shelter. The application of this notion can be extremely vague, but leads nonetheless to the allocation of rare resources levied on the production or earnings of the younger generation.

When the support of children and older people is organized more collectively, by public administrations, then the link between that which is received and that which will be given is both more and less apparent.

- More apparent, in that society leaves adults with no choice: as soon as they enter the working world, they are required to contribute to the support of their elders. This form of collective responsibility knows no exception. After having given, the older generations receive.

- Less apparent, in that mandatory levies are not specifically said to repay contributions previously made. As we will see, the severing of this conceptual link is the source of major problems; the method proposed here for reducing mandatory social insurance levies consists above all in reconstituting this link.

Even if the notion of an exchange is not clearly seen by the subjects themselves, nor by the legal experts who have codified their behaviour, it would be possible to organize this behaviour as a system of exchange. In the diagram below, for example, generation A begins by supporting generation B when these generations are respectively made up of adults and children. Then, 20 to 40 years later, generation B (made up of adults) supports generation A (made up of retired people). And the initial contribution of A to B is the cause of the later contribution of B to A; it is thanks to what the B generation received from their elders that its members are able, some decades later, to work and thus to support the members of A.

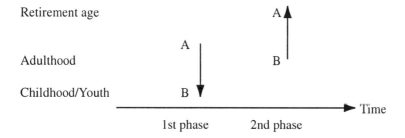

In other words, A begins by investing in B, that is, by spending in order to develop a future production factor. Then A obtains a 'return on investment', in that it can lay claim to part of what is produced by B. B has obligations towards A, and even if it is not explicitly stated that this is because members of A had, in the past, raised and educated those of B, it is because this investment did take place that A can count on B to support them.

We can complete the above with an opposite approach. Suppose that B does not exist: members of A had no children. In this case, they would obviously not have a retirement. They would have to continue working until they died. And the response which consists of calling on workers from other countries only exacerbates the problem: with no investment of their own, generation A may seek to appropriate the fruits of investments made by others. This 'cuckoo' economy (named for the bird species which steals the nests of other birds) is not necessarily a solution: it is generally considered that processes of exchange, and especially commerce, constitute a form of progress as compared to robbery, pillage and other forms of appropriation without payment of another's production.

D   *Exchange between Generations Produces a Deferment of Income*
        over the Course of the Life Cycle

A major challenge for every one of us is that of using part of the income generated by our professional activity, not at the moment that we earn it, but some decades later, once our working life is over. Income, like electricity, is difficult to store. In fact, the only way to massively defer a portion of income to a later time is to let other agents spend it in your stead, or to spend it on their behalf, with the understanding that the reverse operation will later take place. A begins by giving part of its income to B, and later B will give a portion of its earnings to A.

Naturally, for the second part of the operation to take place, it is necessary that B earn sufficient income when the time comes for its contribution. In general, this condition is fulfilled if B has productively spent the income with which A provided it. That is, if B has invested in order to have greater resources later. The deferment thus consists of the following: In a first phase, A allows B to invest, to prepare for the future and, more specifically, for future income; in a second phase, B returns to A a portion of its revenues, as these earnings come not only from B's own work but also from the investment made earlier by A.

Savings constitutes a much-used tool for the deferment of income. That income which members of A save rather than spending at the moment they earn it, is spent by members of B, in theory in order to increase their productive capacity. Later, there may be a reduction in savings, as A spends more than it earns. When the members of A thus begin to use their savings, it implies that others, those members of B whose spending was previously financed by A, now spend less than they earn, leaving A to access part of the available production.

It would be naive to believe that the situation is completely different when this deferment is organized around contributory retirement funds. These funds remove income from the workers of generation B, in order to put them at the disposal of the preceding generation A, which financed the upbringing and education of members of B when they were young. First, members of A contribute part of their resources to the younger generation; then this generation, members of B, accept payment of contributions to retirement funds so that production, *their* production, is partially allocated to their elders.

The mechanism is thus identical in both cases, that of deferment made through savings, and by retirement funds. In each of these cases, if the investment has not been sufficient, there is cause for worry. Borrowers will have trouble repaying their debts, funds will have difficulty collecting contributions. There are two essential differences between the two systems:

- retirement funds rely above all on human capital, on the production capacity of the younger generations. They are based on investment in people, while savings, credit, and the personal financing of economic activity is based more on physical and technological capital: buildings, machines, fabrication methods;

- savings is more a factor of the market economy, retirement funds of the social economy. In the first case we speak of finance; in the second, I use the expression socio-finance. Currently – but this is not fated to last forever – finance tends to be far more 'market-driven', while socio-finance tends to be more administered. The administrative nature of socio-finance allows it to be made to function according to rules which are entirely bizarre from the point of view of the business world, and, in addition, entirely unconvincing from the viewpoint of equity and simple common sense. These negative consequences of the administrative nature of socio-finance are the object of our next section.

E   The Denaturing of Socio-finance by Politics and the 'Courtelinesque' Administration

The French easily make fun of their own faults. Courteline is their preferred author for his mocking of the faults of their administration. When we think of rigid and absurd rules, of behaviour governed by inept texts, Courteline's name comes immediately to mind. Kafka is solemn, tragic; Courteline is light-hearted, his style is vaudevillian. But both are specialists in the absurd.

In what way is the contributory retirement system reminiscent of Kafka or Courteline? Fundamentally, by the separation it institutes between the attribution of retirement rights and the actions which give these rights a content. Jacques Rueff has studied the formation of rights, at the junction of the economic and legal sciences. He has demonstrated that one condition necessary to a smoothly running economic and social system is that the rights to current production be attributed to those who produce it, and that the rights to future production be attributed to those who prepare for it, in proportion to what they contribute to its preparation. Such rights, which are created in close relation to the actions which give them meaning, economic reality and content, are called 'true rights' by Rueff. However, when rights are distributed without any relation to contribution to current or future production, with no relation to behaviours which give them content or which satisfy the expectations of their holders, he speaks of 'false rights'.

Public administration is often attached to false rights. For example, its agents are promoted according to seniority, gaining higher and higher pay the older they get, without addressing the question of whether or not their productivity is rising. Lazy and incapable workers are paid as much as the conscientious and competent functionary, who keeps the service running in spite of the dead weight of certain of his colleagues, and sometimes in spite of conscious efforts on their part to put obstacles in his way. In short, the administration severs the link between the utility of its members and the rights it gives them to national production; it treats productive and nonproductive workers the same way, as long as they have the same diploma or have passed the same civil service exam. This method is universally condemned by all those who aim to provide good administrative service at the lowest cost; if it were generalized, if it were to invade the private sector, the absence of regulation would cause a considerable depression. Witness the situation of those countries dominated for a half-century or more by the Soviet regime, which extended caricatured administrative methods to every sector of the economy.

Contributory retirement funds are unfortunately governed by this administered economy, which ignores the basic rules for regulating economic and social systems. Their basic flaw lies in the fact that retirement rights are attributed, in general, in proportion to the contributions paid into the funds in order to pay benefits to retired people. This method establishes a link between two things with no economic relationship: the fact that workers give part of what they produce to their elders; and the fact that these workers acquire rights over the generation following them, which they will call on for their own retirement.

Alfred Sauvy has tried to explain this many times, without success: 'It is not by paying your contributions that you prepare your retirement, it is by raising your children.' When he was already retired, he said to a journalist:

> Do not believe that the President is putting your contributions into a piggy bank, which will be broken open when you reach the required age. Rather, he gives your contributions to me. I live well on them, thank you very much, but don't count on having them yourself in your old age. However, you can count on those who have children and raise them, because it is their contributions which will pay the pension you are expecting when the time for your retirement comes.

In actual fact, the contributions which we pay to retirement funds are part of an exchange between generations which is coming to an end, an exchange in which we first received (life, education) before giving (retirement contributions). It is an error to see these contributions as creating rights to another exchange, which is just beginning: That in which we begin by giving (financing the raising and education of children and young people, until they enter working life), and which ends when we receive a retirement pension, paid out thanks to contributions made by these children when they become adult workers.

Political responsibility for this conceptual error is considerable. In France, the first retirement funds were not contributory, but based on capitalization: factory workers' and farmers' retirement in 1910, then old-age insurance in 1930. But already at this time, clauses were introduced which, in order to please a certain electoral clientele, denatured the exchange relationship (see Bichot, 1997). Later, during the German occupation, the Vichy regime took control of the old-age insurance contributions in order to pay a new allocation, very useful at the time, the *Allocation aux Vieux Travailleurs Salariés* (AVTS, aging salaried workers' allotment). This gangster operation led to the retirement system contained in today's *sécurité sociale*, or overall social insurance system. After the war, workers continued to receive rights to retirement as before, under the capitalization retirement system, in proportion to the contributions they paid, while these contributions served to pay current pensions directly, according to the method introduced by Vichy. Thus, the origin of today's 'unfounded' contributory retirement system is a misappropriation of funds originated by a collaborationist government and maintained by governments issuing from the Resistance.

Current governmental practice clearly shows what has been done. When the Juppé government, in order to artificially reduce the budget deficit, added a lump sum of 37.5 billion francs paid by France Télécom to current governmental receipts, in exchange for a promise by the government regarding the retirement of telecom agents, the same infringement of normal accounting and management rules was illustrated. The government immediately spent the sum received and, above all, accounted it as a payment in exchange for a promise of counterpayment in the future. In the business world, such an undertaking would be considered cavalier: Imagine a company counting the product of a loan with its sales and other current receipts! In the world of politics, however, this is a practice which even the European authorities, with an eye to the Maastricht criteria, did not dare forbid, although it was severely criticized.

Thus, we have arrived at what Denis Kessler calls a 'magical chain', or what the Americans call a Ponzo system, after the American of Italian origin who introduced money chains and other pyramid schemes to the New World.

F   Reforming Contributory Retirement

Because contributory retirement funds have been built like a house of cards, on fragile foundations and according to absurd principles, should they be done away with entirely in favour of capitalization-based systems? Absolutely not. What is necessary is to reform them, in order to consolidate their structure and allow it to continue to function well and provide satisfactory service throughout the next century, which capitalization would not be able to do in full (see in this context Bourgeois and Pichat, 1978 and 1979; Bichot, 1993 and 1996).

Reforming contributory retirement systems means, above all, changing the rules which attribute an individual's right to a pension. This does not put into question those rights acquired at the time of the reform, which would be maintained, despite the fact that they were attributed according to absurd rules. But those rights acquired as of Day One of the new system would be based on contribution to investment in human capital.

This investment would be made in two ways:

•   by raising and educating children within the family;

•   by paying taxes in support of education, free medical insurance for children, and family or childcare benefits. In different countries, the collection of such contributions and the amounts collected vary. For example, childcare benefits in France are much higher than in Spain, income tax plays a much larger role in Denmark than in either France or Spain, etc. These are differences of form which do not alter the essential point, which is that citizens pay, through the intermediary of public or para-public administrations, so that children and young people can become competent and healthy adults.

For the sake of simplicity, let us suppose that these two components can be considered to have the same approximate overall value: Half of retirement rights would thus be attributed according to the criteria of the children raised by the retiree, and half by financial contributions made towards the health and education of all the children in the nation.

Contributions to retirement funds would, of course, continue to be paid, but they would stop 'earning' points or annuities. They would be considered, rather, as the repayment of benefits already received from the individual's conception through the age of 20 (more or less). According to the usual logic, repayment of a past debt makes the parties even; it does not constitute a savings from which it is possible to draw later.

Currently, contributors are in a situation similar to that of serfs in the Middle Ages: 'there to do their master's bidding.' This means that no limit is set to the contributions which can be demanded of them. If the needs of a fund increase, and if resistance is not too strong, then the level of contributions or taxation is increased. The new system would introduce an important change: A contract would be made with the rising generations, specifying what can be demanded of them. In this way, retirement funds would have to adapt their expenditures to their receipts, and not the reverse. This is the usual way of things in the business world: A debtor promises to pay a certain amount of interest, and not that amount which the creditor might need ten years later in order to easily balance his budget. Introducing this contractual approach into the area of intergenerational relations is what we feel is meant by the political expression 'pact between generations', used by Michel Rocard and others, if indeed this expression refers to anything concrete and is not just a vague concept without operational meaning.

For the rest of this essay, our reasoning takes place within the framework of a point system, like the complementary retirement funds in France. This method has clearly been shown to be superior, from a management viewpoint, to that based on annuities; the value of the point makes it possible to adapt simply and efficiently the amount of retirement pensions paid out to the amount of contributions received. Just as a shareholder in a company holds N shares, that is, has the right to receive N times the unit dividend, which depends on the company's results, so the pensioner holding P points has the right to receive P times the value of the point, this being approximately equal to the contributions held by the fund divided by the total number of points held by pensioners.

In addition, the liquidation of a pension could take place at any age, with the number of points being multiplied by an actuarial coefficient representing life expectancy at the time of liquidation, and by the actualization rate. Take, for example, a member holding 1,000 points. If the actuarial coefficient is 1 for liquidation at age 60, 0.8 at age 56, and 1.3 at age 65, then the monthly pension would be equal to 1000 times the value of the point in the case of retirement at 60, 800 times the point value if liquidated at age 56, and 1,300 times the value of the point for retirement at 65. This actuarial equity ensures that an equal number of points means equal treatment, whatever the age at which the participant decides to cash in his pension. The current value of the pension to be received would be the same in each case. This method would put an end to political manipulations aiming to increase either early or late retirements.

II   Reducing Mandatory Contributions

A   Retirement Point Attribution: An Explanation

As we saw in the system proposed above, retirement points are acquired for raising children, or for contributing financially to the upbringing and education of the younger generation.

Let us look at this attribution in greater detail.

a)   First of all, retirement points constitute a form of property similar to a house or a financial portfolio, and they can be acquired according to two different matrimonial regimes: community of acquired property, or separation of assets. For a couple having opted for community property, points belong to the community as long as the couple is not dissolved by the death of one spouse, or by divorce. In case of divorce, each would keep half of the points acquired since the start of the marriage. In case of death, the survivor also conserves half of the points, unless a specific contract was signed to ensure a higher percentage, supposing payment of an appropriately higher contribution.

We can note that these measures considerably improve the situation of women who, after sacrificing their professional career to the education of their children and, in some cases, to their husband's own career, are later shunted aside in favour of a younger rival. Today, until the death of their husband, they have no rights at all. In the new system, divorce would automatically provide them with half of the points acquired by the couple, if they had not opted for a regime of separate assets.

These measures also serve to do away with the obsolete mechanism of the reversion pension. Now is not the time to undertake a study of reversion, which has rendered significant service but has aged greatly and could advantageously be replaced by another mechanism.

b)   Points given in exchange for children's education could be attributed at a rate of n points per year during which the couple or the individual had effective responsibility, including financially, for the child or young adult. It could be possible to modulate n according to the age of the child, in order to take into account differences in cost between, for example, a five-year-old and an adolescent.

Who receives these points? If the child is raised by a married couple having chosen community property, there is no problem: points are the common property of Mr and Mrs X. If the child is raised by a single person, there is no problem, either: the points belong to this person. If there are two parents, married with a separation of assets, or unmarried, or divorced, where both exercise parental authority, the division of points is to be decided on a case-by-case basis, either by a contract between the parents or by a clause in the divorce judgement. To those who find such formalities extremely daunting, we would remark that problems arising from the absence of clearly defined rules are far more difficult to resolve when, for example, a couple argues or separates.

c)   For the attribution of points in proportion to financial contributions to collective investment in human capital, a sizable reform is necessary. All those contributions, taxes and other payments which, under the current system, support this investment in a very disorganized and often unrecognisable way, must be brought together in one common and clearly identified levy. This single levy would be called the 'Youth Contribution' (*Contribution Jeunesse*, or CJ). For example, a part of current contributions to health insurance funds, or those taxes supporting the National Service in Health and Sanitation should be done away with and replaced by a certain percentage of the CJ, because they serve to pay for care given to children or to young people who are not yet workers.

We will not deal at length here with the legal nature of the CJ: tax, social contribution or intermediate form. This is not, in fact, the essential point. What matters is that this contribution be clearly defined as creating rights; in other words, it is a payment which more closely resembles an obligatory savings fund than a mandatory contribution without return. In our opinion, it would be possible in the long run to move so far towards 'savings' that the CJ logically disappear from the list of mandatory contributions and the calculation of the mandatory contribution rate. A considerable reduction of this rate would thus be obtained; in the French example, around 600 billion francs or 8 per cent of GIP.

d)   We can note that, in the system described above, a person with no children acquires points through the 'channel' of the CJ, and only this channel, while one who raises her own children has two channels for points acquisition, and those acquired through the second will rise with the number of children raised. Given that persons from less privileged social levels tend to have more children than the average, and that a poor child 'earns' as many points as a rich one, it is clear that the new system of retirement could be, compared to the current system, a powerful motor for social justice. A simple example will demonstrate.

Imagine two households with two children each. In each household, both members of the couple work outside the home, but the members of household P earn minimum wage, while those of household M earn twice that amount. Currently, household M's pension is worth double that of household P. With the proposed system, assuming that rights acquired for one child are equal to those earned by the CJ paid on a salary of twice minimum wage, the very modest P household would have pension rights equal to a coefficient of 3, where the rights of the middle class M household would be equal to a coefficient of 4. This ratio of 3:4 is obviously more equitable than the previous 1:2 ratio, from the point of view of both commutative and distributive justice.

In fact, our current retirement systems are fabulous reproducers of social inequality, at least in those countries where pensions are generally proportional to working income; those countries, that is, which do not apply a Beveridgian system ensuring a uniform minimum pension, independent of earnings during the course of a career. The proposed reform would thus replace a system reproducing inequality with a system reducing inequality. That this should be the result of switching from a system with no relation to any logical conception of contribution, to one fully and clearly based on contribution logic, is significant. Infringing the principle of equitable exchange, a consequence of the intervention of 'Courtelinesque' public administrations, has largely negative consequences for those people at the lower end of the social ladder. After having thus spoliated these people, the Courtelinesque administrations naturally must deal with having to assist them, by paying them in the form of charity that which they should have received as a result of their contributions. 'Justice, not charity', could thus be one slogan of the reform of the Welfare State proposed here.

B   *Replacing Childcare Benefits*

That which follows is applicable above all to Northern European countries, including France, in which families receive fairly substantial childcare payments. In Mediterranean Europe (Spain, Italy, Greece, and to a certain degree in Portugal, in spite of its Atlantic character), childcare benefits are much lower. For them, the question is one of achieving just treatment of families without raising mandatory public contributions.

We should recall that when families are exploited, when they do not receive much in exchange for the services which they render to the community, young adults react by reducing their fecundity. Thus, the fecundity index in Spain and Italy is around 1.2. I know that it is popular to affirm that there is no cause and effect relationship between a weak family policy and a low birth rate, but this idea does not stand up under analysis; others, such as Olivia Eckert, will demonstrate this point during the symposium.

How can we reduce the mandatory contributions which finance childcare benefits, without hurting families in any way? What appears a priori to be a challenge becomes easy in the framework of a reformed contributory retirement system such as that described above. We can, in fact, just as easily increase a family's financial comfort by not levying contribution from it, as by giving it something after having taken away.

Consider a couple C with three children and a single woman F with one child. Each earns retirement points, on the one hand by paying the CJ, on the other by raising children. Compared to a couple or a single person with no children and the same primary income (professional income, financial income), and therefore identical CJ payments, C and F would receive more retirement points. It is thus possible to reduce the amount they owe in CJ, and to let them use freely the corresponding sums. It is then no longer necessary to pay them as much in childcare benefits.

The guiding principle here is to adjust the amount of the CJ according to the number of children in a given family (and perhaps also to the children's ages, to the existence of a handicap, etc.), in order to levy less money from those who have more children, rather than to levy equal amounts and pay out childcare support later.

A purely theoretical example will help to illustrate this method. Suppose that the CJ is levied at a rate of 12 per cent of total primary income. Suppose that one retirement point is attributed for one child-month or for FF 2500 of CJ. To simplify, we leave aside the question of age, which would come into play in a more sophisticated example. It could, for example, be decided that the presence of one child each month reduces the amount of CJ due by FF 900, which would naturally imply that less retirement points would be earned through payment of the CJ.

- If the single woman F earns FF 8,000 gross income per month, this corresponds to FF 960 of CJ. If she has one child, the CJ is reduced to FF 60. She would earn almost no retirement points for this lowered contribution, but her child earns her sufficient points, and it is more beneficial for her to have FF 900 at her disposal now than the equivalent amount in 40 years.

- If the couple C earns a total of FF 16,000 gross monthly income, which corresponds to FF 1,920 of CJ, without children, with three children the CJ is reduced to zero. Again, the retirement points earned from raising their own children are sufficient. One could postulate, for this type of family, a sort of negative tax: C could, in this case, receive FF 780, the difference between the 'theoretical' reduction of FF 2,700 in CJ, and the FF 1,920 actually saved on this contribution. Naturally, these FF 780 would be deducted from the retirement points earned for child-raising: C would earn points corresponding to FF 7,500 (3 children) minus FF 780, or FF 6,720, equal to 2.69 points at FF 2,500/point.

- If a couple C′ with five children has the same income, the theoretical reduction of CJ rises to FF 4,500, which is divided into FF 1,920 actually saved in CJ payments, and FF 2,580 of negative tax (or childcare benefits). The points acquired by C' in one month are calculated as follows: 5 x FF 2,500 - FF 4,500 = FF 8,000, or 3.2 points.

- If a couple C″ earns FF 50,000 gross monthly income, it would pay FF 6,000 with no children, or FF 3300 with three children. It earns 3 points per month for the children and approximately 1.25 for its CJ, or 4.25 points, as opposed to 2.69 for the less wealthy couple C: if it wishes to have a retirement pension in proportion to its current earnings, C″ is entirely free to contract a supplementary private pension, a life insurance policy or to save for retirement in any other way.

Within this framework, where the level of CJ paid depends on the number of children in the home, childcare benefits could be significantly reduced. There would thus be, overall, a reduction in mandatory contributions (the CJ would be lower than the taxes and contributions it would replace) and in benefits paid, without any negative effect on families' financial situations.

Certain measures aiming towards more flexibility could be added to this model. For example, there could be some freedom in determining the amounts to be made available immediately, and those to be 'invested' in retirement points. The family C′ could, for example, choose to collect FF 500 or 1,000 extra each month, with its point earnings being correspondingly lowered from 3.2 to 3 or 2.8.

C   *Calibrating these Measures*

It is possible to determine the reductions to be made in childcare benefits, and the rules for calculating the CJ, in such a way that the one exactly cancels out the other. In a country like France, it would, for example, be fairly simple to achieve a reduction of 100 billion francs in mandatory contributions, without any overall deterioration of families' situations. We believe, however, that this reform should also be used as an opportunity for increasing the income of families with children, as current differences in standard of living are excessive, and prevent the renewal of generations.

Another reason to increase the income of families overall is that it is impossible to create a system of reductions in CJ which would be equal, for all families, to the benefits withdrawn with the abolition of childcare support. If only a few families are to lose out in the immediate future (in the long term, all will be winners), it is necessary that the level of reductions in CJ be greater, overall, than the amount of the abolished childcare benefits. All specialists on social issues realize that an overall increase is unavoidable, to prevent the reform from becoming too unpopular due to the large number of 'losers' it would create. Forty billion extra francs provided to families, bringing the reduction in mandatory contributions down to 60 billion francs, could be an acceptable compromise.

Conclusion: the Need for Further Studies and Models

The reform project which has just been presented is not yet meant to be operational. We are convinced of its feasibility, but this must clearly be proven as scientifically as possible, through the use of a variety of simulations, impact and feasibility studies.

We know that in France, new ideas have trouble getting accepted. How many inventors have crossed the Atlantic to find people more inclined to bet on a solid and well-planned, but out-of-the-ordinary project! For example, the microchip payment card (smartcard) was thought up by an engineer whose employer, a major French electronics firm, put the project aside as being of no interest for development. Luckily, this man left his large, conservative company and developed his idea using other sources of support.

In the case of innovation in social finance, however, private initiative can not step in for immobile bureaucratic institutions. It is necessary to convince the administration and the public that a major reform of the retirement system and the system of childcare benefits is both desirable, and socially as well as technically possible. But, although it is often heard in upper political spheres that 'change' is necessary, it is far less easy to obtain aid in carrying out an in-depth and detailed study of the results of a concrete proposal for reform.

The engineering approach to economic, social and employment policy is woefully underdeveloped. We are certain that the country, or group of countries – the European Union, for example – which can improve this situation will gain considerable competitive advantage. Reducing mandatory contributions, while also improving social justice, is the best possible way to bring the growth enjoyed by the rest of the world to an aging Europe. Let us hope that our countries will not choose in favour of ageing and insipid growth.

References

Bichot, J. (1993), *Quelles retraites en l'an 2000?*, Armand Colin.
Bichot, J. (1996), *Retraite et Société*, No. 16.
Bichot, J. (1997), *Les politiques sociales en France au XXème siècle*, Armand Colin.
Bourgeois and Pichat (1978), 'Le financement des retraites par capitalisation', *Population*, No. 6.
Bourgeois and Pichat (1979), 'Répartition du revenu national entre capital et travail; application au financement des retraites', *Population*, No. 1.

7 Toward a Theory of Family Taxation

ALLAN CARLSON

To craft a family-centred theory of taxation, I begin with several assumptions regarding the imposition of taxes.

First, taxation is inevitable, the life blood of all forms of governance. In this age, we cannot choose to ignore taxation. Our only option is to craft it as wisely as possible.

Second, taxation has powerful social effects independent of any measure's ability to raise money for support of the state. Policy architects must be aware of their own social ideologies and build on and around the predictable incentives and effects, aware that there is no possibility of a 'neutral' tax relative to social structures and conventions (see Bittker, 1975, 1395–6).

Third, taxation must be confined to the economy denoted by money and markets. We need recognize that there are two economies that always coexist: *the market economy*, where exchanges take place through the medium of official tender and where competition and the quest for efficiency drive decisions; and *the home economy*, where exchanges occur through the altruistic blending of wealth and services between family members, usually independent of monetary calculation. It is through these latter acts and exchanges – ranging from child care, meal preparation, and home repair to carpentry, gardening, and food preservation – that the institutional life of a family takes form. As the home economy *grows* relative to the market economy, the family's claims on the individual – relative to other institutions – grow as well. Even in the wake of industrialization, these actions and exchanges represent economic activity of considerable value. Working with US data in the mid-1970s, Scott Burns (1977) calculated its overall worth to be at least 50 per cent of the official Gross National Product. Working with a more sophisticated model and Australian figures from 1992, economist Duncan Ironmonger (1996) calculated a 'Gross Household Product' almost *equal* to Australia's 'Gross Market Product,' roughly $350 billion each.

Experience also shows that taxation policy has a direct effect on the degree

116

of household commitment to the two economies. Sociologists Janet and Larry Hunt have shown that the net effect of higher marginal tax rates is to encourage the substitution of home production for market production : with a one-point increase in marginal tax rates, the average woman will work 39 fewer hours annually in the market economy, and devote 29 more hours to home production, as the family defends its living standard (and shelters income from taxation) by turning toward home (Hunt and Hunt, 1982). On this same question, Harvey Rosen (1976, p. 170) has emphasized that '[m]arried women do in fact seem to react to tax rates in the 'rational' manner of standard economic theory'. Unexpectedly, this turn to home production by 'women in families with higher after-tax cash income contributes more to their families' economic well-being than that of women in lower after-tax income families' (Bryant and Zick, 1985, pp. 12–14).

Accordingly, wise and just policy recognizes and defends the boundary between these two economies. At a minimum, and given its radically different methods of operation, the nonmonetized *home economy* must be free of *monetized taxation*. Viewed in a broader context, the taxation of market labour, market-oriented capital, and corporate income can be positively viewed as tariffs on market transactions, protecting the base of the home economy (Sandmo, 1990). This assumption also dictates that the efficiency of state tax collection should normally give precedence to the preservation of this vital boundary between the two economies.

And fourth, the rules of taxation need clean, easily verifiable definitions and lines of accountability. For example, relative to the taxation of households, the existence of a legal marriage is unambiguous in meaning and easily verified through documentation. The cohabitation of unmarried adults, in contrast, bears no equivalent paper trail nor consistent set of legal obligations. To offer another example, the money value of market transactions is calculated with relative ease, while the gains from home production rarely carry an easily calculated value.[1]

As the basis of theory, I need also offer certain assumptions regarding the family.

To begin with, *I hold that the family is a natural and universal human institution*, the primal social bond, rooted both in human biology and in human cultural conventions (on this argument, see Lovejoy, 1981; Guillame and LePlay, 1987, chs 24–30; Zimmerman and Frampton, 1935; Sorokin, 1941; Nisbet, 1976; Murdock, 1949). Men and women as incomplete beings are drawn to each other for coexistence and reproduction. Indeed, the family can be defined in all corners of the globe and in all times as a man and a woman bonded in a socially-approved covenant of marriage, to bear, raise, and protect children, to provide mutual protection and support, to create a small domestic economy, and to maintain continuity with the generations.[2] Families, not individuals, form the natural social units of society. As a corollary, family households – and not individuals – become the proper taxable units. Attempts to tax individuals *exclusive* of their position within families will normally create distortions that harm the family itself.[3]

Of equal importance, *we need acknowledge the enormous and irreplaceable gifts that stable families give to society*. The accumulated evidence from the fields of sociology, psychology, medicine, and criminology shows intact families based on marriage to be far superior to other entities as nurturers of the young and as guarantors of adult well-being. Children reared in such families are significantly – and usually dramatically – less likely to be victims of physical and mental abuse (Daly and Wilson, 1985; Smith, Hanson, and Noble, 1980) to attempt suicide (Stack, 1985 and 1990; Moens, et al., 1988), to use illegal, mind-altering drugs (Chein, Gerard, Lee and Rosenfeld, 1964; Kandel, 1980; Brook, Whiteman, and Gordon, 1983) and to commit other destructive or criminal acts (Pirog-Good, 1988; Figueira-McDonough, 1993; Knight and Prentby, 1987; Marquis, 1992; Beck and Kline, 1988). The children growing up with their natural parents in married-couple households are much healthier in mind and body than children reared in other settings (Kleinman and Kessel, 1987; Davison, 1990; and Saucier and Ambert, 1983) and much more likely to display cognitive advance and to succeed in school (Zajonc, 1976; Santrock, 1972; Biller, 1974; Marjoribanks, 1972).

Married adults, women and men, also lay claim to significantly better health than their never-married or divorced counterparts, and the married are much less likely to commit suicide (Hu and Goldman, 1990; Kisker and Goldman, 1990; Anson, 1988; Rosengren, Wedal, and Wilhelmsen, 1989).

Population growth through the birth of children within married-couple families also generates social progress and long term economic growth (Sauvy, 1969; Simon, 1979). In an era where *every* modern nation has either a zero-growth or (more commonly) a negative total fertility rate, the birth of additional children should be welcomed and encouraged by a tax system. Family advocates of a more social democratic bent might also argue for this as a means of redistributing income across one's lifespan: the 'tax relief' granted when one raises children is compensated for by the payment of higher taxes both before and after the children are present. I would emphasize that tax preferences for dependent children – be they exemptions, deductions, or credits – are the least intrusive way to adjust income in compensation for the 'market failure' regarding children. Competitive wage markets simply pay no attention to the number of dependants a worker might have. While many nations have adopted state child allowances as a response, these tend to draw governments into family life, welfare, and decision making. In contrast, *universal* tax exemptions, deductions, or credits require no investigations, means-testing, or payment schemes, beyond proof of a child's existence. In short, they have the same potential beneficial effects of child allowances, without the consequence of excessive state intrusion.

In the normative absence of stable, two-natural-parent families, the social welfare, criminological, and economic burden on the state becomes unsustainable. Hence, we can conclude that tax preferences in favour of marriage and the birth of children to married couples, as well as tax penalties on divorce and non-marital cohabitation, bear a compelling social logic.

Finally, and for the same reasons, *state or tax driven distortions of the natural family economy deserve compensation*. Most obviously, families deserve relief from the state's prior socialization of their children. Mandatory school attendance laws, child labour statutes, and state old-age pensions funded through taxation all represent, from the perspective of the family, the socializing of children's time and insurance value. One consequence of these governmental interventions into family life has been a sharply diminished birthrate, further weakening the family household. This 'demographic contradiction' inherent to the modern welfare state has long been apparent to observers (see Myrdal, 1940; and, more recently Hohm et al., 1986). An appropriate form of compensation would be massive tax relief targeted on families with dependent children, and increasing with family size.

How might these assumptions be applied in practice? Specifics would include:

- taxation should be confined to the gains of market labour and market capital, entities outside the domain of the family or home economy;

- home labour and home production must be free of taxation. The altruistic, non-monetized exchange of goods and services among family members should never be subject to extraction for state ends. Policy-makers should also avoid the indirect taxation of home production. Such negative strategies would include tax benefits designed to encourage the movement of individuals from home- to market-labour;

- household capital deserves favoured treatment, as well. Ideally, capital-gains and property taxes should be restricted to market capital. Land and homes on and in which families reside should not be subject to tax, nor should capital goods directly employed by family members. Indeed, a strong case from a family-perspective could be made to replace existing property taxes with a value-added tax (VAT). This would stimulate higher levels of home production, encourage the accumulation of capital by families, and strengthen the economic foundation of the home;[4]

- a pure 'flat' income tax, without deductions or exemptions related to family size and marital status, is hostile to the interests of the family, particularly in the encouragement it gives at the margins to market labour over home labour. However, if a single tax rate is offset by large household per-capita deductions or credits, a substantial share of the damage disappears;

- progressive income tax rates can work to the family's advantage, if such progressivity is offset by at least two measures: generous per-capita deductions for family members (such as 20 per cent of median family income); and income-splitting, where a marriage is treated as a partnership, with each spouse holding a claim to exactly one-half of the couple's joint or community income. Within progressive rates, the effects of these measures are : to shift a greater proportion of the tax burden onto single and childless persons; to transform a marriage and the presence of children into the average household's best tax shelters; to encourage marriage and the birth of children;[5] and to discourage divorce.

A Case Study: the United States

Relative to these assumptions and guides, how has the Federal tax burden in the United States evolved since the introduction of an income tax in 1913?

For the first 30 years, the Federal record was fairly dismal. The Revenue Acts of 1913 and 1916 were highly individualistic, with the taxable entity being the individual, rather than a family household. Married couples could file joint returns under the 1916 Act, but gained no real advantage in doing so. Dependent exemptions were allowed during the 1916–43 period, but they had no necessary relationship to family bonds. In short, the Federal income tax ignored the family, in favour of efficiency, progressivity, and individualism (see Bittker, 1975, pp. 1399–404).

However, a dynamic force pushing for change was a 1930 US Supreme Court decision (Poe *v.* Seaborn), which held that in so-called 'community property' states, 'income splitting' for married couples must be the rule. This allowed married couples to file a joint return, where they added up their total income, and 'split' that sum down the middle, with each spouse effectively taxed on his or her half alone. Under progressive rates (and except for those rare cases where husband and wife each earned exactly the same amount of market income), this measure gave a real benefit to marriage. While confined in 1930 largely to those Southwestern states under the residual influence of Spanish law, the community property system began spreading to other states, as legislators responded to married couples seeking to enjoy the marriage-centred tax cut implicit to 'income splitting'. When the US House Ways and Means Committee sought in 1941 to alter the law so that *all* married couples would pay the same tax on their consolidated income as a single person with the same amount of income, the idea was beaten back as 'a tax on morality' and an incentive to divorce (ibid., pp. 1408–11).

Instead, the US Congress began to move in a very different direction. The Reform Act of 1944 created the uniform per capita exemption. In prior decades, personal exemptions had varied widely depending on one's status. In 1925, for example, a married couple received a $3,500 exemption, a single person $1,500, and each dependent $400. For reasons partly of simplicity in administration, Congress adopted a uniform $500 per person exemption in 1944 for the wartime income surtax, and extended it to normal taxation in 1946. Another purpose, though, was pro-family in intent. As a Ways and Means Committee Report explained (House Ways and Means Committee Report No. 1365, 78th Congress, 2nd Session, p. 5; quoted in Seltzer, p. 42), the 1944 Act was expected to impose a 'lesser burden on the taxpayers with a large family and a greater burden on taxpayers with a smaller family'. Moreover, for the first time, the Act limited the personal exemption only to those household members related by 'blood, marriage, or adoption'.

In 1948, a Republican Congress – over President Harry Truman's veto – forced through a new Tax Reform measure. With the Treasury running a surplus that year of $8.4 billion, the primary goal was to cut taxes, and Congress did so in a family-supportive way. Forty per cent of the tax cut was achieved by raising the personal exemption by one fifth, to $600 per person, or about 18 per cent of median household income. Another 13 per cent of the tax cut came through the universal introduction of income splitting, extending to all 48 states the incentive to marriage and the penalties on divorce implicit to this measure.[6]

The 1948 Act also expanded the generous treatment accorded owner-occupied housing: the 'imputed rent' of the home was exempted from taxation; the interest on mortgages was also exempted, as were most capital gains from the sale of a house if a new one was purchased within a given time. Veterans Administration (VA) and Federal Housing Administration (FHA) regulations, in conjunction with underwriters' guidelines, delivered over 90 per cent of these new, tax-favoured mortgages to young married couples (see Fish, 1979, pp. 472–5; Laidler, 1969). Since a woman's market earnings were not counted when lenders calculated a family's eligibility for a mortgage, the incentives encouraged young mothers to become homemakers, with their focus on home production. Econometric analysis showed that about 25 per cent of the growth in home ownership in the 1945–75 period was a direct consequence of the tax system's favourable treatment of owner-occupied housing (Rosen and Rosen, 1980).

Accordingly, by 1948, the United States could claim a powerfully pro-family tax code:

1   the progressivity of tax tables was sharply reduced in a manner that favoured marriage and children;

2   there was a strong financial incentive for adults to marry and a significant, indirect penalty for divorce;

3   the costs of child-rearing were fairly recognized; indeed, the per-capita exemption actually provided a special bonus for truly large families;

4   as the tax code worked in conjunction with other government programs, family housing enjoyed a dramatic boom; and

5   the 'household economy' was encouraged by high marginal tax rates in conjunction with income splitting.

Over the following 15 years, the nation enjoyed both unprecedented economic expansion and remarkable social health. Marriages were more stable than in prior decades, and the proportion of adults who were married reached an historic high. Following a post-war 'spike' in 1946, the divorce rate steadily declined. The 'baby boom' also roared into high gear, with marital fertility nearly doubling between 1944 and 1957. Indeed, demographer Leslie Whittington has shown a 'robust' relationship between fertility and the real, after-inflation value of the personal income tax exemption, calculating an elasticity of birth probability with respect to the exemption of between .839 and 1.31 (Whittington, 1992; Whittington and Peters, 1990). Tax policy, it appeared, had been translated into family strength.

Almost from the beginning, though, critics began to assail the 1948 Reforms. 'Income splitting' drew the loudest complaints. A legitimate concern came from widows and other non-married persons with family dependants. But Congress responded wisely here and extended some of the benefits of 'income splitting' to these categories of taxpayers in 1951, under the category 'head of household' (Groves, 1963, pp. 68–9). But other complaints revealed a deep hostility to the very essence of the plan. One influential analyst claimed to see no virtue in a system which gave a benefit to a person just because he or she had acquired a spouse, rather than spending money in other ways (ibid., p. 59). Another argued that '[a]t the top of the income scale, the major rationale of income taxation is to cut down on the economic power of the family unit,' a goal subverted by the 1948 reforms (Pechman, 1966, p. 83). Economist Michael J. Boskin complained that income splitting 'produces a dead weight loss to society', particularly as it induced 'a larger decline in the market work of wives relative to husbands than is socially optimal' (Boskin and Sheshinski, 1983, p. 284). By the early 1960s, new worries about American 'overpopulation' led to calls for an end to the favoured tax treatment of marriage and children (see Meier, 1958; Pohlman, 1966; Ehrlich, 1968).

For a time, Congress turned a deaf ear to these arguments. The one troubling, although largely invisible development in the 1950s was the slow erosion in the value of the personal exemption, both in terms of inflation, as well as an offset against average household income. According to Treasury analyst Eugene Steuerle (1983, p. 74), this change would become '[b]y almost any measure ... the largest single change in the income tax in the postwar era'.

Direct dismantling of the pro-family tax code began in the 1960s President John F. Kennedy's 1963 tax cut, for example, did not raise the value of the personal exemption, as it should have done if the principles of 1948 had been followed. Rather, the measure implemented the new minimum standard deduction that paid no attention to the presence of children, focusing instead on relief for taxpayers with the smallest incomes (Report of the Committee on Ways and Means to Accompany H.R. 8363, 1963, p. 24).

Later in that decade, complaints that 'singles' were treated unfairly under 'income splitting' reached the ear of Representative Wilbur Mills, chairman of the House Ways and Means Committee. In 1969, he expressed interest in extending tax relief to help 'bachelors and spinsters as well as widows and widowers,' while retaining the 'marriage incentive' for those under age 35. The House-approved bill carried this distinction. Yet the new Nixon Administration's tax reform proposal eliminated the age restriction altogether, deeming it 'arbitrary' (Bittker, 1975, p. 1428) and limited the gains to married couples from income splitting to 20 per cent of total tax. It was this universalized measure that won adoption in the Tax Reform Act of 1969. Not only did this abandonment of true 'income splitting' sharply reduce the 'marriage incentive'; it also created a 'marriage penalty', which affected some two-income couples with particular force. It created a situation where they would, in fact, be better off single, rather than married.

The 1970s were witness to a mounting critique of the favourable tax treatment accorded the 'household economy'. Some critics saw even residual 'income splitting' as giving too much benefit to families with a mother-at-home. As June O'Neill (1983, p. 13) of the Urban Institute explained, 'a system of joint filing is likely to discourage the market employment of married women'. 'Two job couples' became the newest 'Victims of Tax Injustice', demanding compensation for their loss of home production (Bittker, 1975, p. 1431–42). Other critics said that it was unfair to leave 'home production' untaxed, since this encouraged people to produce their own goods and services instead of buying them, which diminished the revenue base.[7] But since it was difficult to measure, and hence tax, home production, policy architects recommended instead that targeted tax cuts be given to households with working wives, which would have the same effect.

Accordingly, in 1972, Congress increased the value and availability of the tax deduction for child care. In 1976, it substituted the Dependent Care Tax Credit, which granted direct tax relief of up to $800 to working parents who put their small children in institutional care. Similarly, Congress' attempt to reduce the 'marriage penalty' in 1981 tax legislation (by permitting a partial deduction on the second income of a two-earner household) also enjoyed the same theoretical justification : this was an indirect way to tax the extra 'implicit income' produced by the additional home labour within the 'one-career' household. At the same time, the housing provisions of the income tax code ceased to have a pro-family effect. FHA and VA eligibility standards were loosened, with the consequence being the funnelling of substantially more loans to non-family households (see Carlson, 1993, pp. 78–84). Indeed, by the early 1980s, some housing analysts suspected that a truly unusual, even perverse process had emerged. As economists George Sternlieb and James Hughes explained (1980, pp. 58–66): 'The very decline in the size of household, with its nominal generation of increased demand for housing units, may in turn be a consequence of the availability and costs of housing units generally.' Put another way, the tax-favoured housing system had now developed a vested interest in divorce and family disruption, where housing supply pushed artificial demand, and where federal housing subsidies – including tax benefits – now served as a substitute for the economic gains once provided by marriage.

Meanwhile, mounting inflation accelerated the erosion of the personal exemption. Even it's increase from $600 to $1,000 in 1969 did little to help. Together with the changes cited above, families with children became the big losers in the income tax sweepstakes. As Steuerle has shown, between 1948 and 1984, single persons and married couples without children showed no real increase in their average net federal tax rate. In contrast, married couples with two children saw their average income tax rate rise by 43 per cent (from 6.9 to 9.9 per cent), while a couple with four children faced a dramatic 223 per cent increase (from 2.6 to 8.4 per cent) (Steuerle, 1983, p. 75).

One countervailing development was the creation of the Earned Income Tax Credit (EITC) in 1975, a modest income supplement made available to low-income families with at least one dependent child at home. It is important to note that the EITC was conceived as a tax rebate to the working poor with children : its maximum benefit level was initially keyed to the combined total payroll tax rate (both employers and employees portions).

This measure aside, though, the 1963–85 period were years of loss for the family, relative to federal taxation. Conscious policy changes, in league with inflation, had these consequences :

1   families raising dependent children faced ever heavier Federal taxes, both absolutely, and in comparison to single persons and childless couples; and the larger the family, the greater the increased burden;

2   'income splitting' disappeared as a guiding concept, reducing the incentive to marriage, creating a disincentive to marriage in its place, and neutralizing the disincentive to divorce;

3   indirect taxation of the 'household economy' appeared for the first time, under the guise of the Dependent Care Tax Credit, followed by the 1981 'correction' to the 'marriage penalty'; and

4   tax incentives to owner-occupied housing ceased to have a pro-family effect; indeed, there was mounting evidence that these incentives (in

conjunction with other policy shifts) now damaged the interests of families, and even encouraged family break-up.

There can be little doubt that these shifts in the tax treatment of families had something to do with the negative turns in family life that began in the mid-1960s. The number of divorces climbed from 393,000 in 1960 to 1,213,000 in 1981, with the divorce rate rising 140 per cent. The rate of first marriage fell 30 per cent in the same period. Among women ages 20–24, the decline was 59 per cent. The US fertility rate tumbled from 118 (per 1000 women ages 15–44) in 1960 to 65.6 in 1978. The number of legal abortions climbed from 745,000 in 1973 to 1,577,000 in 1981. The total fertility rate, which measures the ability of society to reproduce, fell into the negative column for the first time in 1973.

Then came the sweeping Tax Reform Act of 1986. Partly as a response to its inability to balance the competing demands of married persons and singles, and of one-job and two-job families, Congress turned to a radically different approach. Its features included:

- the reduction of multiple tax brackets – ranging from 11 to 50 per cent on regular income – to only two: 15 per cent and 28 per cent;

- an increase in the personal exemption to $2,000 by 1989, and its indexing thereafter to inflation; however, personal exemptions would also now be phased out for higher income households (above $71,900 for joint returns, and $43,150 for singles), creating in effect a 33 per cent tax bracket during this phase-out period;

- a repeal of the 'marriage penalty' deduction;

- modest expansion of the Dependent Care Tax Credit;

- and retention of most tax preferences given to owner-occupied housing.

For the family, there were both gains and losses. On the positive side:

- the near-doubling of the personal exemption, from $1080 to $2,000, was a significant gain, although the reduction in marginal tax rates (from 50 to 28 per cent at the top level) blunted its effects at the upper-middle income level. Nonetheless, the encouragement to child bearing was real.

Whittington, Alms, and Peters predicted in 1987 that this change would result in a direct increase in the US fertility rate of 7.53 births per 1,000 women, ages 15 to 44, by 1990 (Whittington, Alan, and Peters, 1990, p. 553). The real increase turned out to be fairly close to this prediction: 5.5;

- indexing the exemption to inflation was another major achievement, putting a halt to the continued erosion in its value; and

- elimination of the special deduction for two income couples ended this indirect tax on imputed household income.

On the negative side, though:

- in the contest between participation in the market economy and the home economy, the Tax Reform Act of 1986, by bringing tax rates down, generally shifted incentives toward the market. One analysis predicted a direct 2.6 per cent increase in the labour force participation of wives, due to the tax bill (Hausman and Poterba, 1987, p. 108);

- the tax benefit for out-of-home child care, and its indirect tax on the parent-at-home, grew in size and relative significance;

- the phasing out of the personal exemption abandoned the important principle adopted in 1944 of universality. In practice, this phase-out also became a kind of indirect tax on the children of the relatively well-off;

- the significance and probable contemporary negative thrust of housing tax preferences remained unchanged;

- the so-called 'marriage penalty' reappeared in a new form; and

- an increase in the relative value of the standard deduction for 'heads of households' (normally one-parent households) actually created a small incentive favouring divorce and an equal division of children.[8]

In all, for families this Act marked the continued erosion of support. While fertility was encouraged, marriage faced heightened disincentives, as did the operation of the home economy. More births out of wedlock, more working mothers, and a heightened demand for day care were the predictable results.

The summer of 1997 witnessed another significant shift in Federal tax law. Provisions of special relevance to the family were:

- the creation of a new Child Tax Credit, worth $400 per child in 1998 and rising to $500 in 1999. Confined to children ages 16 and under, the credit is phased out for married couples with incomes over $110,000, and for individuals earning above $75,000;

- educational tax credits to pay for college and university expenses : up to $1,500 for the first two years of college; and up to $2,000 thereafter (with a phase out of the latter provision for married couples earning $80,000 or more, and single taxpayers earning $50,000 or more); and

- an increase in the capital gains tax exclusion to $500,000 (for married couples) on the sale of a principle residence (and $250,000 for singles).

Despite the unfortunate phase out of the Child Tax Credit at higher income levels (writing in the early 1970s, tax theorist Boris Bittker (1975, p. 1452) labelled a 'vanishing deduction' such as this a 'drastic remedy'), this provision should be of positive effect, roughly doubling for most families the 'tax shelter' impact of each child. The favoured treatment given to the capital gains from the sale of a family residence should also give positive encouragement to family capital accumulation. On the other hand, past experience suggests that the new credits for higher education will be of ephemeral utility, quickly absorbed by cost increases at colleges and universities.

Conclusion

The American experience points to the pitfalls and promise of a pro-family income tax scheme. Among the discouraging aspects are the 'accidental' nature of several positive measures (such as the victory of 'income splitting' over 'individualism' in the 1930s and 1940s, and the recurring influence of ideas and pressure groups opposed to family autonomy and growth.

On the positive side, though, the American experience in the 1944–63 period strongly suggests that tax policy can play a positive role in family renewal and reconstruction. Moreover, the 1997 reforms – the product of 15 years of conscious pro-family political effort – also show that ideological barriers can be overcome, negative policies reversed, and positive measures advanced for the good of families, and nations.

Notes

1   A compelling case against efforts to measure 'imputed income' from home production is found in McIntyre and Oldman, 1977.
2   This definition comes from The World Congress of Families, which convened in Prague, Czech Republic, 19–22 March 1997.
3   This general orientation was ably summarized in the 1966 Report of Canada's Royal Commission on Taxation : 'We believe firmly that the family is today, as it has been for many centuries, the basic economic unit in society ... [T]he married couple itself adopts the economic concept of the family as the economic unit from the outset' (see Report of the Royal Commission on Taxation (Carter Commission, 1966); cited in Bittker, 1975, p. 1393.
4   While deploring the result, Boskin (1975) documents the powerful effect of this potential change.
5   On this point, see Whittington, 1992.
6   For a detailed treatment of this concept, see Groves, 1963, pp. 56–83.
7   On this point, see Blomquist and McKee, 1986.
8   Noted in Espenshade and Minarik, 1987, p. 119.

References

Anson, O. (1988), 'Living Arrangements and Women's Health', *Social Science and Medicine*, 26, pp. 201–8.
Beck, A.J. and Kline, S.A. (1988), 'Survey of Youth in Custody, 1987', *U.S. Department of Justice, Bureau of Justice Statistics, Special Report*, Washington, DC: U.S. Department of Justice.
Biller, H.B. (1974), *Paternal Deprivation: Family, School, Sexuality, and Society*, Lexington, MA: Lexington Books.
Bittker, B. (1975), 'Federal Income Taxation and the Family', *Stanford Law Review*, 27, July.
Blomquist, A. and McKee, M. (1986), 'Eliminating the "Marriage Exemption" in the Canadian Income Tax: The Erola Proposal', *Canadian Journal of Economics*, 19, May, pp. 309–17.
Boskin, M.J. (1975), 'Efficiency Aspects of the Differential Tax Treatment of Market and Household Economic Activity', *Journal of Public Economics*, 4.
Boskin, M.J. and Sheshinski, E. (1983), 'Optimal Tax Treatment of the Family: Married Couples', *Journal of Public Economics*, 20.
Brook, J.S., Whiteman, M. and Gordon, A.S. (1983), 'Stages of Drug Use in Adolescence: Personality, Peer, and Family Correlates', *Developmental Psychology*, 19, pp. 269–88.
Bryant, H.K. and Zick, C. (1985), 'Household Production, Taxes, and Family Income Distribution', *Human Ecology Forum*, 15, pp. 12–14.
Burns, S. (1977), *The Household Economy: Its Shape, Origins, and Future*, Boston: Beacon Press.

Carlson, A. (1993), *From Cottage to Work Station: The Family's Search for Social Harmony in the Industrial Age*, San Francisco: Ignatius.

Chein, I., Gerard, D.C., Lee, R.S. and Rosenfeld, E. (1964), *The Road to H: Narcotics, Delinquency and Social Policy*, New York: Basic Books.

Daly, M. and Wilson, M. (1985), 'Child Abuse and Other Risks of Not Living with Both Parents', *Ethology and Sociobiology*, 6, pp. 197–209.

Davison, P.A. (1990), 'Family Structure and Children's Health and Well-being : Data from the 1988 National Health Interview Survey on Child Health', paper presented at the Annual Meeting of the Population Association of America, Toronto.

Ehrlich, P. (1968), *The Population Bomb*, New York: Ballantine.

Espenshade, T.J. and Minarik, J.J. (1987), 'Demographic Implications of the 1986 U.S. Tax Reform', *Population and Development Review*, 13, March.

Figueira-McDonough, J. (1993), 'Residence, Dropping Out, and Delinquency Rates', *Deviant Behavior*, 14, pp. 109–32.

Fish, G.S. (ed.) (1979), The Story of Housing, New York: Macmillan.

Groves, H.M. (1963), Federal Tax Treatment of the Family, Washington, DC: The Brookings Institution.

Guillame, P. and LePlay, F. (1987), *Le Reform Sociale*, Vol. I, Bk 3, Tours : A. Mame et fils.

Hausman, J.A. and Poterba, J.M. (1987), 'Household Behavior and the Tax Reform Act of 1986', *Economic Perspectives*, 1, Summer.

Hohm, C.F. et al. (1986), 'A Reappraisal of the Social Security-Fertility Hypothesis: A Bi-Directional Approach', *The Social Science Journal*, 23, December, pp. 149–68.

Hu, Y. and Goldman, N. (1990), 'Mortality Differentials by Marital Status: An international comparison', *Demography*, 27, pp. 233–50.

Hunt, J.G. and Hunt, L. (1982), 'The Dualities of Career and Families : New Integrations or New Polarizations?', *Social Problems*, 29, June, pp. 499–510.

Ironmonger, D. (1996), 'The Domestic Economy : $340 Billion of G.H.P.' in B. Muehlenberg (ed.), *The Family: There is No Other Way*, Melbourne: The Australian Family Association, pp. 132–46.

Kandel, D.B. (1980), 'Drug and Drinking Behavior Among Youth', *Annual Review of Sociology*, 6, pp. 235–85.

Kisker, E.S. and Goldman, N. (1990), 'Perils of Single Life and Benefits of Marriage', *Social Biology*, 34, pp. 135–52.

Kleinman, J.C. and Kessel, S.S. (1987), 'Racial Differences in Low Birth Weight', *New England Journal of Medicine*, 317, pp. 749–53.

Knight, R.A. and Prentby, R.A. (1987), 'The Developmental Antecedents and Adult Adaptations of Racist Subtypes', *Criminal Justice and Behavior*, 14, pp. 403–26.

Laidler, D. (1969), 'Income Tax Incentives for Owner-Occupied Housing' in A.C. Harberger and M.J. Bailey (eds), *The Taxation of Income from Capital*, Washington, DC: The Brookings Institution, pp. 50–64.

Lovejoy, C.O. (1981), 'The Origin of Man', *Science*, 211, 23 January.

McIntyre, M.J. and Oldman, O. (1977), 'Treatment of the Family', in J. Pechman (ed.), *Comprehensive Income Taxation*, Washington, DC: The Brookings Institution, pp. 205–39.

Marjoribanks, V. (1972), 'Environment, Social Class, and Mental Abilities', *Journal of Educational Psychology*, 63, pp. 103–9.

Marquis, P. (1992), 'Family Disfunction as a Risk Factor in the Development of Antisocial Behavior', *Psychological Reports*, 71.

Meier, R.L. (1958), 'Concerning Equilibrium in Human Population', *Social Problems*, 6, Fall, pp. 163–75.

Moens, G.F.G. et al. (1988), 'Epidemiological Aspects of Suicide Among the Young in Selected European Countries', *Journal of Epidemiology and Community Health*, 42, pp. 279–85.

Murdock, G.P. (1949), *Social Structure*, New York: Free Press.

Myrdal, G. (1940), *Population: A Problem for Democracy*, Cambridge, MA: Harvard University Press.

Nisbet, R. (1976), *Twilight of Authority*, New York: Basic Books.

O'Neill, J. (1983), 'Family Issues in Taxation', in R.G. Penner (ed.), *Taxing the Family*, Washington, DC: American Enterprise Institute.

Pechman, J.A. (1966), *Federal Tax Policy*, Washington, DC: The Brookings Institution.

Pirog-Good, M.A. (1988), 'Teenage Paternity, Child Support, and Crime', *Social Science Quarterly*, 69, pp. 527–47.

Pohlman, E. (1966), 'Mobilizing Social Pressures Toward Smaller Families', *Eugenics Quarterly*, 13, Spring, pp. 122–6.

Report of the Committee on Ways and Means to Accompany H.R. 8363 (1963), Washington, DC: US Government Printing Office.

Rosen, H.S. (1976), 'Tax Illusion and the Labor Supply of Married Women', *The Review of Economics and Statistics*, 58.

Rosen, H.S. and Rosen, K.T. (1980), 'Federal Taxes and Home Ownership: Evidence from Time Series', *Journal of Political Economy*, 88, pp. 59–75.

Rosengren, A., Wedal, H. and Wilhelmsen, L. (1989), 'Marital Status and Mortality in Middle-aged Swedish Men', *American Journal of Epidemiology*, 129, pp. 54–63.

Sandmo, A. (1990), 'Tax Distortions and Household Production', *Oxford Economic Papers*, 42, pp. 89–90.

Santrock, J.W. (1972), 'Relation of Type and Onset of Father Absence to Cognitive Development', *Child Development*, 43, pp. 457–69.

Saucier, F. and Ambert, A. (1983), 'Parental Marital Status and Adolescents' Health-Risk Behavior', *Adolescence*, 18, pp. 403–11.

Sauvy, A. (1969), *General Theory of Population*, New York: Basic Books.

Simon, J. (1979), *The Economics of Population Growth*, Princeton, NJ: Princeton University Press.

Smith, S.M., Hanson, R. and Noble, S. (1980), 'Social Aspects of the Battered Baby Syndrome', in J.V. Cook and P.T. Bowles (eds), *Child Abuse: Commission and Omission*, Toronto: Butterworths, pp. 205–25.

Sorokin, P. (1941), *The Crisis of Our Age*, New York: E.P. Dutton.

Stack, S. (1985), 'The Effect of Domestic/Religious Individualism on Suicide, 1954–1978', *Journal of Marriage and Family,* 45, May, pp. 431–47.

Stack, S. (1990), 'The Effects of Suicide in Denmark, 1961–1980', *The Sociological Quarterly*, 31, pp. 361–8.

Sternlieb, G. and Hughes, J.W. (1980), *America's Housing: Prospects and Problems*, New Brunswick, NJ: Center for Urban Policy Research, Rutgers University.

Steuerle, E. (1983), 'The Tax Treatment of Households of Different Size', in R.G. Penner (ed.), *Taxing the Family*, Washington, DC: American Enterprise Institute.

Whittington, L.A. (1992), 'Taxes and the Family: The Impact of the Tax Exemption for Dependents on Marital Fertility', *Demography*, 29, May, pp. 215–26.

Whittington, L.A., Alan, J. and Peters, H.E. (1990), 'Fertility and the Personal Exemption: Implicit Progatalist Policy in the United States', *The American Economic Review*, 80, June, pp. 545–56.

Zajonc, R.B. (1976), 'Family Configuration and Intelligence', *Science*, 192, pp. 227–36.

Zimmerman, C. and Frampton, M. (1935), *Family and Society: A Study of the Sociology of Reconstruction*, New York: D. Van Nostrand.

PART III
THE FAMILY IN THE CONSTRUCTION OF CITIZENSHIP

8 The Australian Welfare State Today: Generational Issues and Family Tensions

ALAN TAPPER

I   Families, Generations and Public Policy

Discussion of the place of the family in contemporary society and in public policy is difficult for a number of reasons. Some matters are relatively straightforward. The general trends in the modern family are well known. They can be summarised as increased diversity and decreased stability, a decline in fertility and a weakened network of intra-familial relationships. The concomitant gains and losses have been much debated. About this, however, some consensus is now emerging: the losses for children brought up in the new family forms, apparent in the large-scale studies of recent times, are now being recognised.

Granting this, many puzzles remain. At one level, we still need to know much more about why the diversified or fragmented family is so much less successful than the biological family. Then we need to construct a coherent history of the modern family, one that goes deeper than a simple story of fragmentation and loss. How much have styles of child-rearing really changed within the family? What has happened in terms of time and attention devoted to children by their parents? What impacts have television, the media, changes in schooling had, for better or worse, within the family? Have neighbourhood networks diminished in significance and socializing impact?

At another level, what is really known about the treatment of the family by public policy? Analysis of that question, which is the main topic of this paper, requires a concept not much discussed in political theory, the notion of a generation. We have commonly assumed that public policy treats each generation much like every other. Recent research has shown just how mistaken that assumption is. Here I want to show how the public role of the family has fared at a time when intergenerational disparities, the product of public policy decisions, have mounted as never before.

135

II   Generations and Governments

A 'generation', as discussed here, is a collection of individuals defined by their year of birth, a bundle of cohorts. It is not a stage of life, such as 'the young' or 'the elderly'.

In recent times, there has been much debate about 'the elderly'. The concept is a slippery one, referring sometimes to today's elderly, sometimes to a category that will always be with us, the group of whoever is oldest at any point in time. The second usage refers to age in the life cycle, a stage of life that almost all will experience. The first usage picks up the end of the life cycle of a particular generation, roughly those born between 1910 and 1940.

Worries about the elderly in public policy slide between these two usages. There is concern that expenditures on today's elderly are presently unsustainable, and quite distinct worries that such expenditures will be even less sustainable when tomorrow's even more numerous elderly reach retirement. Conceivably, today's spending may be sustainable, tomorrow's not; or perhaps today's is unsustainable and tomorrow's commitments will never even begin to be met.

This focus on the elderly arises from the growing demands that today's elderly have placed upon social welfare systems, demands which are only in small degree the product of numerical increases. American economist Lester Thurow (1996, pp. 97–9), speaking of the situation in all OECD countries, states the matter strongly.

> Already the needs and demands of the elderly have shaken the social welfare state to its foundations, causing it for all practical purposes to go broke … Everything else is being cut in government budgets to make room for the elderly … Expenditures on the elderly have fundamentally altered our fiscal systems … Even with rapid economic growth and no new programs, government spending rises faster than tax revenues because of entitlements for the growing population of the elderly.

The problems Thurow describes are undoubtedly massive, in many countries. But what are we concerned about here, old age as a stage of life requiring social support, or the experience of particular generations, some of which will reap huge windfall benefits and some of which will find themselves landed with debts generated by their predecessors? Clearly, modern societies now devote quite disproportionate resources to old age. The beneficiaries today are those born between 1910 and 1940. Later cohorts may also benefit, if spending levels are kept up for the next few decades. If, however, debts mount and cutbacks are required, some cohorts may suffer, taking out less in benefits than they have been required to contribute.

To come to terms with this sort of problem, we need to think not about 'the elderly' as a stage of life, but about generations. Once we make this conceptual shift, however, other questions crowd in. Granting that generational experiences of social security payments and benefits may be quite divergent, what about other areas of public policy? Are expenditures on health, education, and housing intergenerationally equitable? Are taxes, direct and indirect, consistent across time, and proportional to payouts? How do other government policies – on interest rates, employment, public works, capital investment – pan out? The social security story should at least alert us to the possibility of striking inconsistencies. But possibly those inconsistencies will cancel out, with each generation gaining in one area and losing in another. Today's elderly, it may be, are not the big winners they might seem to be.

Only 'generational balance sheets', covering all aspects of government, can offer satisfying answers to such comprehensive questions. And such accountancy will need to reach, speculatively, some decades into the future if we are to make lifetime comparisons between today's worker with today's retirees. Modern governments have made no attempt to construct such records. More surprisingly, until recently academic researchers have done little in this direction. The concept of generational equity has been discussed abstractly but rarely is it assessed quantitatively.

David Thomson, working with New Zealand records, has pioneered the sort of research now so urgently needed here. His results show that intergenerational equity is more than just an interesting philosophical problem. On his account, gains across the board to the generation born between 1910 and 1940 have been massive. That generation's lifetime experience is one of low taxes and high social benefits. Thus, discrepancies favoring today's elderly turn out to be a subset of a much larger issue, favoritism for certain cohorts. The outcome is even more troubling than Thurow's story. As Thomson puts it, 'The twentieth century welfare state is looking disturbingly like a one-generation benefit scheme' (Thomson, 1996, p. 163).

This sort of socioeconomic analysis is new, and of course hasty generalisations are a danger. My own work on the Australian evidence, however, confirms Thomson's account. Australian has kept a tighter rein on expenditure on the elderly than perhaps any other modern welfare state. Even so, intergenerational disparities are very large. In Australia they are the product of three main factors: increased income taxes for later cohorts, cutbacks in income support and tax relief for families with children, and likely declines in pension entitlements in old age for today's workers. The following table shows the lifetime story for two typical couples, one born in 1930, the other born in 1955, using Thomson's New Zealand and my Australian calculations. The unit of measurement is average male annual wages (a unit chosen because it does not disadvantage the earlier-born in the way that a simple CPI-indexed calculation would). In effect, then, by these calculations alone the earlier cohort in New Zealand has benefited by 12 years of average earnings compared with its successor cohort; in Australia, where some aspects of social policy have been more tightly controlled, the discrepancy is still as large as nine years of average earnings. When all taxing and spending are computed, these discrepancies increase even further. Thomson estimates the minimum total disparity to be 18 years of average earnings; I estimate the Australian minimum figure to be 12–14 years.

Table 8.1   Lifetime income taxes, family benefits and age pensions for two cohorts: New Zealand and Australia

Cohort	Born 1930	Born 1950
New Zealand	+ 2.5	- 9.8
Australia	+ 1.9	- 7.2

III   Unit of Measurement: 'Years of Average Pay'

Intergenerational inequity is real and important. Other national studies may reach different results – only time will tell. There are many pointers, however, suggesting that New Zealand and Australia have followed typical welfare state trajectories, and that perhaps other systems, where much more has been pooled and distributed, have been even less successful in imposing cross-generational consistency.

IV   The Family Story

As I said earlier, my aim in this paper is to discuss how the public role of the family has fared at a time when intergenerational disparities, the product of public policy decisions, have mounted as never before. I want to present the generational story and the family story in parallel, and then to reflect on possible interactions between them. In telling the family story I will once again use Australian evidence, but in my judgment that story is notable more for being typical of many societies than for its idiosyncrasies.

In Australia, as elsewhere, family change has been sudden and dramatic. In the 1970s the divorce rate tripled. Since the 1960s, the percentage of births outside marriage has increased fivefold, from 5 to 25 per cent. Many of the new single parent families became dependent of social welfare support, some for short periods, some long-term. Taken together, these figures show that there has been an enormous increase in the proportion of children no longer living with both their biological parents, and in most cases the missing parent is the father. Such children were not long ago a rarity. Now about one-third of Australian children live outside their biological families, two-thirds of them with one parent, one-third in step-families and blended families. Although the divorce rate levelled off in the 1980s, the trend in this direction is continuing, as the proportion of births outside marriage continues to rise. Increased divorce and rising voluntary sole parenthood amount to declines in the social strength and status of marriage, both *de jure* and *de facto* marriage. Remarriage and step-parenthood have provided second parents for many children, though normally this involves a second process of transition and negotiation for a child who has already had to come to terms with the loss of a biological parent.

Families, then, are far more diverse, complex and fissile than in earlier generations. These are external facts about family structure. For some time in Australia it was argued that such external facts tell us little about the success or failure of families as agents of socialization. Research in the early 1980s argued that children in single parent families were achieving levels of social competence equivalent to those of children still with their original parents; only children in step-families seemed to be suffering adversely from the rapid changes. Recent, more sophisticated analysis – the 1993 Western Australian Child Health Survey, carried out by the Institute for Child Health Research in conjunction with the Australian Bureau of Statistics – has overturned that judgment. It is now clear that growing up with both biological parents is one of the three main protective factors making for good mental well-being. Children in the new family types average rates of psychological morbidity (depression, anxiety, aggression, delinquency, withdrawal, obsessions, psychosomatic problems) two or three times higher than their counterparts living in non-disrupted families. The other two factors operating here are the quality of the relationships between the parents and the disciplinary style adopted by the parents towards their children. These three factors together account for more than 80 per cent in the variation in children's mental health problems. No other factor could be found with anything like this influence.

In effect, then, what takes place in the family, both qualitatively and structurally, determines the psychological gains or losses that children experience. Outside forces have relatively little impact. It further follows that a dramatic disruption of family stability, such as has happened in recent decades, must mean a loss for children's socialization. Both family structures and marital relationships have suffered important declines. We know little about how family disciplinary styles have altered in this period. Successful discipline, the Child Health Survey found, involved a combination of consistency and affection, with a minimum of direct coercion. Unsuccessful styles were those which were predominantly coercive or highly inconsistent. Whether in recent decades their have been net gains or losses here is not easy to tell.

The Child Health Survey is distinguished by the careful design of its questionnaires and by the statistical sophistication of its methods. Its final position on mental well-being involved a multiple regression of the factors present at the first level of analysis, demonstrating that each factor contributes independently to the outcomes. Thus, it can not be claimed that family structure is a proxy for other deeper forces – it is on this analysis a force in its own right. In particular, the correlations between family type and psychological well-being are not functions of income changes associated with family breakdown; nor are they explained away by pre-existing family or marital tensions, tensions which themselves lead to divorce. Both of these claims have often been made to show that family structure is not an independent factor; both now seem to be mistaken, at least on the evidence of this study.

The optimistic view has been that the family is diversifying but not declining. The evidence here indicates that family structural change has involved serious decline in children's socialization. Rises in problem behaviour amongst the young, in suicide, delinquency, crime, vandalism, homelessness, drug addiction, sexual abuse – often strongly associated with the new family forms – corroborates the family decline thesis. From here on I will take that thesis as requiring no further argument. It is becoming the standard view amongst family sociologists.

The question which immediately follows is how to explain such a trend. Why has such an historically unprecedented trend emerged in prosperous, fortunate and stable countries like Australia, countries with strong democratic traditions, with no external threats, and with generally successful economies? A great many suggestions have been put forward on this topic, many of them easily invalidated. No strongly developed and widely accepted theories hold the field. We are still guessing, still trying out ideas.

Family decline appeared suddenly, with few warning signs. Few predicted anything of the sort. High levels of family stability were replaced almost overnight by disruption on a scale previously unknown. The changes seem entirely voluntary, a matter of cultural transformation. For many, men and women alike, adult self-fulfilment came to be defined as fulfilment outside the family, a fundamental change in social self-definition. Given the evidence on declines in children's well-being, declines that must have been at least partly visible at the individual level, this changed self-definition amounts to adult gains (or perceived gains) at the expense of commitment to children. It is not easy to make sense of such a loss of parental investment, particularly at a time in which 'child-centredness' has been fashionable.

Family decline is an intra-family phenomenon, a loss in the culture internal to the family. But it does not follow that the explanation of that decline must be internal. It may be that external forces have been operating on the family, so that a consistent desire to succeed as parents and partners has been made more difficult, and for many too difficult, by factors beyond family control. On a first hearing this approach to the problem sounds implausible. What factors might there be? Economic growth in many countries slowed in the 1970s, but in those same countries welfare safety-net expenditures rose strongly, seemingly sheltering families from market forces. New technologies, such as the widespread devotion to television, may have had a strong impact on children, but why should this have reduced parental commitment?

Economic demand, and perhaps economic need, may have taken mothers out of the home more than ever before, and this no doubt has offered women an alternative to the family, while perhaps subtracting from men's traditional role as family providers. However, on my analysis of the Australian evidence (and Catherine Hakim has argued similarly for Britain) we have commonly overstated the force of this trend – since 1965 Australian women's average hours worked per week have increased by only about 20–25 per cent. The trend in hours worked by mothers of dependent children is less clear. Very likely it has increased quite substantially, though from a low base. Its impact on the family – the amount of time and commitment it has taken away from the maintenance of family relationships – remains debatable, in my view. In that same period, the Australian birth rate has halved (a typical trend), so the demands of children are much less than they were, making work outside the home relatively feasible, and not in strong competition with maternal childcare. I know of no evidence that working women are much more likely to divorce than women at home.

V   Families and Governments

Whatever one's view on the trend in women's workforce participation, there seems room for plenty of further explanation. The family revolution may be approached from other angles. Suppose now that we put together the two main themes of this discussion, family change and generational policy. Explanations of family change need to have the appropriate timing, scope, magnitude and causal direction. The turnaround in generational priorities, which in Australia began in the mid-1960s and proceeded rapidly thereafter, has all of those properties in appropriate form. Could it be a major explanation of family change?

Welfare states of today, it now seems, are systems which transfer resources from the young to the old. They favour those who are asset rich over those who are asset poor. They require people who are establishing marriages, raising children, starting careers and buying homes to subsidise those who have completed those common life tasks. Welfare states of yesterday, those of the post-war decades, did exactly the opposite. They were systems of public investment in the young. 'The welfare state' is thus not a single phenomenon. It has had two completely different incarnations, a 'Youth State' and an 'Elder State', to use Thomson's terminology.

The transition from one welfare state to the other coincides with the revolution in the family. Cohort analysis of taxing and spending permits some quantification of these changing social priorities. By my Australian estimates, effective income taxes (income taxes minus family support subsidies) for couples from the 1950 cohort increased by about $200 per week (in current dollars) over effective taxes paid by couples from the 1930 cohort during the child-rearing years (ages 25 to 45). That $200 per week represents about two-fifths of an average after-tax income. The price of participation in the welfare system thus rose very steeply in the period 1960 to 1990, and the social climate for child-rearing was dramatically altered. One can hardly doubt that financial shifts of this magnitude have significant social effects. At the least, these shifts strongly reinforced a pre-existing social tendency.

At the same time, welfare supports for sole parenthood were strengthened and made easier of access. A welfare system designed originally for widows and deserted wives became for many a substitute for marriage. Average stays on sole parent welfare benefits are about 3.5 years. Average lifetime usage of such welfare must be much higher than this, though the figure is unknown. Many children have thus grown up in families dependent on the state and with little male economic input.

The Australian welfare state transformed itself in a decade or two from a system of near-universal family support with little assistance for old age to a system of near-universal generosity towards the elderly with strong supplementary support for couples who divorce or women who choose to have children outside marriage. This transformation is intimately connected to the revolution in the family. That revolution is barely conceivable without an accommodating welfare support system, one that makes non-married families economically viable. Less obviously, and perhaps more importantly, the withdrawal of support from married families in favour of increased payments, services and subsidies to the older third of the population accounts for a large part of the changes in the family. In this way an era of stable marriages and families (and economic prosperity) was replaced almost overnight by a time of family fragility, welfare dependency amongst the young, and unprecedented tax-funded prosperity for the elderly.

VI   Explaining the Generational Story

The argument so far may have helped to account for family change, but it has done so by relying heavily on the apparent enigma of generational transformation. Is this not a case of *obscurum per obscurius*?

The post-war welfare state, the Youth State, was a product of the Depression and war. It was an attempt to construct a stable and secure society, by pooling resources and redistributing the product towards particular phases of economic need. At that time welfare states like Australia put the needs of the young ahead of those of the old. Consistency and equity then required that the benefits enjoyed by those raising children at that time – the parents of the baby boom – be passed on to the next generation of parents, the babyboomers themselves. For a variety of reasons this did not happen.

One kind of reason is political. The elderly are not a small minority, numerically or politically. In Australia, which is unusual in having compulsory voting, those over 50 make up about 40 per cent of the voting population. In the United States, with voluntary voting, the proportion of elderly who vote is twice that of the young, so the over-50s will get an even higher share of the final vote. The interests of children are successfully represented in modern democracies only to the extent that these older voters take the trouble to keep children in mind, and often it is simply a case of 'out of sight, out of mind'. No political parties have been formed to represent those interests; no major parties are committed to redistributing from old to young. Politicians confess to fearing the elderly more than any other active interest group. 'Family citizenship' is thus deeply problematic, even in democracies. If citizens see voting as simply an opportunity to promote their immediate interests, then today's children and future generations will be the losers, even if all current parents were to count their own children as part of their interests when they vote. Only a civic culture in which family interests are high on the public agenda can prevent continued cross-generational asset-stripping.

Another kind of reason is that welfare systems are structured so that there is commonly little or no correlation between contribution and distribution. Arguably, this is true even in many 'contributory' social security or unemployment schemes. The Australian system is entirely noncontributory – benefits and pensions are paid out of general revenue. Tax-funded welfare takes no account of tax contribution when payments are made. The total tax contribution of any generation thus need bear no relation to the benefits reaped or the burdens borne by that generation. Taking no account of contributions creates a vast opportunity for unchecked expropriation by the first generation to pass through the system. The New Zealand and Australian figures indicate that this is exactly what has happened.

'Expropriation' suggests intentionality, and that may be an inappropriate suggestion. The generation that reaped the benefits – the 1910 to 1940 birth cohorts – were, in other respects, civic-minded and public-spirited. They created stable families and a prosperous economy. Nevertheless, they took no account of the intergenerational obligations the welfare state contract imposed upon them.

Conclusion

The argument of this paper is that the fate of the family is bound up with the structure of the welfare state and with the issue of intergenerational equity. Restoring respect for the family, particularly the biological nuclear family, is largely a cultural task, a contest of words and arguments and research and propaganda. But it is also a sociopolitical task. Necessarily, it involves a reversal of taxing and spending priorities. When that sort of proposal is mooted we tend to imagine it can and should be phased in gently, over a decade or two. To take that view is, in effect, to deny the problem any priority now. Both Thurow's and Thomson's rather different concerns are, it seems to me, matters of urgency. It is today's elderly who are the principal beneficiaries of the recent welfare history. As things presently stand, their gains are their successors' losses.

In the last half-century the Australian family has followed a pathway very similar to that of many other countries. It is too early to tell with certainty whether the Australian and New Zealand generational stories are similarly typical or atypical. Generational analysis of welfare state history is overdue. It may provide one of the keys to modern family history.

References

Thurow, L. (1996), *The Future of Capitalism*, Allen and Unwin.
Thomson, D., (1996), *Selfish Generations? How Welfare States Grow Old*, The White Horse Press.

9 The New Citizenship of the Family: Concepts and Strategies for a New Social Policy

PIERPAOLO DONATI

I The Problem: Rethinking the Central Role of the Family

A

The International Year of the Family announced by the UN (1994) provided the opportunity for a vast, worldwide debate that enormously emphasized the central role of the family in society and social policies. However, it does not appear that this event has produced significant fruits in terms of enhanced value of the family *as such*, although it has translated into greater sensitivity toward people's family problems.

At the European Union level, we have witnessed a renewed debate on the meaning, future and social functions of the family in a search for a more precise and effective policy to protect, support and promote the family as such (see Dumon, 1994; Family Policy Studies Centre, 1994). But national and regional governments and the European Union itself have difficulty acknowledging – in facts, not just words – the central role of the family *qua talis* for the purposes of their development model. Uncertainties and ambivalence prevail that make the concept of family policy as dense with misunderstandings as ever (see Hantrais and Letablier, 1996; Commaille and de Singly, 1997; for the Italian situation, see the five *Rapporti sulla famiglia in Italia*, 1989, 1991, 1993, 1995, 1997).

And we wonder: why? The explanation I would like to put forth in this paper is as simple as it is rich with implications. It says that, in a world projected towards globalization and post-modernity, emphasizing the family implies acquiring a new way of considering the family and its presence in society.

Concretely, it implies developing a new concept of 'family citizenship', with all of the theoretical and practical baggage this concept brings along with it.

B

The experts know that a sharp divide is emerging internationally in how the family is considered throughout the world: while non-Western countries tend to increasingly emphasize the family as the basic cell of society (by stressing its nuclear monogamous form even when they share a culture which legitimizes other forms, e.g. poligamy), Western countries on the contrary emphasize the crisis of the family (i.e. its monogamous nuclear form), and thus tend to consider it as simply one of the many forms of living arrangements (see Goldthorpe, 1987; Cherlin, 1988; Glendon, 1989).

Many explain this divide by saying that it occurs because non-Western countries are still 'modernizing', and thus 'behind', while the west has by now surpassed modernity and thus no longer has a need for the family (i.e. the nuclear monogamous form) as a basis for its development. The validity of such an evolutionary philosophy still remains to be proven. For the moment, it only justifies the fact that this is how the west legitimizes exporting lifestyle models to the rest of the world that no longer refer to the family as a basic model for social organization.

In this paper, I start from the idea that these trends should be discussed. It is then a matter of seeing whether the family continues to be a social good, even in our so-called advanced or late-modern societies, and if so whether it is an *optional* or *non-optional* good.

My thesis is that the concept of family citizenship is a valid guiding idea for all countries, worldwide, notwithstanding the variety of legal and sociocultural orders which define the family in a different way. But in particular, this idea may encounter new meanings and operative applications in those countries whose modernization process makes it necessary to prepare responses that can counter the shattering of social fabric, widespread anonymity, mass individualism, solitude, and in general all of the individual and collective pathologies that originate in the failure to acknowledge the *social value* of the family.

Since the most radical challenge to families falls within the later contexts, which are those in the area ranging from North American to Europe, I will concentrate my topic on these countries, especially those of the European Union.

II   Relevancy or Irrelevancy (Difference or Indifference) of the Family to the Civilization Process?

A

Post-war Western society has been characterized by two basic trends regarding the family:

a)   it has assumed the family as something already there, always there, to perform its tasks. In other words, *it has implicitly taken the existence of the family for granted, and in a certain way its 'strength' as well*, as though the dissolution of the institutional aspects of the family had only positive and not problematic consequences. Priority in social protection has been given not to the family in ordinary life, but to disorganized and dissolving forms of the family; and – in any case – privileges have been accorded to the needs of individuals in order to free them from the obligations inherent in families ties. By this way, it has become apparent that the welfare state relies upon the commons (like the families), but it cannot regenerate them;

b)   it has attempted to resolve the problems of the family through social policies that make only *indirect reference to the family*. It was assumed that by giving work, home, and services to people in cash and in kind we could also solve the problems of the family. In agreement with the above attitude, the family has always remained in the background of the welfare state as an implicit reference. It was assumed that the diffusion of public (government) intervention would all fall not on single issues, but on family life as such, and with only positive consequences.

In short, the family *qua talis* has been treated 'residually' (more or less, depending on the national context). We must not be fooled by the fact that governments have granted the population an increasing number of welfare benefits. Even where welfare policies have been very 'generous' from the standpoint of an economic commitment to the population and with full or nearly full coverage of certain risks, even here interventions have been aimed at individuals and 'groups of individuals', without the family being foreseen as an operator (mediator) of their inter-subjective and structural relations. While there has been a considerable effort to protect the rights and needs of individuals, there has certainly been a much weaker (and often nonexistent) effort to protect family relations as a good in itself.

B

The reasons why these trends have dominated until now are undoubtedly complex. But here I wish to emphasize the fact that these cultural attitudes, and the relative societal government directions, have been possible due to the convergence of two strong lines:

- the line of those who thought that the family should not be regulated by the government (for the majority of Western – and in particular European – legal systems, the family is a private sphere into which the state should enter as little as possible, although the opposite often occurs);

- the line of those who thought that the family should change with society's progress, and that its deinstitutionalization represented, all told, a way toward emancipation from a more backward state of humanity, and in any case a positive and generally desirable transformation against the need to guarantee greater social rights for individuals as such.

With quite different but convergent motivations and plans, both *laissez-faire* (pro-deregulation) and welfare supporters have considered the family to be a 'private', 'traditional', 'surviving' social form, a 'primordial' element in social organization that would change within the broader changes of society, in a way that is positive in the end for both people and social life.

All these lines of thought never wondered what social consequences would be caused by the alienation of the family. On the contrary, they have proffered unconditionally positive judgement on the fact that political society – in the form of the welfare state – prevailed over the 'particularism' of family relations.[1] In their opinion, any negative consequences to society due to family transformations could be perfectly managed within the political framework of welfare institutions.

C

But that has not been the case. The family, treated residually, has become an increasingly problematic reality, with heavily negative effects on the entire social framework:

- the publicizing of family relationships (and part of its functions) has increased the privatization of the latter, and the privatization of the family (in the sense of reducing it purely to the sphere of emotions and private interests) has led to *depoliticizing* society as a whole as well, in the sense that individuals now regulate their own opinions, attitudes and interest in every realm of life, without taking the common good into any account;

- the detachment from a solid ideal of the family (in the sense of a sphere having essential, irreplaceable social functions) has led to a widespread *dehumanization* of social, interpersonal and generalized relationships;

- in the end, we must note that *so-called civil society no longer has any idea – much less a plan – of civility*; civil society reveals itself to be uncivil, according to the ideologies of modernity.

The overall result has been – and still is – a deep and at times dramatic disorientation of the so-called life-worlds, with a considerable drop in civility. This may be observed in the lack of motivations and orientations to pursue further significant goals in the process of human civilization.

Among the empirical indicators of this drop we can point out:

- *social-demographic trends*: low birth rate (an increasing part of Europe has fallen below the zero growth rate), rapid and increasing aging of the population, decrease in marriage rates, increase in births outside of marriage, increase in one-parent families, increase in the number of singles;

- *social problems*: children's difficulties in socializing, youthful maladjustment, communication pathologies in couples, isolation of the elderly (in private housing, but also in protected residential structure), child abuse;

- *psychological and cultural reflexes*: diffusion of new mental and psychosomatic pathologies, increased suicide rate (especially among youths, even children, and the elderly), drug use and widespread drug addiction, boredom and the lack of a sense of the meaning of life, weak production of motivations for active, participatory social activity.

D

All of these phenomena denounce a profound crisis in the European model of civility. At the heart of this crisis is the *implosion* of the family. Implosion here does not mean that the family's social functions have disappeared, as they indeed continue to persist and even increase; it alludes instead to a 'shrivelling', a sort of lack of vitality, a loss of meaning of the 'family symbolic complex', as that which binds the genders and generations in a shared life project that goes beyond a single generation ceases to exist.

We must acknowledge that the symbolic complex of the family has been deeply torn and weakened. And this means something very specific: the family has lost its public and social relevance. Its irrelevance to community life has increased.

At the centre of the current disorientation as to what is a family, what 'makes a family', there is an impoverishment of the people's abilities to relate, first of all symbolically. They are only able to represent what they are interacting with at a given moment ('the attractor'). And this is done more through commercials and images than through words and conversation. One is sensitive only to what one sees, touches, that stimulates one's senses – and often not even that. Grown up in a climate of ethical indifference to the family, the new generations of youth are prey to emotionalism, irrationality, and hedonism. For the young people facing our times, the 'other' realities – hidden, latent, long-term, that go beyond visible confines or which do not immediately come to light – such as family relations and what they mean in terms of identity and existential meaning for people, remain unspoken, unimaginable, unexpressed, and in the end unthinkable.

No wonder, then, that the *very idea of family* has become so vague and uncertain. It tends to be assimilated with any form of cohabitation under the same roof. But that is not the case. The family cannot become an undifferentiated relationship that cancels out the confines between the sexes and the generations, or even reverses them (such as when the woman takes on the role of the man or vice-versa; or when the adult acts like a child or, vice-versa, children need to grow up ahead of time) (see Roussel, 1989 and 1991). When this occurs, the primary identity of people is missing and society becomes mired in quicksand. The symbolic complex of the family is the first point of support, the primary glue of society. This is proven by the fact that family counts even when far away, because it is present as a symbolic reality that determines the psychological experiences and existential meaning for people.

The truth is that the family is not a place, a space, a house, even though it takes form in these images and requires a spatial reference, a 'home'. Nor is it simply 'being together'. *The family is the symbolic and structural relationship that binds people together in a lifelong project that intersects a horizontal dimension* (the couple) *and a vertical dimension* (relationships with descendants/ascendants). Thus the family consists of and requires a bind between the sexes as a couple and/or a generative relationship. Family exists if and only if we have a group of people that are linked together by one or both of these types of binds: (i) reciprocity between the genders in the couple, legally formulated as a contract, and/or (ii) reciprocity within the parent-child relationship.

A social policy that refers purely to the *de facto* family[2] would have to be ineffective and destined to fail. I do not mean by this that we should introduce forms of discrimination among the various types of families. Instead, I mean to state that any social policy achieves effective results if and only if it supports those who take on the obligations of reciprocity, rather than make social protection indifferent to people's behaviour (see Mead, 1986). If social policy is indifferent to the assumption of obligations as members of a couple and/or as parents, in the end it penalizes the relationships of social solidarity. The crisis of the European welfare state is indeed the consequence of the fact that, within the *Lib-Lab* arrangement (see Donati, 1977), it has become increasingly irrelevant in terms of social protection whether or not one assumes family obligations.

The legal definition of the family is necessary in order for the welfare state to operate; otherwise it runs into serious trouble. If the family were any form of cohabitation, how could we calculate the contributions and access rights for welfare services based on the relationships of solidarity that must be faced as husband/wife or as father/mother of children? If the definition of family did not require specific relationships as couples and parents, how could we avoid perverse effects in using the benefits related to these roles? For example, one partner could enjoy benefits without any obligation of solidarity towards the other partner. Those who attempt to make the so-called 'free unions' (hetero- and homosexual) equal to the family need not to look for such a solution. One can maintain that this equalization is not necessary, since we can acknowledge the human rights of the individuals that live in different types of relationships without thereby abandoning the idea that the full reciprocity between members of a couple and between parents and children is a specific common good that should be protected and promoted as such (see Donati, 1990).

In my view, without denying that people enjoy their inalienable individual and subjective rights in civil, political, social and cultural terms,[3] *family rights as such* should be defined and promoted today. Legally, the family exists if and only if there is a contract of reciprocal responsibility within the male-female couple or a parent-child relationship (and, more generally, an ascendant/descendant relationship, such as between grandparent and grandchild). It should be noted that even those states that acknowledge the so-called 'living together arrangements' ('common law family') never make families based on marriage fully equivalent to those that are not, nor do they give common law mates the same rights as the mate. There is indeed a tendency by legislation to attribute natural parents the same duties as legal parents, thereby demonstrating that the existence or lack of marriage is irrelevant in terms of the obligations that natural parents have towards their children.

Conjugal and parental relationships are certainly not easy to impose and carry forth. We are often not even able to see and define them. We are in any case ambivalent towards them, since we experience them as binds that limit us, while we then use them as resources. We generally see and confront them only from one side. For example, we see the costs of marriage and children, but not what they give us. We see the restrictions that family relationships force on us, but not the resources they offer and the opportunities they open up to us.

Certainly it is difficult to manage family relationships. But what I want to emphasize is the fact that European society in the last fifty years or so has done very little to build a culture (and social policy) that helps us to manage family relations in a synergic manner, and intergenerational relationships in particular. The negative consequences and reflections of this lack of development are increasingly evident.

E

Today's society has reached the point where the family is increasingly a form of life 'indifferent' to the public sphere, meaning that social institutions make no differentiation as to what family a person lives in. It sees no connection between lifestyle and internal family organization on the one hand, and social, non-family problems on the other, except when pathologies and outcasts appear.

Experts are well aware that the impoverishment and weakening of the symbolic complex of the family is the first cause of societal collapse. This collapse is normally long and painful, and does not take place over a few years, but leads to a deterioration that continues for several decades and at times for centuries.

We are faced with such a turning point in history. We must rethink our model of civilization. Civilization must find a new meaning of family, or it will be lost.

But how is this possible? The dilemma is truly among the most crucial and difficult to solve. We are still struggling between residual and institutionalizing orientations toward the family: on the one hand, family is an assumption or in any case left to the mercy of events, on the other it is thought that it may and must be somehow controlled and directed.

The tendency to make residual social policies toward the family still persists because, in some ways, it is impossible to do otherwise. Even when one does not intentionally wish to follow this path, in practice it is difficult to see how to address the family since one would need to refer to a specific, normative model of family relationships (based on marriage). But this model appears difficult to practice. Thus one takes refuge in the comment, 'we take note that this is how people live'.

The only alternative to mere residual pragmatism appears to be a new public commitment by individual nations for institutional welfare policies that attempt to meet the broadest possible spectrum of needs of the population, by addressing individuals and large categories (defined according to professional occupation, such as the self-employed, or by gender, or by age: children, young people, the elderly, etc.) (see Donati, 1993b). But even this road has become (or is becoming) unsustainable, not only because it involves increasing economic costs, but also because it does not reduce social problems – and often multiplies them or shifts them elsewhere. In many cases it produces the very weakness or dissolution of the family that lies at the origin of the problems being fought. The crisis of the welfare state in Europe is well known. It came well before and goes far beyond what is known in the public domain following the need to standardize the public accounts of member states to the famous single currency requirements (Maastricht Treaty).

So what can be done? Herein lies the drama of today's social policies towards the family, forced to be residual even when they want to be institutional, and in any case nearly always with limited – if not perverse – effects.

To escape from this stalled position, we must view the situation from another perspective and ask new questions. We must get out of this dilemma that obliges us to choose between residual and institutional policies.

III   The Directions of Social Policy as a Concept of the Family/ Society Relationship: a Relationship to be Entirely Reviewed

A

The following have been characteristics of the dominant family social policies from the 1950s to the 1990s in Europe:

a)   there has been a substantial tendency to publicize the family's functions, in particular by transferring them to the welfare state. In other words, vis-à-vis the increasing social weakness of families, most countries have decided to meet the family's needs simply by offering newer and more widespread public provisions and services for daily life needs, from full-time schools to leisure services, by this way enlarging the eligibility for social rights and collective facilities on an individual basis;

b)   at the same time, widespread and profound privatization of family values has been encouraged, in the sense that the politically organized community has given up on selecting the common values to follow, and has made it increasingly irrelevant what type of cohabitation unit one lives in;

c)   policies for the family have been undertaken mainly in an indirect way, since provisions have privileged generic social needs, from the house to employment, from income to services, without taking into account the structure and specific needs of the family nucleus, or with little regard for them (absence of selectivity aimed to favour the most disadvantaged nuclei, overloaded with tasks and socially weak, as nuclei and not as individuals);

d)   implicit policy choices have been made toward the family, as the relationships were never addressed but merely the individuals as such and/or generic social categories (defined in terms of gender and age, like children, women, elderly people, etc.).

B

What have these tendencies produced? We can generally say that they have not been to the advantage of the family.

a)   The publicizing of family functions has led to an increasing difficulty for generations to recognize each other (as generating and generated) and to elaborate rules of social exchange between them. In addition, the diffusion and growth of government services today show signs of difficulty not only and not so much from an economic standpoint, but for their inadequacy to meet user (citizens') needs in terms of family needs, especially the life cycle of the family.

b)   The privatization of family values has produced lifestyles that depend excessively on mass consumption and are characterized by high risk, which in many ways reverberate on the family, producing problems that add to its crisis.

c)   Indirect policies have often ignored the family rather than support it, and in any case we must admit that the criteria of these policies (including the idea of equal opportunity between the genders) do not have immediately positive reflections on the family *sic et simpliciter*.

d)   Implicit policies have increased the rights – or, vice-versa, the obligations – of some at the expense of others. They have taken for granted that intervention on an individual (or age category) would be beneficial to family solidarity and a significant shared life-world; but this does not happen automatically. A relational perspective has been missing.

C

The need therefore arises to change tracks. In what directions ? Generally speaking, I would say the following (see the summary diagram in Table 9.1):

a)   publicized functions must be replaced with a clearly understood *principle of subsidiarity* according to which the broader social formations must not take the place of smaller ones, but support their independence by providing the rules and means necessary for them to perform their specific tasks on their own. More generally, the state must not absorb the functions of intermediate social formations, but help them – including through additional forms of association (such as family-based associations, for the family) – to manage the services that concern them (consider family counsellors, nursery schools, care for children and the elderly, home services, etc.);

Table 9.1   Dominant trends thus far and new directions for family social policies

Dominant trends from 1950 to 1990	Need to revise towards
a) Publicizing family functions	a) Implementation of the principle of subsidiarity between government and family
b) Privatization of family values	b) Processes to highlight the family as a relational good
c) Indirect policies (centered around the generic needs of daily life: such as housing, employment, food, health, education, etc.)	c) Direct policies (centered around the family nucleus as such: i.e., the tax liability of the family, services for the entire nucleus, etc.)
d) Implicit policies (centered around individuals, for individual needs differentiated along the individual life cycle)	d) Explicit policies (centered around relations between genders and between generations for the mediating functions they perform)
= family as residual	**= family as subject**

b)   the privatization of sociocultural values must be replaced with processes of inter-subjective '*relational emphasis* ' of what are the 'valuable goods' in life. This is a path of dialogue that encourages human contact, the care relationship. In the family, rights are not individualistic in nature, but relational. Indeed, what happens in the family, especially how the family is socially designed and constructed, cannot be indifferent to the community. Every vital community develops a culture of whether or not such relationships are 'civil';

c)   indirect policies must leave room for policies *directly aimed at the family nucleus as such*; they must speak the language of 'family care work', 'home for the family', 'services for the family', 'family income', and aim in this direction for *ad hoc* operative measures;

d)   implicit policies must be replaced with *explicit policies for family relations as such*, within the framework of intergenerational exchanges. When working with a generation, they must consider what the effects will be on other generations: the state may benefit or be detrimental to a generation based not only on those measures taken directly for it, but also through the effects of measures taken for another generation. Positively speaking, a new 'social pact' is required between generations, both within the family and in the collective sphere (employment, the distribution and redistribution of resources, and especially citizenship relationships).

In short: *the change must be made from social policies based on the residual nature of the family to social policies centred around the social subjectivity of the family.*

IV   The Family is a Social Subject Requiring a Citizenship of its Own

A

We must first of all leave behind the idea that the family is a special commodity, a 'private world', that each person chooses according to his or her own tastes and inclinations, as preferred, in terms of how to configure relationships between the genders and between the generations.

On the contrary, the family is a relational good shared by all. What happens in the family is not without its consequences for everyone else living in a territorial community. The problems of the family are also problems of the entire surrounding community. The relationships between the genders and the generations forge the character of a society, civil or uncivil.

Only those societies that hold these truths firm, and thus make sure to have a strong and well-defined symbolic family code, are capable of confronting the challenges and surviving. If the prohibition to reverse the sexes and generations in the family fall by the wayside, the family falls into dissolution and drags the entire society down with it.

It is the quality of the symbolic family code, elaborated in dealing with the challenges inside and outside the family, that decides the quality of life, on one hand, and, the psychological and social pathologies on the other hand, always with consequences in every other sphere of life (economic, political, etc.).

B

All of this may be stated in another way: the family is a 'social subject'. It is in a very precise way. That is, the family is an originative social formation that has its own autonomy in its internal relationships. People form couples and generate children by autonomous choice. Autonomy, however, does not mean absolute independence, because every healthy, vital society must place requirements for social legitimacy on these relationships. In other words, it must always be seen whether or not these relationships conform to human rights. It cannot be otherwise, because the family is a specific type of shared good, which I call *relational common good*.[4] It is so for both those who belong to it and those who enter relations with it.

The family is not a private life form that can give itself just any norms. The family, as I have mentioned elsewhere (see Donati, 1989), has an auto-poietic nature that is ambivalent in itself, since the family generates itself, but cannot do so if it is not in constant connection and regulation with the outside, with the surrounding society (the norms that regulate the internal and external boundaries of the family can never be purely private).

C

Now there is a brand-new and positive way in which the family becomes a social subject in the above sense, more than ever. This is the empirical fact of the new social mediations that it concretely puts into practice. These are mediations between genders, between generations, between the private sphere of its internal relations and the sphere of the surrounding community. As a matter of fact, in the couple one partner mediates his/her own social world to the other. One generation transfers (or fails to transfer) something to the other, even unintentionally. The problem of the generational debt remains always, even when refused. In addition, we must observe that one participates or does not participate in civic and social life, and in many different ways, depending on the type of family one has.

The family counts more and more, and not less and less, in mediating relations between each of its individual members and the world outside the family: this is true for children, but even for adults and the elderly, though obviously in different ways.

These mediations are invisible relationships that society can keep hidden (fail to acknowledge and support) or render explicit (acknowledge and reward). Until recently, these mediations were handed down and shared, fully implicit and taken for granted. The social changes in recent decades have made them more invisible and problematic. Today they must be made more explicit and have their own voice. This voice is the *citizenship of the family*. Family citizenship means, as I have explained at length elsewhere (see Donati, 1993c), that the family *as such* must enjoy its own set of rights-obligations, as a reality of solidarity and not simply as the sum of the rights-obligations of its individual members.

Now more than before, if we want to not only protect the family legally but also concretely promote it and support it in its social functions, we must give more importance to all of those associative forms that families create to organize shared actions, both to promote rights and manage services, for its own good and for the community at large. Thus, by extension, we must also acknowledge a new set of citizenship rights-obligations for family associations within a new configuration that I call 'societal', because citizenship here is an expression not of the state as an entity above, but of the pluralism of social autonomies (see Donati, 1993a).

D

What does 'family citizenship' mean, and what kind of social policy change does it imply?

When I first coined the expression 'family citizenship' and supported it at the European Union (see Donati, 1992) I did not think it would receive all the attention it did. But, as happens in these instances, it is not enough to coin an expression with strong theoretical and practical connotations and provide data and arguments to support it in order for it to be adopted and applied. Misunderstandings and instrumental or misshapen reinterpretations are always lurking. Thus, today, we must say more to make the concept and its implications more explicit.

To clarify: the concept of family citizenship *does not mean*, as many have interpreted it, asking for additional aid for the needs of people's daily life – women, children and the elderly in particular. *Nor does it mean* asking for special attention to single-income families and those with several children, which are penalized compared to others. Basically, it does not mean asking for more protection for the type of families that statistically fall or risk falling into the area of poverty. The expression means a lot more, and a lot else.

First of all, it means recognizing the social value of the family for the functions of solidarity and social reciprocity that it performs. The family does not ask for a 'reward', but asks instead to be treated with social justice for the functions it must carry out as an ordinary agency in everyday life. Indeed, the current mechanisms of welfare distribution and redistribution (in many aspects) penalize rather than acknowledge what it does, or could or should do. Here is where the concept of family citizenship begins to have its first and most correct meaning. How can we expect more solidarity among people and more care for infants if both of these behaviours are made more difficult and less convenient than the more selfish and individualistic behaviours of those who do not take on any family obligations? And how will it be possible to achieve solidarity among the citizenry if the government itself makes family solidarity indifferent, when it should be the first guarantor?

Within a broader perspective, the concept implies a radical change that puts an end to the concept of the welfare state as it has been constructed throughout the entire modern era. This is no small turning point. The welfare state has been built on the idea that a government is more socially oriented to the extent to which it includes a growing number of individuals – classified by social category – within the state's guarantees. The concept of family citizenship overturns this view, in at least two ways. First, because it asks for citizenship not only for individuals (as such or as members of social classes or categories), but also for an intermediate social formation – the family – with everything this involves (this concretizes the passage from 'state citizenship' to 'societal citizenship'). Secondly, because it sees the social state as a system of decisions and intervention serving the autonomy of the family, and not vice-versa, where the welfare state has until now worked in an assistance mode, to relieve individuals of their family responsibilities (this concretizes the principle of subsidiarity).

Obviously, to acknowledge the principle of family citizenship means changing a few support structures of the entire organization of society. This is certainly no small thing.

E

Generally speaking, to grant citizenship means recognizing the relevancy of a subject, be it individual or collective (i.e. consisting of certain relationships, such as the family), for the public dimension of social life, within a complex of rights and obligations between the associates. In the case of the family, it means recognizing that the family-subject has relevancy for the public dimension of human life (see Donati, 1994a).

We cannot create a social policy (in the much larger sense than public policy) without a definition of the family, since it is essential to know whom one is referring to when deciding on concrete measures of intervention (as policy-makers and administrators are well aware). And definitions are not all equal, since each definition leads to different effects. If one adopts a vague definition of the family, as some proposed bills do, or if one defines it simply as people who live together, there are two negative effects: first, there is no policy to support those who spontaneously take responsibility within the couple or towards the children; second, since responsibilities are ignored or merely imposed by law, the welfare state goes bankrupt morally and financially. International experiences prove this, and that is why in no state is the family yet defined in the vague terms that some would prefer today.

When we speak of the family-subject, we are referring to that primary unit that is linked by marriage and/or parenthood according to ascendant/descendant and collateral lines specified within certain thresholds; thus consisting of relationships of mutual and explicit commitment between the people who join themselves in a heterosexual couple and/or between the generations intertwined and/or derived therefrom.

One cannot emphasize enough that the family must be identified not on the basis of an aspect extrinsic from people, such as the place-home of cohabitation (residence or domicile), or wealth or other instrumental characteristics (spatial, economic, etc.), but based on its internal relationships. Even those who do not share living quarters or wealth can be a family. What identifies a group of people (at least two) as a family is the existence between them of fully reciprocal relationships between genders and generations.[5] To the point where, if these requirements are not satisfied, the family becomes something else. It dissolves into a primary social group of informal relationships that can have a wide variety of connotations. Because these are free and spontaneous arrangements, it is often useless and counterproductive to want to regulate them externally. In these cases, what is prominent is the type of private agreements made between the individuals, based on their individual civil rights. The state must be very careful in how it intervenes to regulate and/or help people living in these conditions. In the first place, any recognition and support of these living arrangements must take place in terms of a principle of reciprocity referred to the relations between the persons involved and between the private and public aspects of the situation. No one should simply be guaranteed certain rights without the responsibility of correlated obligations, both towards the other person based on whom the benefits are expected and the community around. Thus, an informal group may be helped by the community to the extent to which it takes on correlated responsibilities towards the latter. In addition, any welfare policy must take into account the fact that each intervention produces unexpected – and often undesired – effects which are often distortions: if aid is provided to those who do not make a commitment, it becomes an incentive for lifestyles which lack any social commitment.

I remember the case of financial assistance to single teenage mothers with children. Experiences in this regard show that the partner and a whole series of other people end up living off that assistance, making the assistance damaging for the girl herself, who finds it to be an obstacle to marriage or in any case to a fully reciprocal relationship with her partner. In this case, as in others, the welfare state becomes an impediment to the formation of a couple responsible for its own ménage (see Murray, 1993: more generally, Opielka, 1997). The same occurs with so-called 'gentlemen's loans', which are often publicized as a policy measure for the family, but are actually a form of aid to individuals for daily life expenses. Certainly, they may also be used to pay the rent or buy furniture for an informal couple or and entire group, but this is precisely one of those indirect measures of social policy for the family which, as I said earlier, do not necessarily have positive effects on the family. Indeed, in many cases they serve to create alternative forms of cohabitation.

I do not mean by this to say that there should be no aid to single mothers or people in trouble in their interpersonal relationships. Not at all. What I mean to say is that the aid should be configured as an incentive and reward for social binds, rather than vice-versa as is the case today.

The nature of the family specifically consists of that stability of expectations, which normally translates into a pact (legally regulated contract) which is a guarantee for all concerned, and allows this social subject to exercise precise social functions that informal groups cannot exercise – or exercise in much less foreseeable, less secure, less reliable ways, and without the necessary guarantees for the surrounding society. The family demands that mutual and stable formation of reciprocal expectations which is also a civil way of facing life together, as people in a relationship rather than as individuals who do not make specific commitments with and for others.

Family citizenship is therefore bound to the reliability of certain functions or tasks that may be ensured by the existence of a certain reciprocal relationship within the couple and/or between parents and children. Mere cohabitation or free unions do not provide these guarantees, although in certain cases they may show a certain stability and solidity, because they are lacking explicit contractual elements both within (between their members) and without (the public sphere).

Some people today propose so-called 'solidarity pacts' between unmarried hetero- and homosexual couples, which should be recognized by the local authorities through a special register, as a tool for giving certain benefits to the hetero- or homosexual partner (reversibility pensions, transfer of rental contracts, etc.). Here again, these measures have nothing to do with a family policy, but serve other purposes.

It is important to emphasize the difference between the old and new forms of family citizenship. Many of the criticisms made to the idea of family citizenship are centred around two points: that it would privilege a certain model of family, and that such a social policy would bring with it a preceptive type of social order. I can confirm that neither is true.

In order to understand the historical discontinuities I am referring to, we can recollect that, generally speaking, the relations between families and governments have followed two typical *patterns* or *stages*.

a)   In the first half of the twentieth century, European welfare states *used to address families and children mainly in terms of social control*: families were granted economic, legal and material provisions in exchange for men's control over women and children. *Family rights embodied individual rights* so that people (in particular children) suffered from bonds which were too compelling. Children's rights were greatly restricted: they were almost completely subsumed under the family coverage. In case of family failure, total institutions were delegated to pick up the children.

b)   Since the Second World War, European welfare states have, in a sense, reversed the pattern: they have acknowledged an increasing number of social rights and provisions for individuals and social categories (in particular women, handicapped people, old people, and children), but have left the family apart. The rights of the family as a social group and institution have been undermined in many respects. In a certain sense, *the family has lost its citizenship*. The overall outcome has been the decline of fertility and the creation of a social environment unfavourable to the reception of the newly born (be it a direct or an indirect effect).

c)   Nowadays the 12 countries of the EC are entering a stage (or pattern) which is very different from the previous ones under many aspects.

On the one hand, the new trends contradict the pre-war pattern in so far as the family cannot be considered and handled as a social control agency which acts on behalf of the state: the family has acquired an increasing autonomy (*autopoiesis*) and is oriented towards managing its generational problems even more privately.

On the other hand, the new trends must differ from the post-war pattern in so far as it becomes clear that the multiplication of individual rights is only a partial solution: we have to find new means to deal with the uneasiness and the disfunctionality in family relationships, particularly the breaking down of the social web, which deteriorates the relationships between generations. If we want to have a social environment which is more sensitive to children's needs, then we must give proper *consideration to the repercussions that the lack of social support for families has on children*. Families should become valid interlocutors of societal institutions and governments, at every level (regional, national, and European).

In the perspective of the development of citizenship rights, the new issues revolve around the need for a better *compatibility between individual and family rights*: both kinds of entitlements must be secured, and the pursuit of this target should be done in such a way as to foster relations of social solidarity and equity between generations.

This is our topic. From the point of view of the development of families and children rights the last decade has been one of lost opportunities. But, at the same time, it has been fruitful, since a new awareness has arisen and grown up precisely in respect to the need of introducing the 'generational' issue into the welfare state.

The new family citizenship is essentially different from the old form. In patriarchal society, the family was recognized and supported with specific benefits to the extent to which the family head accepted the delegation of functions from the state for the social control of women and children. The new family citizenship, on the contrary, consists of access to certain rights, which are positive and relational rights granted to the family nucleus as such, in addition to and without reducing individual rights. The rights of family citizenship refer to the functions of the family as a social relationship of mediation. The family has a few more rights than individuals, its own rights as a relationship – or rather, as a social mediation relationship. This implements the dictates of national and international declarations that recognize the rights of the family as such, and not simply the rights of the individuals within the family.

We must carefully consider the idea that the family is a shared good to be promoted *ex novo*. This cannot and must not mean reduced efforts for women and children, and for all of the weaker members of the family and society. Individual rights may not be questioned. Instead, social policies must aim to resolve the problems of individuals and various social categories (children, the elderly, women) within a relational view of the rights-obligations of each and all, taking into account that these rights-obligations have a relational structure (are exercised in relationships) and live within/by a relational context.

In Europe as in America, it is by now clear that the modern arrangement of society based on favouring the individual-state axis has reached its limit. Many nations, parliaments and governments have realized this in recent years. If we continued in the direction of the past we could only produce deep breakdowns. We must instead take the best of the consequences of the past and place them within a new philosophy of society that sees the family – as well as other social formations known as 'intermediate' – the protection and ferment of an authentic process of civilization.

F

The concept of family citizenship helps to redefine the field of social policies, as it pushes to make new distinctions.

First Family policy differs from other, similar types of policy. It is not a demographic policy (to increase the birth rate). It is not a policy against poverty (which requires other measures). It is not simply a policy for social or other services. Family policy is the set of measures that make families better able and more independent in managing family relationships. Certainly, this also means supporting fertility according to the couple's desires. But this target is a different matter. The same holds true for the consideration accorded to the family dimension in many kinds of measures proposed to fight poverty. These measures are merely forms of income and resource redistribution based on the objective of increasing equality in the amount of income individuals can spend (and this is why calculations are based on the number of people who live together): but what does this goal have to do with family policy? Only very little, and only indirectly. Finally, welfare service policies are not family policies if they operate on individuals or individual problems. In order to be real family welfare measures, they must operate on family mediations (for example, in the new services that help maintain parental relationships when the marriage relationship has broken up). Today, this is the case in only a few instances.

Second We must review the welfare state, from the taxation system to social security, so that families are recognized for their solidarity functions rather than penalized for them. The family must be made a fiscal subject and a subject of social security and pensions. More generally, we must discuss in terms of a school for the family, a home for the family, a minimum family income, and so on.

Third At the local level, all of this may be translated into a 'package' of measures centred around the family (which I cannot describe in detail here due to space limitations) that emphasize the care of people within the family and organizes external social services based on this objective. The entire system of local taxation and tariffs, especially for community services, should be regulated according to family equity indexes. This is not a question of providing 'assistance' to families, but of redefining social equality by making the family an *active*, not passive, social subject.

Fourth We must review all social policies from a generational standpoint, in light of the following criterion: whether they increase or decrease reciprocity between ascending/descending generations.

Fifth Family policy strictly depends on the fact that families have a voice, their own social, cultural and political representation. This means promoting family associations in all forms, at the local, regional, national and supranational levels. And then create federations or confederations of these family-based associations.[6] It is important that these associations and their federation or coordinating bodies not be considered equivalent to old associative forms, all of which in some way depend on other institutions. Thus they should be promoted both by universal facilitation measures, especially tax advantages, as well as by granting them autonomous consulting and representative powers through special consulting committees permanently established with central and local governments.[7]

V New Social Policies: Choosing the Family as a Basis for a New Model for the Quality of Life

A

European society needs to completely rethink its model of development not only in terms of science or technology, models of production, consumption and communication, forms of transportation and so on, but especially concerning the very foundation of its society, as a *civil* society. The rest somehow follows as a consequence.

When we talk about the foundations of civil society we are talking about family. And the arrangement of local communities must be rethought beginning from the family, since local communities are *networks of families, or networks of relationships between families*.

B

I have spoken of the crisis of civilization. Wherein lies the basic problem? I believe that the heart of the matter may be grasped by saying that the family is not put in a position to properly carry out its functions as a network of relationships within the more general network of relationships in which it exists. There are undoubtedly many difficulties in the family. Most people cannot even manage to see any logic to it. I believe we can understand all of these difficulties if we view them from a perspective that somehow gives a unitary meaning to family problems.

The basic difficulty in the family lies in the fact that *the family is unable to act as a mediating subject for relationships between its 'internal' and the 'external' environments*: school for children, work for the adults, services for children, services for the elderly, even recreational places. The fact is that all of these environments outside the family have become increasingly 'self-referential', thus operating increasingly in relation only to their internal needs, without taking the needs of the family into account. It is easy to understand how, faced with external worlds that 'revolve around themselves', that see only their own instrumental goals, hours of operation, economic, technical and organizational problems, the family is unable to organize responses to its needs in a sufficiently coherent and autonomous way.

Many of the weaknesses in transmitting a historic memory, in dialogue between parents and children, and in socialization between generations in general derive from this new pattern of relationships that leaves no room and time for the family, although broader processes of changes in values and lifestyles are also responsible. Discomfort grows where, and the more that, external environments do not see the difficulties of the family as a life system with its own logic, its own culture, its own need for dialogue. This trend in the overall systemic process must be reversed.

We might say that social policies must make a 180° turnaround from the past, in the sense that the relationship between the government (or political community) and the family must be re-observed and re-implemented from the side of the families themselves. But it is more correct to state that we must redefine the relationships between state and families in terms of *reciprocity*, thus of symmetry and equal involvement, with the utmost cooperation between the private and public spheres without one predominating over the other. This can be concretized through a few strategies and related measures and interventions.

a) Social policies must overcome the dilemma between the residual welfare state and the total welfare state by adopting a new strategy based upon what I call '*societal* policies'. The guiding idea is a *triangulation* between the state, market and third (non-profit) sector as symmetrical and functionally specific poles of social organization (this is summarized in the idea of 'societal citizenship').

   In terms of concrete measures: we must take care not to make any of the three poles residual, and in particular not to outcast the third sector, especially those with a family basis (associations, voluntary agencies, social cooperatives) which should instead be promoted through systemic and social measures (see point b); *ad hoc* social legislation is required for the third sector, in particular for family-based associations.

b) Social policies must *distinguish between system intervention* and *social intervention*; i) the former have to do with impersonal mechanisms (such as the taxation system, the pension and insurance system, etc.); ii) the latter have to do with the production of personal, solidarity services in the life-worlds, and must therefore be aimed at local communities by adopting a 'community care' philosophy.

   In terms of concrete measures:

   i) systemic mechanisms must consider the family as such, for example by taxing family income so as to take into account the number of members and their particular needs according to personal condition and stage in the life cycle (which splitting and quotient systems achieve in good measure, but not yet fully satisfactorily);

   ii) social intervention must adopt procedures that reinforce primary and secondary forms of association, adopt network strategies and network intervention through specific methodologies (for example: foster families, *tagesmütter*, good neighbours, flexible day care, respite care, etc.).

c)   Social policies must be directed towards *all* families, and not pursue only or as a priority those *ad hoc* measures developed for fringe and/or pathological forms. Targeting families usually end up with blaming the victim, and/or producing vicious cycles of deprivation. The problems of the weakest or most difficult family forms must be resolved within the framework of a social policy for 'ordinary' family life.

In terms of concrete measures: people must be supported and promoted in their own families within a framework of tax measures (taxation based on a family quotient, tax deductions, etc.), income integration (aid, various benefits), services offered (consultations, home services, etc.) aimed at the family system as such, i.e. at all families regardless of their particular features, then taking specific measures for the weaker, fringe forms within this common framework.

d)   Social policies should be conducted on the *family life cycle*, not to negate the individual cycle, but to place the right emphasis on the life cycle of generations. Generations need to see paths and support each other mutually in order to experience them as plans. In other words, an 'intergenerational policy' is required (see Bengtson and Achenbaum, 1993; Donati, 1995).

In terms of concrete measures: focus intervention on family needs in its most critical stages, and in relation to the specific critical types of that stage. For example, young couples require special assistance when they begin creating a family (adequate housing, infant care services, educational financial aid, etc.), assistance to families with adolescents, assistance to adult families responsible for elderly members, assistance to elderly families. And these measures must not be unrelated, but take into account the effects – of solidarity or otherwise – that they may have between generations.

Conclusion

In the future, the welfare society (as distinct from the welfare state of the past) shall start over from the idea that the quality of social life basically consists of the quality of primary (family) and secondary (associative) relationships in local, territorial and 'personal' communities, from the smallest to the largest. This quality is measured based on its ability to produce meaning in daily life; an ability that is measured in a sense of peace and self-control, rather than experiences of stress and self-alienation. Here, in these life-worlds, is where the family can and must become the protagonist of the model of civilization as a mediation subject (base-cell) for a *new* civil society: not the mercantile society inaugurated in the eighteenth century, but the social society that must characterize the near future. A society that certainly cannot and must not return to the past, but must find a new social philosophy and new tools to avoid the fragmentation and opposition of separate spheres of life – or between family and non-family dimensions of existence – that cannot totally go their own way, leading to continuous tensions and forms of alienation. We need a social organization that is at the same time more differentiated and more integrated among its various spheres of daily life, all of those that regard our life-world.

The family can be at the centre of such a culture, as a moment of necessary mediation between the various environments and dimensions of daily life. Otherwise cultural regression is ensured. Indeed, the family persists as the only 'multi-generational' place in society, thus as the only social sphere where the generations meet and confront one another, while all other places tend to be single-generational, and often separate the generations from one another.

Only today can we begin to see the possibility of a real family citizenship on the horizon. The idea that the stakes are that of an entire civilization may act as a stimulus. Indeed, the choice does not concern personal tastes, but is actually the dilemma between taking a step forward in the process of civilization or falling into a collective regression that could have frightful results.

Notes

1   Particularism of the family here means its characterization as a closed community (*Gemeinschaft*), as it is usually defined in sociological theory: see Parsons, Bales et al., 1955; Finch, 1989.
2   A *de facto family* is a set of people who simply state that they live under the same roof, regardless of the social and legal relationships among them.
3   On the distinction and scope of these rights, see Donati, 1993a.
4   On the concept of 'relational good' see Donati, 1991 and 1993a, ch. 2.
5   I realize that this definition is very broad. But, in fact, it is meant to be so, for it tries to generalize as much as possible what a family consists of. In my view, it consists of social relations and not of individuals or other 'things'. That is why a family exists even when a child has left his/her parents and lives somewhere else (for instance in a college) without living together and sharing a common wealth with his/her parents. In that case, to say that 'fully reciprocal relations' exist between the parents and the child means that there is a latent principle of symbolic exchange (reciprocity) which can be activated if necessary (on reciprocity see Godbout, 1992 and 1994).

6   A specific reflection has just begun in this regard. On the Italian situation, see Donati and Rossi, 1995. On the English situation see Bernardes, 1995. At the European level, see Donati, 1994b.
7   These measures are not entirely absent. One need simply recall that many national governments have Committees to represent families and their associations, as does the European Union (remember the role of Coface at the Brussels Commission). But generally speaking these bodies have a weak role with little effect at the political institutional level.

References

Bengtson, V.L. and Achenbaum, W.A. (eds) (1993), *The Changing Contract Between Generations*, Hawthorne, NY:, Aldine-deGruyter.

Bernardes, J. (1995), *Family Organizations and Associations in the United Kingdom: A Directory*, London: Family Policy Studies Centre.

Cherlin, A. (ed.) (1988), *American Family and Public Policy*, Washington DC: The Urban Institute Press.

Commaille, J. and de Singly, F. (sous la direction de) (1997), *La question familiale en Europe*, Paris: L'Harmattan.

Donati, P. (1977), 'Freedom vs. Control in Post-modern Society: a relational approach', paper presented at the 33rd World Congress of Sociology of the IIS, University of Cologne, 7–11 July.

Donati, P. (1989), 'L'emergere della famiglia "auto-poietica"', in P. Donati (ed.), *Primo Rapporto sulla famiglia in Italia*, Milano: CISF, Edizioni Paoline, pp. 13–69.

Donati, P. (1990), 'Le "famiglie di fatto" come realtà e problema sociale oggi in Italia', *La Famiglia*, No. 139, pp. 3–20.

Donati, P. (1991), *Teoria relazionale della società*, Milano: Angeli.

Donati, P. (1992), 'The Development of European Policies for the Protection of Families and Children: Problems and Prospects', in *Child, Family, and Society*, Commission of the European Communities, Brussels, February, pp. 103–130 (proceedings of the EU Conference 'Children, Family, and Society', Luxembourg, 27–29 May 1991).

Donati, P. (1993a), *La cittadinanza societaria*, Rome-Bari: Laterza.

Donati, P. (1993b), 'I sistemi di protezione sociale in Europa: concetti e strategie', in P. Donati (ed.), *Fondamenti di politica sociale. Teorie e modelli*, Vol. 1, Rome: Nis, pp. 79–110.

Donati, P. (1993c), 'Le nuove mediazioni familiari: le "relazioni invisibili" portatrici di nuovi diritti', in P. Donati (ed.), *Terzo Rapporto sulla famiglia in Italia*, Cinisello Balsamo: Edizioni San Paolo.

Donati, P. (1994a), 'Le nuove frontiere della politica sociale: l'Europa delle famiglie', in P. Donati and F. Ferrucci (eds), *Verso una nuova cittadinanza della famiglia in Europa*, Milan: Angeli.

Donati, P. (1994b), 'Family Associations in Europe: A General Outlook and a Typology', in W. Dumon and T. Nuelant (eds), *National Family Policies in the Member States of the European Union in 1992 and 1993*, Leuven-Brussels: European Observatory on National Family Policies, October, pp. 42–65.

Donati, P. (1995), 'Il malessere generazionale della famiglia: dove va l'intreccio fra le generazioni?', in P. Donati (ed.), *Quarto Rapporto Cisf sulla famiglia in Italia*, Cinisello Balsamo: Edizioni San Paolo, pp. 27–87.

Donati, P. and Rossi, G. (eds.) (1995), *Le associazioni familiari in Italia*, Milan: Angeli.

Dumon, W. (ed.) (1994), *Changing Family Policies in the Member States of the European Union*, Brussels: Commission of the European Communities, DG V.

Family Policy Studies Centre (1994), *Families in the European Union*, London: FPSC.

Finch, J. (1989), *Family Obligations and Social Change*, Oxford: Polity Press/Basil Blackwell.

Glendon, M.A. (1989), *The Transformation of Family Law: States, Love, and Family in the United States and Western Europe*, Chicago: University of Chicago Press.

Godbout, J.T. (1992), *L'esprit du don*, Paris: Éditions La Découverte.

Godbout, J.T. (1994), 'Y a-t-il encore une économie de la parenté?', *Ethnographie*, Vol. 90, no. 1, pp. 13–23.

Goldthorpe, J.E. (1987), *Family Life in Western Societies*, Cambridge: Cambridge University Press.

Hantrais, L. and Letablier, M.T. (1996), *Families and Family Policies in Europe*, London and New York: Longman.

Mead, L. (1986), *Beyond Entitlement. The Social Obligations of Citizenship*, New York: The Free Press.

Murray, C. (1993), 'Welfare and the Family: The U.S. Experience', *Journal of Labor Economics*, Vol. 11, No. 1, pt 2.

Opielka, M. (1997), 'Does the Welfare State Destroy the Family?', in P. Koslowski and A. Follesdal (eds), *Restructuring the Welfare State. Theory and Reform of Social Policy*, Berlin-New York: Springer, pp. 238–74.

Parsons, T., Bales, R. et al. (1955), *Family Socialization and Interaction Process*, Glencoe, Ill.: Free Press.

Rapporti sulla famiglia in Italia (1989, 1991, 1993, 1995, 1997), ed. P. Donati, Edizioni S. Paolo.

Roussel, L. (1989), *La famille incertaine*, Paris: Éditions Odile Jacob.

Roussel, L. (1991), 'Les "futuribles" de la famille', *Futuribles*, No. 153, April, pp. 3–22.

10 Family Citizenship or Citizenship for Children? Childhood Perspectives and Policies

HELMUT WINTERSBERGER

This paper was written for the International Foundation for Human Sciences in the context of the International Symposium on 'The New Citizenship of the Family: Comparative Perspectives' held in Granada in early October 1997. As the title suggests, I question the approach of extending citizenship from individuals to families. On the other hand, I share with other participants in the symposium a number of concerns as to recent developments involving families and children in modern societies. However, I am convinced that extending citizenship from adults to children would be a better approach for making the needs of children and their families more visible as well as for searching for solutions.

My way of arguing is predominantly influenced by my affiliation with the European Programme on Childhood, in particular with the research project 'Childhood as a social phenomenon'. Therefore in the first pages of the following paper this approach to studying childhood will be introduced. In the second section, some phenomena which constitute a concern to most participants in the workshop are presented. The collection of concerns about modern childhood is neither original nor complete. On the contrary, it is redundant and selective, it serves, however, the purpose to debate them in a child-centred perspective. The third part is dedicated to some tentative and preliminary, practical and political conclusions.

I Childhood as a Social Category

In the project 'Childhood as a Social Phenomenon' (Qvortrup et al., 1994), childhood was analysed from a macro-sociological perspective. For this reason, we did not apply the concept of the 'child' in the developmental sense, but rather chose to think in terms of 'childhood' instead. Children were seen as a collectivity, and the purpose was to describe and explain the main contours and architecture of childhood.

Childhood was not looked at as a transient phase in the life time of one single individual, but we rather suggest that childhood be seen as a permanent social category: even if each child eventually becomes an adult, the category of childhood remains as a structural segment of society to be continuously filled up with new members.

Childhood is to be seen in a generational perspective. In this connection, major groups of reference are adulthood or old age, since age is one of the describing dimensions whose social correlates we attempt to disentangle. Yet, adulthood is not the only possible group of reference; if childhood may be understood in terms of marginalization or as a minority group in the sense of a 'group of people who because of their physical or cultural characteristics are singled out from others in the society in which they live for differential and unequal treatment' (Wirth, 1945), also other minority groups might be used. Applying this notion of a minority in the study of childhood caused us to focus our attention on the common characteristics that distinguish its members rather than on their individual characteristics. On the other hand, the use of this concept forced us to consider the relationships between childhood and other social groups, and therefore, to more carefully evaluate the possible forms of inequality that characterize it at the level of juridical status, power, distribution of resources and economic and social opportunities (Saporiti and Sgritta, 1990).

Childhood is theoretically similar to other structural segments in society, also in the sense that it is in principle exposed to the same societal (economic, political, cultural, technological, environmental and social) forces as other segments (such as adulthood). These forces may, however, influence children in other ways than adults and the groups or classes they belong to. Childhood is regarded as an integral part of society and its division of labour (contrary to seeing the developing child as an individual to be integrated into society). In many and partly subtle ways, childhood interacts with other segments in society: it is influenced by these other segments while influencing them itself. Children are themselves co-constructors and subjects in history and society.

To use children as central unit of observation is of major importance. This injunction is not merely technical in nature. The observation that children are overwhelmingly perceived through the prisms of adult variables is itself of theoretical importance. The nature of childhood's representation in social science as such contributes to the perception of childhood and the way it is looked upon in modern society.

Plenty of material relevant for the study of childhood is available in all developed countries. However, when this material was traced and analysed in line with theoretical and methodological guidelines above, our incipient ideas about childhood as excluded or marginalized or dependent in real life were immediately confirmed, since children were also excluded, marginalized, and dependent in the available material. Even in child studies, children are sometimes invisible in the sense that they are perceived as 'becoming adults'. Information is scattered, because it is collected from viewpoints of the family, the school, women's activities and opportunities, professional and/or bureaucratic interests, etc., and is therefore adult-centred. The nature of children's representation in research and documentation thus becomes a significant token of the nature of children's participation in real life. Children's near absence in public statistics and social accounting signifies their lack of importance in the minds of authorities and adult society in general. A description of children which takes seriously their own life expressions, might question the validity of conventional wisdom.

II   Perspectives on Modern Childhood

Childhood in modern society is affected by many sociocultural, -economic and -political trends. The demographic transition, changes of family forms and functions as well as shifts in the intergenerational distribution of resources are three pertinent examples briefly elaborated in the following section. Modern childhood is conceptualized as a stage of ambivalence emanating from belated and incomplete subsumption of childhood under the modernization process.

A   *The Demographic Transition: Ageing of Society*

The most visible demographic phenomenon concerning childhood in developed industrialized countries is the shrinking number of children, in absolute terms and as a proportion of the total population. This trend affects practically all industrialized countries. Though the respective levels may be different, the trend is the same everywhere. In spite of extremely low infant mortality rates below and around 1 per cent, the fertility rates for most Western European countries nowadays are far below the replacement level. On the other hand, the number and proportion of elderly people is steadily growing due to the increasing life expectancy. While in the past the few elderly people were by far outnumbered by children and youth, today their share is approximately the same, and tomorrow elderly people will outnumber children and youth. Basically, three groups of concerns could be discussed in connection with this transition: population decline, generational imbalance and marginalization of childhood.

In Western civilization, development models are generally growth-oriented; this holds true for economic as well as for population development. However, if one accepts the proposition that there are limits to growth, one has to include also decrease and stagnation in the various models of economic and social development. The transition of total fertility rates in Western countries from above to below replacement levels may be interpreted as a turning point towards either decline of Western civilization or transition from – in the long run – unsustainable to a more sustainable population development. In other words, there are many possible explanations of population development between the extreme scenarios of extinction due to over- or underpopulation. The problem is that on the one hand population development is often discussed ideologically, irrationally and emotionally. Consequently there is a lack of political space for debating population development in a more rational way. From a child-centred point of view this whole perspective is of rather limited relevance, because it is focusing rather on 'hypothetical children' who were not conceived and/or born rather than on the condition of existing children.

The second group of concerns has to do with the changing intergenerational balances. What impact will the demographic transition have on social security, when a shrinking active population will have to raise the pension funds for a rapidly increasing number of retired persons? In which way the function of bringing up children should be shared between parents and society, or more explicitly, between households with children and households without children? This raises obviously the question of sustainable development of pension schemes and of a new generation contract. Again, as for EU countries which belong to the richest societies in the world, the problem seems to be solvable. It is, however, important to see that the premodern interpretation of children as assets for old-age security is valid also for modern societies, the intergenerational solidarity pact has just to be shifted from the family level to society. Once this is recognized politically, the problem is to reformulate pension regulations in accordance with actual economic and demographic developments.

From a child-centred point of view, however, the most relevant question concerns the consequences for children themselves. Will fewer children have better access to the same resources, which had to be shared among a greater number of children before? Or will society reduce the resources made available to children and families with children, because in democracy the mechanisms of political exchange tend to discriminate against those who do not have a voice or the right to vote, as well as those, whose numerical weight is vanishing? Existing studies unfortunately confirm rather the latter hypothesis: in most Western countries there is a tendency towards neglecting the needs of children and young people rather than those of other age groups (Preston, 1984; Cornia, 1990).

B   Familialization and Institutionalization of Childhood

In all developed industrialized countries family instability is on the increase. However, we do not have sufficient information about the (quantitative and qualitative) relevance of this phenomenon for children. While it was often assumed that the phenomenon of family instability would affect to a larger degree families without children and to a lesser families with children, more recent ones underline that an increasing number of children actually experiences in one way or the other family instability.

Often we do not know the exact number of children, because – for instance in the case of divorce – statistics usually account for the number of divorces, and consequently also for the number of adults, but not always the number of children, involved. While answering this question would not raise any principal methodological difficulties, the distribution of children according to different family arrangements would require some conceptual and methodological clarification. In Austria it is estimated that since the Second World War more than half a million of children have experienced the divorce of their parents (Haller, 1996), and that today around two-thirds of children live in traditional nuclear families while one-third lives in other arrangements, such as three-generational, single-parent or reconstituted families (Wilk and Bacher, 1994).

The picture becomes even more unclear, when we move our attention away from quantitative to more qualitative aspects: Which is the impact of different family forms child welfare? It seems that the poverty risk is present in a majority of lone-mother families, while in reconstituted families – due to unclarities concerning the roles of family members – the subjective well-being of children might be affected.

However, in spite of increased levels of family instability, never before, in Western countries, childhood has been familialized to a similar degree as today. Childhood is for nearly 100 per cent of children in Western societies family childhood, in the sense that children live in some kind of family arrange-ment (be it a nuclear, lone parent, step or foster family). At the same time, we observe also an increasing level of institutionalization. At a first glance this seems to contradict the trend towards familialization. Actually it does not. While in the past institutionalization referred to substitute care, nowadays institutional child care is predominantly of a complementary nature. Children spend more time (hours and years) in schools, in child day-care centres, crèches and in other organized extracurricular activities, but during the evenings and nights they are at home mostly with at least one of their parents.

In addition to changes in the composition of families, there are also shifts in the functional profile of families to be observed. This is a consequence of economic and social changes, like industrialization and urbanization. As Hernandez (1993) shows for the US, this goes back more than 100 years already, when the Two-parent-farming family was replaced by the Father-breadwinner/mother-homemaker family, which in the second half of this century was again replaced by the Dual-earner family. These functional changes had a major impact on children in the sense that both shifts in family function caused a child care revolution, the first leading to scolarization of childhood, the second to the introduction of day-care for children in preschool age.

It seems that children usually do not have a say on family and child-care arrangements; their wishes and preferences are not taken into consideration a great deal; they are generally treated not as subjects but as objects and affected by decisions and actions of adults. Only recently reforms were initiated in a number of countries, which aim at hearing and involving children themselves in legal procedures. Giving priority to the best interest of the child is a nice wording, but it is not always easy to define it in the concrete situation. While it was proved in some studies (Wilk and Bacher, 1994), that a nuclear family arrangement is a comparatively good arrangement for the development of children, one cannot follow automatically that in the best interest of the child, any family disruption has to be prevented. In some cases separation might be the lesser evil. Day-care centres and schools, are increasingly determining the everyday life of children. Therefore it is of utmost importance that these institutions are really focusing on the needs and expectations of children primarily and not on those of teachers, child care workers or parents. The problem should not be restricted to the quantitative dimension of available places but quality should be a most relevant dimension, too. As for the goals of the education system as a whole, a proper balance between children's interests as children and socialization-oriented goals directed to children as future adults has to be searched for.

C   *Generational Distributive Justice and Equity – Increasing Child Poverty*

In most modern societies children and families with children are economically disadvantaged as compared with adults or families without children respectively. As a consequence, child poverty has become a widespread phenomenon. In Austria, the risk of living in poverty is 21 per cent for children, while only 9 and 11 per cent for adults and elderly persons respectively (Steiner and Wolf, 1994). According to a study by the Italian National Bank (Cannari and Franco, 1997), the situation is similar in Italy. But even in Denmark and Norway, which – from a continental perspective – are among the more egalitarian and welfare-oriented societies in Europe, children are clearly over-represented in the poorest strata of the population, and under-represented in the richest. The situation for adults in working age is different: they are clearly over-represented among the richest, while under-represented in the poorest part of the population. Elderly persons fare much better than children, but they are not as privileged as adults of working age (Jensen and Saporiti, 1992).

In this respect, it is, however, interesting to consider the development over several years. In 1970, a larger proportion of elderly people than of children was living in poverty; today, the situation has been reversed: a much higher proportion of children lived in poverty. (see Preston, 1984, for America and Cornia, 1990, for European countries such as Germany, Ireland and Sweden). The reasons for this shift in poverty from old age to childhood have not been sufficiently studied. Various distributive dimensions are to be considered simultaneously.

First of all, there is the horizontal distribution. During the transition from traditional domestic economy to modern national economy, children have seemingly lost their economic productivity; therefore, in modern societies households with children are disadvantaged as compared to households without children. Usually, larger families have larger income, but smaller per-capita income, than smaller families; children are more likely than adults to live in larger families; from there it follows that children are statistically concentrated in families with smaller per capita income (Kuznets, 1989). These findings can be confirmed for practically all European countries, and the number of children in a family mostly correlates very well with poverty (Wolf and Steiner, 1994).

A second dimension is the generational or relational distribution between different age groups. It is affected by the horizontal distribution, but not at all identical with it. It has been demonstrated above, that, for Western European countries in general – the poverty risk for children is higher than for other age groups, and that the gaps between child poverty on one hand and adult as well as old age poverty on the other hand are on the increase.

A third dimension refers to generations in the sense of cohorts. In the current debate about adapting pension systems it is often argued that the present generation of pensioners is the one who reconstructed the economy after the Second World War. It would therefore be inappropriate to cut pensions in line with the increasing generational imbalances. Some argue also, that the welfare state might be a one-generation phenomenon only (Sgritta, 1991; Thomson, 1991); in other words, it would disappear together with the generation, with which it has emerged and expanded during the last decades.

In contrast to the previous macro-dimensions, the fourth refers to the micro-economic distribution between adults and children within the family. We do not know very much about this, however economic theory provides models and concepts, such as the equivalence scales. The general assumption is that children get a constant share of the household income, that means that expenditures for children increase along with the economic status of the family.

Fifthly, there is also the distribution of income over the life cycle. Generally, children do not have an income at all. According to the principle of seniority, younger workers and employees get lower wages and salaries than older ones. In the period between 25 and 50, when children live still at home, the household income has to be shared between more persons, than at a later age. Pension income is generally smaller than income from employment, but not necessarily smaller than standardized per-capita income in the period of family formation. On the whole, the same life income might be distributed in different ways over the life cycle. In addition to the five dimensions affecting directly the synchronic and/or diachronic generational income distribution, there are also other dimensions with indirect consequences. The vertical distribution between the rich and the poor, for instance, is not necessarily neutral with a view to child poverty. In particular, if – following the slogan 'The rich get richer, and the poor get children' – poor families have more children than rich ones, this would lead to structural child poverty. In this case, the struggle against child poverty has to be embedded in the struggle against class-bound poverty as such. Also the gender distribution is of interest, if the probability for children to live with a lone mother is greater than to live with a lone father, or if – at the household level – mothers and fathers are sharing resources with children differently.

To find an equilibrium between all these dimensions is not an easy task, because any change with desired consequences in one dimension might have undesired ones on the remaining ones. The present controversial debate about child poverty and distributive justice for children and their families is a symptom for the complexity of this task. Reviews of the mechanisms of horizontal redistribution in favour of families with children in European countries (Dumon, 1993; Ditch, 1996), show that there are as many approaches as there are countries. However, the generally high levels of relative child poverty in Europe suggest that there is not a single country which has actually succeeded in solving the problem.

The problem demands for an efficient system of transfer payments to children or families with children. Approaches to this problem range from universal to means-tested systems, from tax allowances to direct benefits or a mixture of both, from rather symbolic to substantial transfers. It seems, that on the whole universal systems are more effective than means-tested measures. Some studies prove that substantial economic transfer payments are likely to reduce the burden of child poverty. Selective measures for particularly vulnerable families, such as families with three or more children, lone-parent families as well as families with one earner only might also be considered. Although these measures usually address families with children and not children themselves, they should be child-centred nevertheless. While for instance a child allowance may be supposed to be of immediate benefit for children, in the case of a tax allowance for non-working spouses the benefit for children is only mediated by a statistical correlation between the phenomena of non-working spouses and the number of children.

D   Structural Ambivalence of Modern Childhood

The notion of 'ambivalence' appears in de Mause's (1974) article on the 'Evolution of Childhood'. There, it characterizes only one specific period in the evolution of childhood (or rather of parent-child relations), namely the period between the fourteenth and seventeenth century. According to de Mause, this period is preceded by periods of much lower modes as infanticide and abandonment, and followed by such of much higher modes, as intrusion, socialization and the helping mode. Although de Mause expresses the view that the different concepts are not to be seen in a strictly consecutive way, but that they may coexist simultaneously in one and the same period, the basic message of the evolutionary perspective of childhood is that of a 'linear' development from a stage of uncivilized, cruel and/or indifferent parent-child relations to one of supportive relations.

However, the De Mauseian view of modern childhood as an almost paradise-like situation is an over-optimistic interpretation of the current reality.

By shifting the level of analysis from family to society and by applying a generational perspective we can show that the term ambivalence is perfectly adequate for describing the basic condition of modern childhood, too. Infanticide is still a widespread phenomenon as a consequence of war, poverty, traffic, and pollution, even in our times. According to UNICEF data, during the last 10 years only in wars two million children were killed, five million mutilated and 12 million became homeless. The same holds for other phenomena, e.g. abandonment, sexual abuse, physical punishment and all other forms of child abuse. If we do not restrict our attention to the improved material living standard of children only, but extend it also to qualitative dimensions and compare the gains of children with those of adults, we can show that, while all age groups have benefited from economic growth and from the expansion of the welfare state, adults and elderly people have benefited much more than children.

The ambivalence concerning childhood in developed industrialized countries, is the consequence of incompatibilities, tensions and contradictions between childhood and the process of modernization. It emanates from a contradiction between the rules of a modern society and the basically premodern characteristics determining childhood still today. The development of society as well of its agencies at the micro-level is characterized by the trend towards individualization. However this process was not carried through to its end.

If modernization may be interpreted also as a process of extending citizenship rights and responsibilities to an increasing part of the population, children are, however, still awaiting this process of extending citizenship rights. To an increasing extent the everyday life of children is determined by social interrelationships in the broader sense and not at all exclusively by the family. But familial paternalism has retained its dominant place in children's life. And also in other institutions but the family children are mostly treated in a paternalistic manner. So on the one hand, children are confronted with expectations and responsibilities which are not too different from those, adults are confronted with, on the other hand children do not have the corresponding rights. As to responsibilities children live in the twentieth century, as to their rights they live still in the age of feudalism. There can be no doubt that this ambiguity is generating tensions not only for children and adolescents, but above all for the relations between children and society, children and adults.

III   Citizenship for Children

While in traditional society the (extended) family used to be a rather compact and autonomous unit in the society, this does not hold true for the nuclear family in industrial and post-industrial society, where the parents' domain is predominantly outside the home, and childhood is characterized by increasing individualization and institutionalization (Näsman, 1994). It is therefore difficult, if not impossible, to clearly define the sphere of the modern family. If we define it strictly as the intersection of the father's, mother's and children's sphere, we end up with a small residual area of exclusively intrafamilial relations, which can hardly reflect the complex nature of tasks of the modern family. If we conceptualize it broadly as the union of the three spheres mentioned above, we get a relatively big, but, at the same time, heterogeneous area in which practically all the conflicts and contradictions of society at large are contained (Beck and Beck-Gernsheim, 1990).

This increasing complexity of the modern family is reflected in both, the complexity of interrelationships actors (fathers, mothers, children) and sectors (education, employment, health and social services), as well as the emerging tensions, conflicts and contradictions, which may be of exogenous (e.g. the conflict between the economic and social logic) or of endogenous nature (the relation between child protection, provision and participation). As for the division of power, resources and responsibilities, there is no great mystery about the male dominance. Men used to dominate women and children, and although today male aspirations to dominate women cannot be made explicit as in the past, men are certainly interested in defending at least some of the privileges they used to have. Women want equal opportunities as compared with men, and consequently their closer (biological, psychosocial and cultural) relations with children may constitute a major handicap in this struggle for equal opportunities. But what about children themselves? In this situation, it is more than appropriate to make also children, their aspirations and their needs, more visible, and to assess the compatibility between both, modern adulthood or parenthood on the one hand, and modern childhood on the other hand.

A   *Children's Rights*

There is a shift in the perception of childhood from objectivity to subjectivity, i.e. children individually are increasingly seen as persons with their own rights and responsibilities, and children in the sense of a collectivity as a population group competing with other population groups (e.g. adults and elderly persons) for the resources of a given society. The UN Convention on the Rights of the Child itself has contributed to the understanding of the child as a subject, in particular also as a legal subject. The content of the document has been explained with five principles: survival, development, protection, provision and participation. While the principle of survival as a basic human rights dimension is often interpreted as particularly useful in the context of either historical analysis or research on child condition in Third World countries, the shift of analysis to the structural level, as introduced before, has shown that the principle of survival can be appropriate also for the study of childhood in modern societies. At a first sight, the following two principles, development and protection, appear to be rather child-specific. However, neither development, in the sense of learning and adapting to changing social environments, nor protection, i.e. the right to be cared for and to be shielded from abusive acts and practices, are to be seen as tasks and privileges exclusively reserved to children. Neither can the need for development and protection be taken as a pretext for denying civil rights to children nor should adults be denied to right to develop and to be protected. The principle of provision refers to the right to possess, receive or have access to certain resources and services, to a fair distribution of resources between the generation of children and adult generations as well as to making available resources to children at risk. Participation means the right to do things, express oneself and have an effective voice, individually and collectively, as well as creating social spaces and practices for active participation of children.

The Convention on the Rights of the Child is on the one hand the result of a process which has taken place under the conditions of childhood ambivalence, i.e. it reflects this stage of ambivalence. On the other hand there are definitely indications that the Convention (or some parts of it) is an adequate instrument for gradually overcoming this stage of ambivalence by extending citizen rights to children. This ambivalent nature refers to both its content as well as the process of its implementation. The Charter of Human Rights forbids any discrimination according to gender, race, religion, etc., but not according to age. The Convention on the Rights of the Child extends the same anti-discriminatory regulations from adults to children, but does not mention age either. In doing so it rightly approaches the problems of discrimination, e.g. between girls and boys, poor and rich children, of children with a disability and children from minorities, but it neglects the main dimension of child discrimination: the discrimination between children and adults. On the other hand the Convention extends quite a number of rights contained in the Human Rights' Charter to children, e.g. the freedoms of thought, expression and association (Art. 12, 13, 14 and 15), and in doing so, children are recognized – for the first time – as legal subjects and citizens.

On one hand, the process of preparing, adopting and implementing the Convention constitutes a most remarkable case in human-rights development ever since the foundation of the UN. The fact that – within a few years 185 governments, i.e. practically the entire international community, have signed and/or ratified the document is rather unique. On the other hand, the extraordinary acceptance of the Convention to governments might raise some doubts: governments may have thought, they actually did not commit themselves heavily by signing this document. Therefore the value of the Convention for children has still to turn out, and the process of implementation has to be monitored very carefully. In this connection it is interesting, that European parliaments and governments have increasingly recognized the relevance of the Convention also for children in Europe; the European Strategy for Children, as adopted by the Parliamentary Assembly of the Council of Europe in early 1996 is a good example for this development at the European level (Wintersberger, 1996).

B   *Political Focus on Childhood*

Growing conceptual autonomy of childhood, a number of societal trends concerning childhood as well as the main thrust of the UN Convention on the Rights of the Child demand also for a radical shift in the political paradigm. Pleading for child-centred and -focused measures in political terms means emphasizing childhood policies as a political arena distinct from family and women policies. Representatives of family organizations often claim that the best policy for children is a good set of family policy measures; and similarly, feminist leaders argue that good women's policies are the best prerequisite for the well-being of children. There is some truth in both assertions, though it is not the whole truth. Family policies may coincide with childhood policies to a large extent, and this may also be the case for women's policies. But there are areas and issues where the interests of children, fathers or mothers do not fully coincide. Both family and women organizations tend to instrumentalize children's needs for promoting parents' and women's interests.

Therefore, childhood policies have to be conceptualized as an own political arena: They have to be comprehensive by not only covering explicitly child-related policies, but also the effects of measures taken in other political spheres. The interest of children must at least be given the same priority as the interests of other population groups. The approach has to be generational in so far as it takes into account intergenerational distributive justice. Childhood policies should be universal, i.e. primarily address all children as a population group and only select specific groups of children in a second step. Childhood policies should take children for what they are, and not only see them as prospective adults. Last but not least, modern childhood policies has to regard children as subjects, thus addressing the crucial question of their active participation in all decisions affecting them, be it on the individual or on the societal level (Wilk and Wintersberger, 1996).

The shift in the paradigm from objectivity to subjectivity of childhood leads also from a dual interpretation of childhood responsibilities to be shared between the state and the family, towards a triangular structure of negotiations between society and the institutions of both parenthood and childhood. At the level of the family this requires a better distribution of parental tasks between men and women as well as a development towards a negotiation family (between parents and children). As long as we see this as a zero-sum game between children and their parents this might be interpreted as an erosion of traditional parental or paternal power. However, if we take this as an opportunity for also renegotiating the balance between rights and duties of both parents and children with regard to society the outcome might rather strengthen than weaken the institutions of parenthood and the family.

References

Beck, U. and Beck-Gernsheim, E. (1990), *Das ganz normale Chaos der Liebe*, Frankfurt a.M.: Suhrkamp.

Cannari, L. and Franco, D. (1997) *La povertà tra i minorenni in Italia: dimensioni, caratteristiche, politiche*, Banca d'Italia, Temi di discussione No. 294.

Cornia, G. A. (1990), *Child Poverty and Deprivation in Industrialized Countries*, Florence: Innocenti Occasional Paper No. 2.

De Mause, L. (1974), *The History of Childhood*, New York: Psychohistory Press.

Ditch, J. et al. (1996), *A Synthesis of National Family Policies 1995*, Commission of the European Comminities.

Dumon, W. (1993), *National Family Policies in EC-Countries in 1991*, Commission of the European Communities.

Haller, M. (1996), *Kinder und getrennte Eltern*, Der österreichische Amtsvormund.

Hernandez, D. (1993), *America's Children, Resources from Family, Government and the Economy*, New York: Russel Sage Foundation.

Jensen, A.-M. and Saporiti, A. (1992), *Do Children Count? A Statistical Compendium*, Eorosocial Report 36.17.

Kuznets, S. (1989), *Economic Development, the Family and Income Distribution. Selected Essays*, Cambridge: CambridgeUniversity Press.

Näsman, E. (1994), 'Individualization and Institutionalization of Childhood in Today's Europe', in J. Qvortrup et al. (eds), *Childhood Matters. Social Theory, Practice and Politics*, Aldershot: Avebury.

Preston, S.H. (1984), 'Children and the Elderly in the U.S.', *Scientific American*.

Qvortrup, J. et al. (eds) (1994), *Childhood Matters. Social Theory, Practice and Politics*, Aldershot: Avebury.

Saporiti, A. and Sgritta, G.B. (1990), *Childhood as a Social Phenomenon*, National Report: Italy, Eursocial Report 36/2.

Sgritta, G.B. (1991), 'Iniquità generazionali e logica della compatibilità', in *AA.VV.: Politiche sociali per l'infanzia e l'adolescenza Milano*, Unicopli.

Steiner, H. and Wolf, W. (1994), *Armutsgefährdung in Österreich*, WISO No. 2, 17, Jahrgang.

Thomson, D. (1991), *Selfish Generations? The Ageing of New Zealand's Welfare State*, Wellington, Bridget: Williams Books.

Wilk, L. and Bacher, J. (eds) (1994), *Kindliche Lebenswelten. Eine sozial wissenschaftliche Annäherung*, Opladen: Leske & Budrich.

Wilk, L. and Wintersberger, H. (1996), 'Paradigmenwechsel in Kindheits-forschung und -politik. Das Beispiel Österreich', in H. Zeiher et al. (eds), *Kinder als Außenseiter? Umbrüche in der gesellschaftlichen Wahrnehmung von Kindern und Kindheit*, Weinheim und München: Juventa.

Wintersberger, H. (ed.) (1996), 'Children on the Way from Marginality towards Citizenship', *Childhood Policies: Conceptual and Practical Issues*, Eurosocial Report 61.

Wirth L. (1945), 'The Problem of Minority Groups', in R. Linton (ed), *The Science of Man in the World Crisis*, New York: Columbia University Press.

11 Which Family for Which Citizenship? The Diversity of French Conceptions of the Family and Citizenship

SOPHIE DUCHESNE

I   Towards an Empirical Approach to the Relationship between Family Roles and Citizen Roles

What place does the family occupy in the definition and functioning of contemporary citizenship? Or to be more precise, how do family roles – of mother, father, spouse, child – fit in with the specific roles of the citizen, even if only in the way the people involved perceive them? Few studies on the subject offer an empirical answer to these questions. The results of readily available surveys are too sketchy,[1] qualitative data too rare. Whereas on the one hand much research has been carried out on the theories of citizenship, reflecting the opinions of academics, be they lawyers or political scientists,[2] on the other very little is known about how citizens, the people who actually occupy the roles theorists define for them, perceive the matter.

This paper is based on the results of a study on the perceptions of citizenship.[3] The family was not at the centre of the research, but it clearly came out in the findings, in this case the interviews. The aim of the study was basically to try and understand how 'ordinary' citizens perceive their citizen role.[4]

The study first of all shows that 'ordinary' citizenship, as described by the people questioned on the concept, is slightly out of sync with the 'scholarly' perception of citizenship that academics deal with on the theoretical level in that it appears more civil than civic. Conceptually speaking, citizenship is defined, in the political sciences in particular, as belonging to a democratic political community. The word citizen has two antonyms: outsider – someone who does not belong to any political community, and subject – someone who belongs to a political community but not a democratic one. The important idea behind this definition of citizenship is consent. The question asked by political theorists with regard to citizenship is the following: under what conditions, to what extent and in what way can the members of any given society perceive themselves as consenting – and conversely dissenting if need be – to the norms imposed on them and the decisions taken by those in power; in other words is it possible for each and every member of a political community to voice their opinions on matters that concern them, and for these opinions actually to be taken into consideration? The theoretical definition of citizenship concentrates too much on the relationship between citizen and government.

By comparison, 'ordinary' citizenship as described by the interviewees when asked if they would like to talk about what being a citizen means, puts much more emphasis on the relationship *between* citizens. What is at stake in the relations between fellow citizens? How is the bond that unites citizens forged? How can this bond be kept alive, respected, made stronger? These are the questions at the heart of 'ordinary' citizenship that can be defined in the following way: 'being a citizen means wanting to enter into the ties with one's fellow citizens.' This definition was apparent in all the interviews, varied as they were, and they were extremely varied. You are only really a citizen if you realize that citizenship has to be gained and entered into through strong ties with others, with your fellow citizens. 'Ordinary' citizenship is also essentially a moral category. Over and above the different possible conceptions of citizenship that came out of these interviews, the demands of citizenship are each time defined as moral: recognizing the existence of specific bonds between fellow citizens and demonstrating by one's actions the will to partake in them.

It is easy to see how roles of a more private nature, that is family roles, can be encompassed within this dual characteristic – civil and moral – of 'ordinary' citizenship. And yet few of the interviewees made reference to this type of role in the course of the interviews. For example, the children's upbringing was mentioned by less than a quarter of the people questioned,[5] and only three people thought of it explicitly as one of the features of citizenship.[6] The lack of frequency with which parental roles were referred to in these interviews is in contrast with the results obtained in the pioneering study carried out by Robert Lane.[7] According to his interviews, citizenship brings together four groups of attitudes: the idea of a moral man who is unselfish, pious, honest, kind, cheerful, tolerant and who carries out his duties; the idea of a good family man who provides for his family, procreates and rears children and is concerned with raising family standards of living; the idea of a good member of the community who is sociable, helps the unfortunate in the neighbourhood, avoids appearance of snobbishness, goes to church, gives blood and money to charity; the idea finally of a good member of the political community who cares about public affairs, keeps informed, expresses opinions, but preferably 'orthodox' ones, obeys laws, votes, pays taxes, participates in military service and is loyal to his country.

But the very normative and 'traditional' nature of the attitudes expressed to Robert Lane – in comparison with what emerged from the French discussions – is perhaps not only ascribable to the place, the people and the timing of the study; it is no doubt also due to a particular form of questioning that relates the conception that the interviewees have of their role as citizen to the concept of the ideal citizen.[8] Robert Lane emphasizes the strength of the 'tension' which permeates his findings. He attributes this to the great variety of guilty feelings that the vagueness of the citizen role, combined with a substantial degree of demands with regard to inadequately defined behaviour, provoked in the people questioned. He however rejects any notion of 'role conflict', in other words of any conflict between the different conceptions of the citizen role.

The findings of the study carried out in France are markedly different. It has been seen that family roles, and particularly educative roles, appear much less important. Above all, although the two elements are linked, the French interviews are to a great extent centred around a conflict of roles. Two conflicting views of 'ordinary' citizenship are evident in the corpus as a whole. Both, which will be referred to as 'inherited citizenship' and 'scrupulous citizenship' imply not only a different relationship between the roles of the citizen and family roles, but even in a wider sense two different conceptions of the family and family roles.[9]

II   Civic Bonds as an Extension of the Family Bond: 'Inherited Citizenship'

The first model is entitled 'inherited citizenship'. Citizenship here is defined in relation to nationality. 'Citizen' and 'national' are synonymous or at least analogous. The citizen is perceived as a person who is embedded in a history, the history of a nation. The citizen has inherited his citizenship from his ancestors just like the rest of his patrimony. The citizen 'naturally' takes up his place in the national community because he is the fruit of his ancestors, just as the nation is the fruit of their labour. He feels he has inherited this nation because he knows that prior to his existence there was an accumulation of efforts, of suffering also perhaps, and, above all the will to construct something that he is now part of.

It is thanks to the will of his ancestors that the citizen is the way he is; he legitimizes himself through the respect for and the recognition of what was done before his time so that he is who he is and where he is and for the circumstances in which he lives. His self-respect depends on the respect he has for his ancestors, and on the way in which he values everything that they created before him. He will perpetuate, continue, pass on this history that was made for him, in which a place has been kept for him. He is by birth destined to exercise his citizenship. He is embedded in a history that began well before his time and which will continue well after his death. He is a page, an episode in this history and his duty to his ancestors, his fellow citizens and especially to himself is to keep it going.

In this model, this conception, not to want to take on one's citizenship, not to want to acknowledge one's essence, not to want to act as a citizen is very serious indeed, a rejection that amounts to betrayal. It is the betrayal of the love of the people who have lived before you, of the love of previous generations, it renders all the combats and all the suffering meaningless; and in refuting the value of what they achieved the citizen who rejects his role refutes his own worth.

The roles of the citizen, still within this model, are described essentially in terms of duty. They are based not so much on the fellow feeling that this 'inheritor' has towards his fellow citizens, but rather on the debt he has incurred from previous generations simply by being born. It is the past, history, that forges the bond between citizens: each and everyone has duties because he has ancestors who did a great deal for him. It is for this reason that he in turn owes something both to the people who have also inherited from the same ancestors and to subsequent generations. Given the fact that this first conception of citizenship is based on the passing on from generation to generation of the feeling of belonging to a national community, the family clearly plays a central role.

The citizen's duties are described as a total daily commitment by the citizen to his family, his town, his region, his country, following a system of concentric circles with the family at the heart of it all. The citizen's commitment is a very daily commitment, very much orientated towards the private sphere and close relations. However, it is a world of very non-political roles and commitments. Why is this? Because in this model politics is seen above all in terms of parties and conflict. For this type of citizenship aspires to the unity of the community to which the citizen belongs. Consequently, everything to do with political parties and politics in general, which conjure up images of division, repel the citizen. The family image comes up repeatedly in this context: the citizen does not get involved in politics for the same reasons as he avoids speaking about politics with his family: politics causes discord. The people questioned whose interviews corresponded to this first model recognize that politics and political parties are of course necessary; but it is not a matter of concern for the citizen.

Being a citizen is a daily occupation. It entails acting in one's immediate surroundings, in one's region, for the people one associates with, for the people one meets. It is through the accumulation of very daily actions that the national bond is conserved which in a way reproduces or rather extends the family bond. The family is at the core of this model. Citizenship originates in the family, it is passed on like the rest of one's heritage, it is an essential element of all patrimonies, even the most modest. Citizenship takes on the features of the family – the sense of duty, the importance placed on unity and solidarity, the very daily and concrete dimension of the commitment, the preference for all that is close by, the inscription in time and space. Citizenship takes on the roles of the family: the father's or the mother's role in particular – since this ensures the perpetuation of the nation through the reproduction of its members, but also through the passing on of its economic and cultural patrimony – is obviously one of the crucial roles that the citizen must devote himself to.[10] Citizenship is part of the national bond which itself is nothing more than a kind of extension of the family bond.

III The Family, Refuge from a Subjected Citizenship: 'Scrupulous Citizenship'

The first model – 'inherited citizenship' – is the easiest to describe because it is the one that each of us knows the best, because it is the one that goes the furthest back in French culture: it stems from both the Catholic tradition and the republican tradition in France. However, it is the complete opposite of another model of citizenship which was just as important in the interviews but which is more difficult to formalize. This second model will be referred to as 'scrupulous citizenship'. 'Scrupulous citizenship' is a very different model from the previous one in that it believes that citizenship and nationality are not, or at least should not and must not, be one and the same thing. Otherwise, state the people questioned whose interviews corresponded more closely to the second model, if citizenship is nothing other than nationality, why talk about it so much? And we get the very strong feeling that they want to express something that they cannot at first quite get to grips with.

Whereas in the first model the citizen heir finds justification for his existence in the national history that distinguishes him, that explains who he is and what he is like, similar to his close family and different from others; the second model looks on the contrary for the justification of the citizen in his unique and universal nature. Citizenship in this case is to be conquered for the sake of humanity and not for the sake of the nation. Only the standard of interpersonal and individual relations is really legitimate in this model. It is clear that the interviewees whose discussions corresponded more closely to the second model are only able to portray themselves in a clear and positive way when referring to interpersonal relationships. They are only comfortable when speaking about their relationship with a person or people individually. As soon as they try and speak about people collectively their descriptions become negative and their expression less flowing, more hesitant.

Collectivity is seen firstly in terms of crowds of people; the images associated with it are the supermarket, the subway, where one is uncomfortable, jostled, handled roughly. It also conjures up images of the masses which are oppressive and potentially frightening. Finally, in the extreme, collectivity conjures up a marching army which symbolizes the indoctrination that threatens people who have abdicated their own free will and who have let themselves be drawn into a movement over which they have no control. This second model of citizenship is therefore the opposite of a familiar and friendly world in which individuals are seen in a very personal way, mix with one another, get together, exchange experiences; it is a world of the masses, of collectivity where the citizen is lost, knowing neither who nor where he is, constantly afraid of being denied a personality. The relationship between these two worlds shapes the defining purpose of this 'scrupulous citizenship': the search for universality. The citizen is legitimized by his ability to realize his humanity; this involves the ability to communicate on equal terms with every other human being, to recognize that everyone is equal, to understand, to respect every other human being as much as he respects himself and even to base the respect he has for himself on the respect of others.

The term 'scrupulous citizenship' is intended to stress the high moral imperatives that form the basis of this model and which often go unnoticed. For the two models of citizenship described here are in permanent opposition and the conflict is almost political in nature, if by politics we mean the conflicts concerning the nature of the city-state. It is therefore very difficult to judge the two models on an equal basis because we tend instinctively to side with one or the other. It is easy to see how the first model is moral because so much emphasis is placed on duties; the second model which puts the stress on rights is nevertheless just as moral. But the demands the citizen places on himself are different in the two models. On the one hand, out of respect for his ancestors, the citizen wants to prove that he is their equal by carrying out the duties they have set out for him, the aim of which is to keep his national community alive even if this means he has to sacrifice himself; on the other hand the citizen expends a great deal of energy in extirpating his prejudices, in overcoming the 'distortions' generated by his upbringing. The people questioned who fell more into the second model say things like: 'I know that I am not myself when I hear myself making racist or xenophobic remarks, exclusionary remarks about people who are different from me because simply I do not really understand them. I feel that prejudices have accumulated in me that do not belong to me.' They feel that there is a human being deep down inside them that they would like to 'set free' from the a prioris, the distinctive characteristics that are suffocating it.

For all that, this search for universality is not without a certain recognition of everything that the citizen benefits from as being part of the city-state. There is undoubtedly no room on this earth for people who want to live alone. As one of the interviewees said with a laugh, to live on a desert island you would have to be able to buy it. The obligation to live in a city-state means that the citizen does not owe it anything because constraint does not justify duty, only will can be the basis for it. At the same time the interviewees who corresponded more closely to the second model know that living in a given country, particularly in France, brings a great many advantages and opportunities that would not be available on a desert island. It is true that these advantages are bestowed on him by the state but they stem essentially from the efforts of the other citizens, their exertions, the exertions of everyone who lives in a society that they also have not necessarily chosen; even if they feel lost in the crowd amongst the others, that does not stop them from working in order to create a pleasant environment in which to live. As a result each citizen owes a minimum to the others – his participation. This is based on the scruples he would have in taking advantage of others, because they are nothing other than his equals. To be up to the search for universality which is the essence of 'scrupulous citizenship' implies respecting what each individual does for his country. As far as this second conception is concerned, a lack of public-spiritedness no longer signifies betrayal as in the 'inherited citizenship' model, but is seen rather as taking advantage of the situation, as being a profiteer. Each citizenship model has a different idea of what a lack of public-spiritedness means.

In this model of citizenship there is also a detachment where politics is concerned, but this is based not on the fear of conflict but on the fear of commitment. This concept of citizenship integrates the notion of conflict: the more opposition there is, the more ideas there are and the more new things are created. This second model is entirely concerned not with passing things on but on the contrary with the idea that everything has to be constantly reinvented. Conflict is not a problem. However, *commitment* causes resistance. Political engagement is associated with the idea of parties which does not as before conjure up images of division, but rather images of 'belonging', of having a card, of joining up, of being a member of an organization, a group, all notions that recall the repulsive realm of collectivity. This model resonates with the idea clearly expressed by several of the interviewees: 'I hate belonging.' If the 'scrupulous' citizen hates belonging to his nation, he equally hates belonging to a political organization of any kind.

And what about the family? It is clear that the family is not at the heart of this kind of citizenship, because citizenship is first and foremost an individual quest. The family, instead of being a link with the city-state – the family to the local community to the region to the nation – falls within the private sphere and is a matter of choice. The family bond is not as before at the origin of the ties that unite citizens. It is perceived as a refuge from this citizenship that we embark on only out of a sense of moral duty and not out of a sense of pleasure, of essence.

'Scrupulous' citizenship entails being daring, trying to go out into the crowd, penetrating the masses, accepting to take part in this collectivity that is perceived a priori in a negative light. This venture that we partake in only out of a sense of moral responsibility, out of a feeling of respect for others, out of self-respect, is a real effort for the person involved. For the citizen the family is a group of people that he has chosen to live with, that has not been forced on him by society: the spouse he has chosen, the children they wanted together, within of course the limits placed on this commitment in the long term, the changes that family ties can and must be subjected to by the hazards of life and chance encounters. The 'scrupulous' model reminds us in many respects of the conception of society that Jean-Jacques Rousseau developed in the *Social Contract*. Did Rousseau not write the following about the family: 'The most ancient of all societies and the only one that is natural, is the family: and even so children remain bound to the father only as long as they need him for their preservation. As soon as this need ceases, the natural bond dissolves. The children, released from the obedience they owed to the father, and the father released from the care he owed the children, return equally to independence. If they remain united, they continue so no longer naturally, but voluntarily; and the family itself is then maintained only by convention'

(Rousseau, 1966, Book 1, ch. II, p. 42). The 'scrupulous' citizen hates belonging to any kind of group; the same goes for his family. He feels comfortable only where he himself has chosen to be and to stay and as long as he can question his commitments if he so wishes.

IV   Different Families for Different Concepts of Citizenship?

The concept of the family as far as the 'scrupulous' model is concerned is to all intents and purposes quite different from the family which is the basis of the 'inherited' citizenship model. In the first model, the family runs for generations, its purpose is transmission from one generation to another, and it exists only when three generations are taken into consideration. It exists when there are at the same time ancestors and children, that is the generation from which the citizen received his citizenship and the generation to which he is going to – and must – pass it on. The 'scrupulous' family is on the other hand centred around the couple and the children; it is the nuclear family in the strict sense of the term. It forms a shield which is certainly protective in nature but which also in a way forms a shield to action and commitment by the citizen in the city-state.

The duality of the conceptions of the family and the ambivalence that their equally valid nature causes the people involved is particularly noticeable in women. It is clear that as far as women are concerned the bond with the child is sometimes part of a logic of transmission just as their role as a mother is seen as an essential part of their citizenship; sometimes, however, when talking about the difficulties of fulfilling their educative role while at the same time having a fruitful career, taking a stance in the public sphere, expressing themselves outside the private sphere, they evoke the way in which the family can form a barrier between themselves and their citizenship.

How are these two models of citizenship that appear to be completely irreconcilable, in that the people involved differ considerably, divided between the interviews? The people interviewed cannot simply be slotted into one category or the other – with is rather fortunate, otherwise the tensions that exist within French society would be insurmountable. It was on the contrary seen that almost every interview carried out for this study encompassed to varying degrees each of the models. The majority fit in with one of the two models, either the 'inherited' or the 'scrupulous' model, but all of them had in some way or another elements from the other model of citizenship. It is of little importance how the elements from each conception are concretely combined in the interviews. It is, however, interesting to note the extent to which this configuration of representations which combine the incompatible is essential for democracy.

Neither model, as antagonistic as they both may be, is in fact more valid or more moral than the other; both are, however, equally necessary for the development of a modern democracy. Why? Because the first model permits cohesion, work in the long term, commitment, transmission, whereas the second makes mobility, flexibility, and inclusion – which has become essential for modern day societies since borders have evolved, since social, professional, geographical and political mobility has increased – all possible.

Both models are necessary for the good working order of democracy and yet as far as the theory is concerned nobody is really capable at the present time of elaborating a model of democracy that would allow the combination of both strong cohesive capacities and strong inclusive capacities, for this combination includes logically inconsistent and irreconcilable principles – a holistic conception and an individualistic conception of existence.[11] The individual, 'ordinary' perceptions do not face the same demands for logical coherence as the theoretical side. This is why 'ordinary' citizenship enables the combination of roles that the theory cannot reconcile.

The conceptions of the family inherent in each of the models of 'ordinary' citizenship are similar to the two models presented by François de Singly (1996: cf. p.16, n. 6 and pp.159–60). The so called 'modern' family that developed from the eighteenth century onwards when the emotional logic took precedence over economic accumulation, is characterized by the unity of the family group – and its persistence – as well as by the existence of varied roles depending on age and gender – to which social status could be added – that the upbringing aimed to instil in the child. The 'contemporary' family that has developed since the mid twentieth century from a decline in gender and age-related cleavages with the blossoming of each member of the family becoming the essential principle that justifies the evolution of their relationships. François de Singly emphasizes the necessity of not envisaging this type of binary modelling on an alternative mode, opposing one with the other, only being interested in proving that one has replaced the other:

> We tend to think too often in terms of revolution, in terms of 'all or nothing'.
> Understanding contemporary societies necessitates a different conception of
> change: the changes in the significance of what is at stake and the possible
> transformation in the order of priorities, the ways of creating a balance. For
> several decades the evolution of the family has been characterized by a

considerable increase in the demand for authenticity, for self-realization without for all that doing away with the more classical functions of the family such as the provision of services – manifest in the hidden economy of the family, in the solidarity between generations. A new balance (although an unstable one) has been created. Personal identity is formed at the crossroads of two principles – that of roles, positions, status and that of the subjectivistic ideal (ibid., p. 223).

The conceptions of citizenship are undergoing a similar type of evolution, an adjustment in the balance between holistic and integrationist tendencies and individualistic and inclusive tendencies, which leads to an instability in such a way that the balance often threatens to break down and dangerously favour one or the other, integration or inclusion to the detriment of the other and therefore to the detriment of democracy. The evolution of family roles and the roles of the citizen are closely linked. There is, conceptually speaking and as far as political theory is concerned, no definition of citizenship that is universally applicable, just as in the representations there is no view of citizenship that is universal. This is one of the essential paradoxes of citizenship: it is evoked every time we try to rally people together even though its meaning is a constant matter of conflict. Who should be a citizen? What is a citizen? These two questions are amongst the most controversial in the history of Western society, especially in the history of France. It is only in retrospect when a period of time becomes part of history that we can say which conception of citizenship was characteristic of the period. There is no such thing as 'good' citizenship. The same is probably true of the family.

Notes

1   SOFRES is one of the rare institutes to have asked on several occasions a series of questions on the roles of the citizen. As well as a question on the importance attached to being a 'good' citizen, the questioning was formulated in the following way: which of the following statements correspond the most to your idea of a 'good' citizen (numerous answers given, totals in each column add up to more than 100)?

	December 1976 %	March 1983 %	May 1989 %
Keeps up to date with what is happening in country	59	57	54
Obeys rules	56	56	48
Brings children up well	54	50	45
Votes regularly	51	43	38

	December 1976	March 1983	May 1989
	%	%	%
Minds own business without making a fuss	37	31	32
Pays taxes without trying to cheat the tax man	35	31	28
Is a member of a union	11	7	5
Is a member of a party	5	3	3
No opinion	3	2	2

Source: SOFRES, 1990, p. 170.

In 1991 the CSA (French broadcasting regulatory body) in turn questioned the French on their conception of the roles of the citizen, but the part relating to the family focused this time on 'having children' rather than bringing them up. The results were, however, more or less the same: the element 'children' was in the top four highest scoring answers.

2   The bibliography on citizenship in the political sciences is much too vast to give an exhaustive list. I will therefore only cite two pieces of work which give an idea of the extent of the questions debated on this subject: the Reader edited by Turner and Hamilton, 1994, and the review article by Kymlicka and Norman, 1994.

3   The results of this study have been published in my book *Citoyenneté à la française* (1997).

4   The study consists of about 40 so-called 'non-directive' interviews carried out between 1989 and 1990 on people living in the Greater Paris area chosen for their socio-demographic and political diversity.

5   It should be borne in mind that the interviews were 'non-directive' and that consequently the subjects discussed were brought up at the initiative of the person being questioned who set the boundaries on the topics proposed to them.

6   They were an unmarried woman with no children and two fathers. However, it should be noted that these three people were questioned while the woman conducting the interview was visibly pregnant.

7   See Lane, 1965, which gives an account of the same interviews which form the corpus of his book *Political Ideology: Why the American Common Man Believes What he Does?* (1962): 17 interviews each lasting about 10 hours, held in 1957–58 based on a long interview guide on white, married fathers living in Eastport on the East coast of the USA.

8   The questions in the interview guide are the following: 'Think for a minute about what a 'good citizen' in a democracy would be like. Regardless of whether there is such a person or not what kinds of things would he do? What kinds of attitudes towards politics would he have? How close do most people come to this ideal? How close do you come to this ideal? (Lane, 1965, p. 485).

9   The very succinct nature of the presentation I am going to give of each of the models will make them seem abstract models and therefore in a way theoretical. It should not be forgotten that it is empirical models that are being dealt with, constructed from accounts gathered in interviews.

10   It is no doubt unnecessary to reiterate the terms of the 'Declaration of the rights and duties of man and of citizens' as formulated during the French Revolution: 'You cannot be a good citizen without being a good son, a good father, a good friend, a good spouse' (article 4).

11   Jean Leca, starting from two theoretical models that he refers to using the terms naturalism and artificialism and which logically correspond to the empirical models of 'inherited' and

'scrupulous' citizenship writes: 'there is no inclusion without artificialism, no solidarity without naturalism; this imperative is a real challenge for Western politics and political theory' (Leca, 1990, p. 60).

References

Duchesne, S. (1997), *Citoyenneté à la française*, Paris: Presses de Sciences Po.

Kymlicka, W. and Norman, W. (1994), 'Return of the Citizen: a Survey on Recent Work on Citizenship Theory', *Ethics*, 104(2), January, pp. 352–81.

Lane, R. (1962), *Political Ideology: Why the American Common Man Believes What he Does?*, The Free Press.

Lane, R. (1965), 'The Tense Citizen and the Casual Patriot. Role Confusion in American Politics', *The Journal of Politics*, 27.

Leca, J. (1990), *Nationlité et citoyenneté dans l'Europe des migrations*, text prepared for the Giovanni Agnelli foundation, March.

Rousseau, J.-J. (1966 [1762]), *The Social Contract*, Paris: Garnier-Flammarion edition.

de Singly, F. (1996), *Le soi, le couple et la famille*, Paris: Nathan, coll. Essais et recherches.

SOFRES (1990), *L'état de l'opinion*, Paris: Le Seuil.

Turner, B. and Hamilton, P. (1994), *Citizenship. Critical Concepts*, Vol. 2, London: Routledge.

12 The Role of the Family in Establishing the Social and Political Link: The Double *Defamilialization*

JACQUES COMMAILLE

The subject put forward for this international symposium is conducive to taking a step back from what is known in the social sciences as 'the family'. Indeed, the question of the social and political link raises a fundamental question: first, about the passage of the individual to the social group and then about the crucial question of the structuring of the social sphere, of society. It is then possible to reintroduce the issue of the family and the role it plays, that it is capable of playing, in the fundamental schema of the construction of a social and political order. This is the same angle taken by Norbert Elias in *La société des individus* where he studies the relationship between the individual and the structuring of society and refers to the family as one of the many factors.

Such an approach does not treat the family as a fixed entity, a method often taken as scripture. It is based on a critical attitude towards the social sciences and on the need for a necessary vigilance with regard to ideologization when dealing with the family that is obvious, for example, in the process of the universalization of the family which leads to:

- disregarding the part played by social influences (inequalities between social classes, social risks that individuals are unequally exposed to depending on the class they belong to, their sex, their age);

- linking the family to the preservation of a traditional social and political order.

The basis of our argument is that there is a crisis of the social and political link and that this is happening within the framework of a reversal of perspective where the family becomes one of the effects of a more general phenomenon. In this context the problems of the family in establishing the social and political link are related to this more general crisis.

This can be seen in:

i) the confusing nature of the family;

ii) a defamilialization[1] in the social sphere;

iii)a defamilialization through politics.

These are the aspects that will successively be dealt with below.

I   The Confusing Nature of the Family and the Tension between the Individual and the Familial

It is generally accepted that the 1970s marked the end of a kind of 'golden age' of the traditional family in Europe. The organization and running of the private sphere entered the modern era and this was viewed with much delight. This was evident at different levels.

Family practices initiated this transformation, the effects of which are fully evident today. Without systematically reiterating all the changes which have time and again been underlined in demographic and sociological studies on the family, it is possible to sketch a status of the family that is characterized by the following principal features which are manifest in all the countries of the European Union and, on a larger scale, in all so-called industrially advanced societies:

*   couple-forming no longer necessarily involves marriage. This is clear not only in the decrease in the number of marriages, but also in the increase in non-marital cohabitation, including with children (there has been a drop in the number of marriages in all the member states of the European Union: there was a decrease of 25 per cent between 1970 and 1994; the number of births out of wedlock in the European Union increased from 5.1 per cent of live births in 1965 to 21.8 per cent in 1993);

- the couple as a unit is less and less an indissoluble union and its precarious nature is increasingly viewed as a constituent component of its formation as can be seen, for example, in the number of divorces which is about one marriage in three in the European Union;

- procreation is less and less the principle vocation of couples as can be seen by the discernible drop in fertility, a fertility which is itself increasingly being controlled (between 1965 and 1994 there was a decrease of 46 per cent in the fertility rate in the European Union, dropping to 1.45 children per woman in 1994, the lowest level in the world with Japan);

- the couple is more often than not a couple where the man goes out to work and the woman stays at home (the number of working women in the European Union is catching up on the number of working men: between 1986 and 1994 the number of working women increased from 40 per cent to 44.2 per cent whereas the number of working men decreased from 69 per cent to 66.6 per cent, which certainly constitutes one of the most major changes but also one of the causes: the massive entry of women into the labour force turns the economy of internal family relations and the social functions that this fulfils upside down, in that this change in the behaviour of women, in altering their relationship to society, alters at the same time their relationship to the family.[2]

All of these changes are evidence of the advent of a model of the family that coexists in an increasingly persistent way with what was the reference model for family policy in its genesis and formation in certain European countries: the family was above all an *institution* which was supposed to fulfil social functions such as biological reproduction, interpersonal solidarity within the family, the rearing of children, socialization with regard to the values of society and in so doing social reproduction ... In this postulated model a holistic conception prevails in which individuals do not exist as such, but rather in accordance with the social group they belong to. In opposition to the concept that the individual is an end in himself, he is here subject to the superior ends that the institution he has entered in to is said to pursue. It is understood that, in this model, marriage may be considered as 'the ritual that combines individual time and social time, a personal history and the history of others' (Auge, 1985). In fact, what is increasingly developing alongside this model is conversely a model where marriage or other ways of forming a couple are no longer a way of becoming part of the social group, but a choice made by two individuals who in so doing are going to constitute a 'relational family' where the partners, in using their cultural, socio-professional and even aesthetic (de Singly, 1994) 'capital', are going to try and achieve the tricky compromise between self-fulfilment, 'self-concern' and respect for the other person, the fulfilment, the obligation of a common undertaking that is married life (de Singly, 1996).

For a time this kind of reciprocity between political conceptions and the conduct of citizens that was evident during the 'golden age of the family' continued, but this time centred around another model of the family. In this period at the end of the post-World-War II boom, the entrance of the family into the modern era was almost triumphant when, for example, the liberalization of divorce could easily be associated with the idea of the liberation of the people involved and in particular the liberation of women. This was the period in which there was a huge upheaval in legislation concerning the family committed in particular to equality between men and women, between children whatever their origins (illegitimate or legitimate), the liberalization of divorce and the recognition of other ways of forming a couple other than by marriage, the legalization of abortion etc. These concrete and very real changes in the legal-political regulation of the family attest to the concern of the political world not only to adapt to the 'evolution of moral standards' but also perhaps, following processes of influence that it would be appropriate to look at in closer detail, in response to the new demands of the 'Market'.

We are going to put forward the hypothesis that this reciprocity between political representations and the conduct of citizens where the organization of their private lives is concerned, no longer exists and that for various reasons, the relationship between the two is much more complex.

The reality of the family is itself much more complex. The advent of a 'contemporary family' arising out of a relative eroding of gender and age-related cleavages is based on a crucial principle: the personal fulfilment of each member of the family, which has not completely replaced a more traditional model of the family following what would be a binary modelling traditional family versus the 'contemporary family' and a principle of linear development.

Thus, above and beyond what counts in the economy of internal family relations, the social functions of the family, that is to say the functions that render the family an element in the structuring of the social sphere, have not disappeared ... or are being rediscovered. The same can be said of solidarity between generations, this 'hidden economy of the family' that still seems to exist: through donations of money from the middle generation to the younger generation and from the older generation of grandparents to these two generations, through the exchange of services between the three generations: a French study on solidarity between generations shows that 64 per cent of the middle generation (49–53 year olds) questioned said they had given money to the younger generation (19–36 year olds); 33 per cent of the generation of grandparents (68–92 year olds) had done the same thing for the middle generation and 33 per cent for the younger generation; among people who have young grandchildren 83 per cent look after them either during the holidays or during the day and 34 per cent do this regularly on a daily or weekly basis (Attias-Donfut, 1995). Of course this form of intrafamilial solidarity is closely linked to the make-up of society as a whole. First, it cannot be separated from social status: generally speaking, the better-off the family, the stronger the solidarity between generations. Second, if the rediscovery of this solidarity is a positive point in the social sciences, its promotion is not always without an ulterior motive, having something of the nature of a wish to reactivate solidarity in the private sphere in the context of a will on the part of the state to disengage as far as solidarity in the public sphere is concerned. As an Italian expert from the European Observatory on National Family Policies (European Commission) said: 'in certain regions of Southern Italy [in certain regions of Europe it could be added], the family is increasingly being asked to regulate poverty.'

In the same way it is appropriate to remember the still as important role of the family in social reproduction, the reproduction of a hierarchical and inegalitarian social order, therefore in 'reproducing the structural information of the global social context' (Schultheis, 1997): be it for access to education and a socio-professional status (with the help of strategies which have nothing to be jealous of those concerning familial patrimony under the *ancien régime* (ibid.)), be it to assimilate cultures marked by confessional or linguistic specificity (ibid.).

If the family is in its essence more complex, juxtaposing or combining practices stemming from its modern and its traditional aspects, it is just as complex in the way that individuals perceive it and in the way they perceive the relationship between the family and society. Surveys regularly show the importance that continues to be attached to the family and often in the most traditional of ways (the value placed on marriage and fidelity for example) (Eurobarometer, 1993). But Sophie Duchesne in her contribution to the present publication and in her work on citizenship (1997a and 1997b), highlights a kind of ambivalence on the subject which would appear to be more apparent in women, who, it seems, are more divided than other groups between a conception whereby their role in the family takes precedence and a conception whereby their personal fulfilment as an *individual* prevails.

The reality of the family and of its representations that have become less clear-cut where citizens are concerned corresponds to what we shall call a sociopolitical and institutional status of the family that can in certain cases be full of ambiguities to say the least. Thus, if we take the example of French society, looking at the trace of the fundamental old division that makes it 'a split society' (Rheinstein, 1972), we were able to see that while feminism was part of the individualistic tradition in the 1970s–80s, it was only able to juxtapose feminist issues with the family-oriented conception still firmly entrenched in the institutions. Nothing demonstrates this better than the setting up in France in the same year, in this case 1995, of administrative-political mechanisms completely foreign to one another: one to celebrate the International Year of the Family, the other to prepare for the World Conference on Women in Peking. This was an extreme example of what has been observed for many years, that is the juxtaposition of governmental bodies devoted respectively to the family and to women's issues. The variations in the organization of the DG V of the European Commission as far as the family is concerned on the one hand, 'equal opportunities' on the other, seems to follow the same logic or rather the same ambivalence at the European level.

In fact, if both the demands of feminist movements and the changes in the behaviour and aspirations of women had institutionally and politically to be taken into account, just as citizens had to adapt to the upheavals in the ways of organizing and running their private lives, for a country like France it was inconceivable to get rid of all the institutions and organizations set up in the period of the 'golden age' of the family and the place that these occupy continues to be extremely important. In addition to social administrative bodies that still – directly or indirectly – have the family within their scope of activities there are in France organizations like the *Caisse Nationale des Allocations Familiales* that secures via the *Caisses d'allocations Familiales* a joint administration of family benefits[3] with the representatives of beneficiary families, employees' and employers' unions. The presence of family associations in this organization, as in others (the *Conseil Economique et Social* for example) and the systematic consultation of them by administrative bodies and the government, is revealing of the persistent influence of this form of representation of family interests in all political processes concerning the family. This is one of the elements that best distinguishes what remains a French exception on the matter compared to other member states of the European Union. *L'Union Nationale des Associations Familiales (UNAF)* that proclaims itself the 'Parliament of Families' is thus the expression in France of a 'representation that is guaranteed, indeed encouraged by the state'

(Martin and Hassenteufel, 1997).[4] If the representativeness of these family movements appears at times weak, their capacity for expertise at the national level has undoubtedly increased which allows them to maintain, if not reinforce, their power of influence, even if what is exchanged between family associations, semi-public institutions and political-administrative circles 'remains to a great extent ideological; representations (points of view) and at the best of times a highlighting of the problems of what the correct definition of the family should be' (ibid.).

The persistence of this very family-orientated tradition in French society most probably explains the prudence of political circles as a whole on all matters that concern the family and the sacred way with which the family is referred to in the pubic arena. In fact, the old left-right split on the matter of the family is less and less obvious and does not exist other than in rhetorical terms. It is true that the family issue is traditionally one of the pillars in the political positioning of the right, in that the family is associated with the perpetuation of the social order, 'the recognized importance of the family unit in the organization of society [remains] to the present day one of the strongest indicators by which to recognize the upholders of the political and social status quo' (Remond, 1982).[5] It is this status of the family on the political spectrum that makes the left suspicious of it and seemingly reinforces the doctrinal conception of a socialist left whose attachment to secularity is expressed in this case by a wish to be neutral in relation to the ways that individuals perceive the organization of their private lives. But the fact remains, as noted by specialists on the history of the right in France, that

> it is curious that [in the 1960s and '70s] it was ... right-wing governments ... that revolutionized the institution of the family by introducing the principles of liberty and equality, liberty to marry, not to marry and to divorce, complete equality between spouses, of children born out of wedlock and children born of adultery; not to mention the right to abortion (Dupaquier and Fauve-Chamsoux, 1992).

At the same time, the status of the family is still such in French society, and the influence of a strongly family-oriented tradition still so important, that the socialist governments between 1981 and 1994 did not depart from the, at least, formal celebration of the family and developed a policy that consisted less of imposing a doctrinal conception than of dealing tactfully with the diverse forms of family interest groups.

II   A Defamilialization in the Social Sphere

Apart from partisan confrontations embodied in public discourse and declarations of intent (like those more or less explicit in certain European right-wing factions who believe a woman's place is in the home) all political movements are confronted with a set of transformations and constraints which make political voluntarism in relation to the family even more uncertain and would in any case make the implementation of such voluntarism, if it existed, in practice increasingly problematic.

The confusion with regard to the social status of the family and the ambiguities of its political status have only become more pronounced in the wake of economic mutations: the crisis in, or the 'eroding' of, the labour force. These changes have in fact social consequences which allow us less and less to speak about the family on its own and force us increasingly to deal with it in its socioeconomic dimension. For example, the social functions of the family can no longer be referred to without taking into account the disruptions caused by unemployment and socially-related insecurity in the fulfilment of these functions.

The irruption of unemployment in a family is not only synonymous with financial difficulties but also with a disorganization in the exercising of family and social roles, their transmission and consequently their perpetuation. When highly qualified workers become unemployed, their status within the family is all the more altered because they were not simply 'financial providers' but also the bearers of a professional model, the possessors of a trade or profession that they may well have passed on to their own children:[6] 'we see ... the ... passage [by which] children tend naturally to exercise the same professional activity as their parents ... towards a crisis situation whereby the trade or profession, previously much sought after (or at least accepted) by young people and an object of pride for everyone, is brutally devalued.'[7]

If young people are living longer and longer with their parents, it is of course in relation to the longer time spent in education and training, but it is equally due to the problems of professional insertion which constitutes as much of an obstacle to independence for young people, that is to say finding a place to live and ... starting a family: in France, between the generation born in 1963 and the one born in 1970 the average age of children leaving the parental home went up by about two years (half of those born in 1963 had left the parental home by the time they were 21, for those born in 1970 the age had gone up to 23); the number of young people aged 20–24 who cohabit decreased from 1982 to 1995 and fell from 31 per cent to 19 per cent; the number of young people living alone increased at the beginning of the 1980s (in 1995 14 per cent of 25–29 year olds lived alone compared to 8 per cent in 1982) (Galland and Meron,1996).

It can be said that there is increasingly a knock-on effect between the crisis in the employment sector, the aggravation of social problems and the weakening of the family economy: in its make up and the way it functions. In other words, the increase in the number of socially-related risks is directly linked to family-related risks. At the European level a close link is perceived between unemployment and conjugal isolation and between unemployment and the break-up of marriages without it being possible to decide on the direction of the causal relationship, 'one [factor] leads to the other and vice versa' (Kauffmann, 1993).[8] In France, for example, 'three quarters of the people on RMI (a minimum guaranteed income) are unemployed and single' (ibid.). That is why 'the descent into poverty should really be seen as the result of a combination of factors. Unemployment is the catalyst; it is however the family situation that then, on top of unemployment, explains the most unexpected falls into precarious situations' (ibid.).

The reappearance of the social question can only accelerate a 'socialization' of family policy in relation to the family already firmly anchored in the traditions of several European countries. Developments in France are in this regard exemplary. The number of means-tested benefits as a percentage of all benefits increased (13.6 per cent in 1970, they represented 42 per cent of family benefits in 1996; if all the benefits paid out by the *Caisses d'Allocations Familiales,* including the RMI, are taken into account, this number, according to the *Caisse Nationale des Allocations Familiales,* increased from 12 per cent around 1970 to 60 per cent today (Join-Lambert et al., 1997). Benefits aimed at specific needs (handicaps, widowhood, more generally social isolation, etc.) have increased and the proportion of family benefits in relation to social welfare as a whole has decreased: from 40 per cent in 1946 to slightly more than 12 per cent today, this decrease being explained by the increasing importance of new categories such as those dealing with the aged and unemployment (Commaille, 1997a). In fact, it could be said that to a crisis of faith in the virtues of family policy has been added a growing uncertainty as to the objectives to aim for in the face of the spread of poverty along with a crisis in public finances, resulting in an increasing deficit between the progressive increase in social security payments and the decrease in incoming revenue: 'during the decade 1980–90, social security payouts increased, in real terms, by an average of 3.3 per cent, while the labour force increased by less than 2 per cent a year' (Hirsch, 1994). In fact, France, although so family-oriented, can no longer afford an ambitious system of horizontal redistribution along with a system of vertical redistribution which is increasingly vital for certain categories of the population, in a European context where, precisely, it is an exception: distributing one of the highest proportions of family benefits in Europe and continuing to formulate a family policy inspired in particular by pro-natalist objectives (Gauthier, 1996). When the great majority of European Union member states are mobilizing their public finances more in the social policy domain and this trend may become more pronounced if we consider 'the shift in the orientation of public action [in the European Union] in favour of individuals (children, mothers, fathers, employees and workers, men and women), rather than global categories such as the family' (Ditch et al., 1996).

III   A Defamilialization through Politics

We are emerging from a historical era during which the status of the family in relation to politics could vary, in time and geographical space, but was nevertheless viewed in a positive manner. In relation to our theme of the social and political link, nothing better illustrates the definite functionality between the family and the political link than the fusion model, that is to say the claimed homology between the family order and the political order: one should be in the image of the other and vice versa. But two other models can be cited:

- *the tutelage model*, the family must be controlled in view of the social functions it fulfils to the extent that the state can act as a substitute for the family which is to all intents and purposes legally incompetent;

- *the contract model*, members of the family are partners bound by a contract. This private contract is not in the least incompatible with the 'social contract', because in this 'civic city-state' model the individual is all the more a citizen, all the more attached to the political world precisely because he enjoys rights within his private sphere. We will refer to the idea of model in time and space. It should be noted here that this is a model that is very much like the one in force in Northern Europe where, for example, the stress is placed more on equality between men and women than on the family institution.

If we are talking about a defamilialization through politics, it is because there is currently a void in the models of relation between the family and politics, whatever the models may be. In a country like France, with a firmly established family-oriented tradition, it is particularly significant that a kind of impossibility in formulating any kind of policy is evident other than an administrative policy aiming especially at economizing public finances and at coping with the most acute expressions of the social crisis (Commaille, 1998 and 1994).

The diversity of the attitudes of the European Union member states makes a similar assertion at European level more difficult but it is, however, certain that it is not within the framework of the European Union that a reversal in this trend of government to 'governance' will happen, because there is no family policy at the European level (Commaille, 1997b).

This trend as far as the family is concerned is part of a move from government to governance in politics in general. For example, the gradual substitution of an administrative logic for a political logic as far as social protection is concerned is only one of the symptoms of the increasing difficulty experienced by the political world to take a stance in relation to the 'market', to economic imperatives. The mutations in the economic sphere and the increasing influence of an international logic *(globalization)* have contributed to the generation of a kind of fatalism and a submission of politics to the 'free market philosophy', at a moment when all economic policy must be accompanied by a *Weltanschauung* . This is evident particularly through the stance taken by the state. As a French theorist on the state said: policies no longer correspond to 'a strong conception of the state'. 'The state ... is becoming "weaker" in the sense that it was coherent, adapted to "its" society, animated by an integrationist project of great significance.' The state would appear increasingly, in fact, to be 'acceding to social heterogeneousness [of behaviour and situations] which is no longer considered *a priori* as an anomaly to be reduced'.

The disappearance of the models discussed above is the sign of an absence of a political project. It is undoubtedly within the framework of a political project, if one were to exist again, that the respective places of the citizen and the family, the role of the family in the transmission and the construction of the social and political link, could be discussed.

The example of Europe is in this instance interesting. Europe as a political entity implies a political project and citizens to promote it. With regard to this, it is noted that the Commission of wise people set up by the European Union to look at the social dimension of Europe, as well as the Committee on Employment and Social Affairs of the European Parliament are jointly concerned with having a reference to social rights, political rights and the rights of the family (or familial rights to keep in line with the other types of rights) listed in article 119 of the Treaty of Union. This is the expression of a new interrogation on the place not only of individuals in the construction of citizenship, but also on the possibilities open to them in the organization of their private lives and also perhaps in their duties on the matter in relation to their duties as citizens.

Is this a return of the family as a public fact? Does the family have a role to play in the construction of Europe as a political entity?

Conclusion

We are back at the starting point: there is a danger in isolating the treatment of the family with regard to the question of citizenship in general, to the social and political link in general. If a phenomenon of defamilialization is apparent, it does not stem from the 'private' sphere, from the behaviour of families and the attitudes of citizens with respect to the family, which, as we have seen, are much more complex than what is often denounced as a loss of values and individual responsibilities on the question.

On the second matter that we proposed to look at – the family in the construction of the social and political link – the social and political link is dependent on a social and political sphere that disrupts, threatens or even excludes the family or uses it as a simple pawn in the political game.

As a result, the rehabilitation of the social and political link does not first of all pass by a rehabilitation of the values of individuals with respect to the private sphere as we increasingly hear (with a wish to restore the 'father' and limits, which is so well illustrated by the reactionary movement, in the etymological sense of the term 'Back to Basics').

Here are two examples:

- the wish to reactivate the obligation to provide maintenance, the duty of solidarity between family members. But this is forgetting the fact that when we look at who cannot fulfil this obligation, it is often the people who are economically and socially deprived;

- the desire to reactivate family solidarity with regard to social solidarity. But, as Giovanni Sgritta said, this is asking families in some cases to 'regulate poverty'.

Finally, asking the question of the role of the family in establishing the social and political link, is not the same as asking the question of the re-establishment of family *duties* with respect to society but is more a question of thinking about the sociopolitical and economic factors that favour the smooth running of individuals' private lives, with reference to what should be a political project that defines the new founding principles of a form of citizenship... why not of a European citizenship?

Notes

1   By *defamilialization* is meant the process of the weakening of the status of the family as a dominant type of organization of the private life of individuals which also implies the question of the organization, the structuring of society as a whole.
2   For a more detailed study of these developments see Begeot and Fernandez-Cordon, 1996.
3   Progressively, the French *Caisses* have had their scope of activities increased to incorporate the administration of more socially-related benefits: first, social welfare to families, then in 1988 the *Revenu Minimum d'Insertion.*
4   For family groups see also: Chauviere and Bussat, 1997; Millard, 1995.
5   On the question of political positioning with regard to the family see also Dupaquier and Fauve-Chamsoux, 1992.
6   Relating to this, see work on the crisis in the iron and steel industry, Nezosi, forthcoming.
7   Patrick Champagne, 'La reproduction de l'identité', *Actes de la Recherche en Science Sociales,* 54, cited by Gilles Nezosi, op. cit.
8   On the interrelations social insecurity - family insecurity see Martin, 1997; Commaille, 1996.

References

Attias-Donfut, C. (ed.) (1995), *Les solidarités entre générations. Vieillesse, Familles, Etat,* Paris: Nathan, coll. 'Essais & Recherches'.
Auge, M. (1985), *La traversée du Luxembourg,* Paris: Hachette.
Begeot, F. and Fernandez-Cordon, J.-A. (1996), 'La convergence démographique au-delà des differences nationales', in J. Commaille and F. de Singly (eds), *La question familiale en Europe,* Paris: L'Harmattan (English edition: *The European Family,* Dordrecht: Kluwer Academic Publishers, 1997).
Chauviere, M. and Bussat, V. (1997), *Les intérêts familiaux à l'épreuve d'une comparaison France-Angleterre. Etude sur les enjeux d'une catégorie d'action publique,* CNAF-GAPP.
Commaille, J. (1994), *L'esprit sociologique des lois. Essai de sociologie poltique du droit,* Paris: PUF.
Commaille, J. (1996), *Misères de la famille, question d'Etat,* Paris: Presses de Sciences Po.
Commaille, J. (1997a), *Les nouveaux enjeux de la question sociale,* Paris: Hachette, coll. 'Questions de politique'.

Commaille, J. (1997b), 'L'avenir politique de la question familiale en Europe', in J. Commaille and F. de Singly (eds), *La question familiale en Europe*, Paris: L'Harmattan (English edition: *The European Family*, Dordrecht: Kluwer Academic Publishers, 1997).

Commaille, J. (1997c), 'La famille, un traitement politique en trompe-l'oeil'. *Raison présente*, 125.

Commaille, J. (1998), 'La politique française à l'égard de la famille', *Regards sur l'actualité*, La Documentation Française, January.

Ditch, J. et al. (1996), *Synthèse des politiques familiales nationales en 1994*, European Observatory on National Family Policy, European Commission.

Duchesne, S. (1997a), *Citoyenneté à la française*, Paris: Presses de Sciences Po.

Duchesne, S. (1997b), 'La citoyenneté', *Les Cahiers du CEVIPOF*, 18.

Dupaquier, J. and Fauve-Chamsoux, A. (1992), 'La famille', in J.-F. Sirinelli (ed.), *Histoire des droites en France*, Vol. 3, *Sensibilités*, Paris: Gallimard.

Eurobarometer (1993), *Les Européens et la famille*, Brussels: Commission of the European Communities, December.

Galland, O. and Meron, M. (1996), 'Les frontières de la jeunesse', *Données sociales*, Paris: INSEE.

Gauthier, A.-H. (1996), *The State and the Family. A Comparative Analysis of Family Policies in Industrialized Countries*, Oxford: Clarendon Press.

Hirsch, M. (1994), *Les enjeux de la protection sociale*, 2nd edn, Paris: Montchrestien, coll. 'Clefs-Politiques'.

Join-Lambert, M.-T. et al. (1997), *Politiques sociales*, Paris: Presses de Science Po.

Martin, C. (1997), *L'après-divorce. Lien familial et vulnérabilité*, Rennes: Presses Universitaires de Rennes.

Martin, C. and Hassenteufel, P. (eds), *La représentation des intérêts familiaux en Europe*, European Commission, September.

Millard, E. (1995), *Famille et droit public. Recherches sur la construction d'un objet juridique*, Paris: LGDJ.

Nezosi, G. (forthcoming), 'Vie et mort d'une identité professionnelle. L'idéologie de l'homme de fer sur le bassin sidérurgique de Longwy', *Revue Française de Science Politique*.

Remond, R. (1982), *Les droites en France*, Paris: Aubier-Montaigne.

Rheinstein, M. (1972), *Marriage, Stability, Divorce and the Law*, Chicago: The University of Chicago Press.

Schultheis, F. (1997), 'La contribution de la famille à la reproduction sociale: une affaire d'Etat', in J. Commaille and F. de Singly (eds), *La question familiale en Europe*, Paris: L'Harmattan.

Singly, F. de (1994), *Fortune et infortune de la femme mariée*, 3rd edn, Paris: PUF.

Singly, F. de (1996), *Le soi, le couple et la famille*, Paris: Nathan, coll. 'Essais & Recherches'.